LIFE IN SHAKESPEARE'S ENGLAND

A BOOK OF

ELIZABETHAN PROSE

The Queen as patron of Letters

George Gascoigne, poet and dramatist, presenting his *Hemetes the Heremyte* (c. 1579) to Elizabeth

LIFE IN SHAKESPEARE'S ENGLAND

A BOOK OF

ELIZABETHAN PROSE

COMPILED

BY

JOHN DOVER WILSON, M.A.

FORMERLY SCHOLAR OF GONVILLE AND CAIUS COLLEGE, CAMBRIDGE

BARNES & NOBLE, Inc.

NEW YORK

PUBLISHERS & BOOKSELLERS SINCE 1873

First published, 1911
Reprinted, 1969
By Barnes & Noble, Inc.
By Permission of Cambridge University Press

Printed in the United States of America

THE CAMBRIDGE ANTHOLOGIES *are intended for the general reader, who, whilst he is familiar with the greater masters, has little leisure, and, it may be, little inclination, to become a professed student of literature. They seek to provide such a reader with first-hand knowledge of the literary atmosphere and social conditions in which these masterpieces were created. At present, this need is satisfied only by reference to histories of literature, which have too many preoccupations to deal justly with it, or to authorities even less accessible.*

It is the object of this series to let each age speak for itself, and to give coherence and prominence to what seem to be its significant features. Thus, the thought, temper, manners and activities of the period of Shakespeare, which is the theme of the first two volumes, are exemplified in selections from contemporary poetry and prose. The former illustrates the literary interests, models and aspirations, as well as the lyrical and rhetorical quality of the time; the latter gives a picture of the Elizabethan Englishman, painted by himself, in pursuit of his business, sport or roguery.

Volumes dealing in like manner with other periods will follow, and the series will include a history of English literature for general readers.

J. DOVER WILSON

W. T. YOUNG

October 1911

v

PREFACE

A REFERENCE to the table of contents will acquaint the reader with the plan of this book. That meagre framework of facts which we call the life of Shakespeare has been made its basis, and the various extracts are so arranged as to illustrate the social atmosphere which surrounded our greatest poet at different periods of his career. The country lay at his door in infancy, with its shepherds and milkmaids, its witches and fairies. Stratford had its grammar-school, which he probably attended, and, though he did not proceed to college nor as far as we know ever leave the kingdom, sections on the university and travel have been added to complete the picture of an average Elizabethan gentleman's education. With the youth of twenty-two we then journey to London, noting on our way the vileness of the roads and the comfort of the inns, we see the chief sights of the capital, we stand amazed at its turbulence and gaiety, we catch glimpses of the temptations that beckoned the future dramatist to enter that " primrose way to the everlasting bonfire " down which his predecessors Marlowe and Greene had wandered to their undoing. Next we pass to the conditions which surrounded Shakespeare as author, actor and playwright, concluding this stage of our itinerary with a visit to the court, which was the constant supporter of the theatre against a puritanical civic government and the true centre, though not always the kindly patron, of all literary activity. In the last three chapters of the book we follow the dramatist, now crowned with fame and prosperity, to the retirement at Stratford which terminated with his death. William Harrison and others give our fancy the entry to his house, his garden and his orchard, and even allow us to picture him at his table or in his bed-chamber. Moreover since this was the period when Shakespeare's dramatic genius played around the land-rogues and water-rogues which add so much that is splendid and picturesque to Elizabethan life, it seemed proper to insert here chapters on vagabondage and seafaring. Finally the varied activities of the age are summarized in a charming and little known passage from Breton, giving an account of a single Elizabethan day. It will be noticed that from this list of topics one, the greatest and to Englishmen of that day the most engrossing of all, has been omitted—I mean religion. The omission, it might be said, is really Shakespeare's. Nothing is more remarkable in his work than its silence concerning the religious life and violent theological controversy of his time. And since this collection professes to deal with Shakespeare's England and not Elizabeth's, it is at least excusable if religion finds no special treatment in it. In point of fact the subject deserves a prose anthology to itself, and I hope some day to undertake one.

With this striking exception, the life of sixteenth century England pulses through all Shakespeare's plays, not excluding those whose scene is laid in Italy or ancient Rome. This book, therefore, is intended as a commentary on the work as well as the life of Shakespeare. The section on roads, for example, has a direct bearing upon the escapades of Falstaff, the passage on "witches in Scotland" throws an interesting and, I believe, a new light upon the weird sisters in *Macbeth*, Autolycus is the hero of the chapter on rogues, and so on. Partly in order to increase the utility of the book in this direction, all the chapters and a large number of the extracts have been prefaced with quotations from Shakespeare. But considerations of space have compelled me to make them as brief as possible, and they are sometimes little more than hints to remind the reader of scenes and speeches which he should look up for himself. It will be frequently observed how closely Shakespeare's thought and phrase resemble those of his contemporaries.

Such being the general aim of this volume, there has been no attempt to make it an anthology of the best Elizabethan prose. It contains no Hooker and very little Bacon, but, in so far as it draws considerably upon a number of excellent writers of the second rank such as Nashe, Harrison, Stubbes, Earle and Markham, the main characteristics of sixteenth and early seventeenth century prose are, I hope, sufficiently exemplified. I hope also that the reader will not be too conscious of the compiler's scissors, to which, as a matter of fact, Elizabethan prose authors lend themselves with great readiness. There are, for example, the "character-writers," Earle, Overbury and the rest, whose work has been laid under full contribution, while most of the earlier pamphleteers are continually dropping into the "character" vein and are full of such admirable little vignettes as the portrait of the bookseller from Nashe on p. 153. This, however, is not always the case, and that more use has not been made, for instance, of the work of Greene is to be set down to the fact that interesting passages are not easily detachable from the main body of his text. In collecting material for this scrap-book, I have in all cases given the preference to those specimens which are at once entertaining and complete in themselves. The majority of the extracts, it should be added, have been taken from books or documents written between 1564 and 1616, the dates of Shakespeare's birth and death, out of the sixty-nine used only four being earlier and some half dozen later than this period.

Finally, since the collection has been made primarily in the interests of the general reader and the student rather than of the professed scholar, I have striven to make it as attractive and as easy to read as possible. The text has been modernised throughout, an undertaking which has convinced me that Elizabethan editors save themselves a vast deal of trouble and risk by adhering to the original spelling, and, while not shirking the labour, I fear I cannot altogether have avoided the dangers. Free changes also have been made in the punctuation where sense or the modern eye seemed to require them. The glossary at the end ought to explain most of the names, strange words and difficult passages, and the reader will find it more useful if he remembers that words which have a modern look have often altered their meaning since Shakespeare's day. The text of all extracts is based upon the originals, except in the cases for which acknowledgement is here made and in a very few others where the British Museum contains no early edition. The word Rye in brackets following a title indicates that the passage has been taken from W. B. Rye's *England as seen by foreigners in the days of Elizabeth and James*, a translation from the journals of distinguished visitors to the country. In these instances, of course, the English is modern and not Elizabethan. My thanks are due to the following gentlemen for kind permission to use their text or illustrations ; to my friend Mr R. B. McKerrow for the extracts taken from his edition of *Nashe*, to Dr W. W. Greg for the contract on p. 161 from his *Henslowe Papers* and the letters on pp. 92 and 179 from the *Collections* of the Malone Society, to Professor Gollancz and Messrs Chatto and Windus for the last six passages in Chapter X taken from *Rogues and Vagabonds in Shakespeare's Youth* in *The Shakespeare Library*, to the last mentioned firm again for the illustration facing p. 208 from their edition of Harrison's *Description of England* and to Dr Victor E. Albright for permission to reproduce his interesting sketch of the Elizabethan stage. Nor can I close this list of acknowledgments without confessing my obligation to Mr A. R. Waller and to the readers of the University Press for much care and assistance in the production of the book ; and to my wife without whose patient help the task could never have been undertaken.

J. D. W.

September 1911

TABLE OF CONTENTS

xii

TABLE OF CONTENTS

TABLE OF CONTENTS

xiv

TABLE OF CONTENTS

LIST OF ILLUSTRATIONS

CHAPTER I

ENGLAND AND THE ENGLISH

This royal throne of kings, this scepter'd isle,
This earth of majesty, this seat of Mars,
This other Eden, demi-paradise,
This fortress built by Nature for herself
Against infection and the hand of war,
This happy breed of men, this little world,
This precious stone set in the silver sea,
Which serves it in the office of a wall,
Or as a moat defensive to a house,
Against the envy of less happier lands,
This blessed plot, this earth, this realm, this England....

Richard II., II. i. 40—50

England

The air of England is temperate, but thick, cloudy and misty, and Caesar witnesseth that the cold is not so piercing in England as in France. For the sun draweth up the vapours of the sea which compasseth the island, and distills them upon the earth in frequent showers of rain, so that frosts are somewhat rare ; and howsoever snow may often fall in the winter time, yet in the southern parts (especially) it seldom lies long on the ground. Also the cool blasts of sea winds mitigate the heat of summer.

By reason of this temper, laurel and rosemary flourish all winter, especially in the southern parts, and in summer time England yields apricots plentifully, musk melons in good quantity, and figs in some places, all which ripen well, and happily imitate the taste and goodness of the same fruits in Italy. And by the same reason all beasts bring forth their young in the open fields, even in the time of winter. And England hath such abundance of apples, pears, cherries and plums, such variety of them and so good in all respects, as no country yields more or better, for which the Italians would gladly exchange their citrons and oranges. But upon the sea coast the winds many times blast the fruits in the very flower.

The English are so naturally inclined to pleasure, as there is no country wherein the gentlemen and lords have so many and large parks only reserved for the pleasure of hunting, or where all sorts of men allot so much ground about their houses for pleasure of gardens and orchards. The very grapes, especially towards the south and west, are of a pleasant taste, and I have said, that in some counties, as in Gloucestershire, they made wine of old, which no doubt many parts would yield at this day, but that the inhabitants forbear to plant vines, as well because they are served plentifully and at a good rate with French wines, as for that the hills most fit to bear grapes yield more commodity by feeding of sheep and cattle. Caesar writes in his Commentaries, that Britanny yields white lead within land, and iron upon the sea coasts. No doubt England hath inexhaustible veins of both, and also of tin, and yields great quantity of brass, and of alum and iron, and abounds with quarries of freestone, and fountains of most pure salt; and I formerly said that it yields some quantity of silver, and that the tin and lead is mingled with silver, but so, as it doth not largely quit the cost of the labour in separating or trying it. Two cities yield medicinal baths, namely Buxton and Bath, and the waters of Bath especially have great virtue in many diseases. England abounds with sea-coals upon the sea coast, and with pit coals within land. But the woods at this day are rather frequent and pleasant than vast, being exhausted for fire, and with iron-mills, so as the quantity of wood and charcoal for fire is much diminished, in respect of the old abundance; and in some places, as in the Fens, they burn turf, and the very dung of cows. Yet in the meantime England exports great quantity of sea-coal to foreign parts. In like sort England hath infinite quantity, as of metals, so of wool, and of woollen clothes to be exported. The English beer is famous in

Netherland and lower Germany, which is made of barley and hops ; for England yields plenty of hops, howsoever they also use Flemish hops. The cities of lower Germany upon the sea forbid the public selling of English beer, to satisfy their own brewers, yet privately swallow it like nectar. But in Netherland great and incredible quantity thereof is spent. England abounds with corn, which they may transport, when a quarter (in some places containing six, in others eight bushels) is sold for twenty shillings, or under ; and this corn not only serves England, but also served the English army in the civil wars of Ireland, at which time they also exported great quantity thereof into foreign parts, and by God's mercy England scarce once in ten years needs supply of foreign corn, which want commonly proceeds of the covetousness of private men, exporting or hiding it. Yet I must confess, that daily this plenty of corn decreaseth, by reason that private men, finding greater commodity in feeding of sheep and cattle than in the plough requiring the hands of many servants, can by no law be restrained from turning corn-fields into enclosed pastures, especially since great men are the first to break these laws. England abounds with all kinds of fowl, as well of the sea as of the land, and hath more tame swans swimming in the rivers, than I did see in any other part. It hath multitudes of hurtful birds, as crows, ravens and kites, and they labour not to destroy the crows consuming great quantity of corn, because they feed on worms and other things hurting the corn. And in great cities it is forbidden to kill kites and ravens, because they devour the filth of the streets. England hath very great plenty of sea and river fish, especially above all other parts abundance of oysters, mackerel and herrings, and the English are very industrious in fishing, though nothing comparable to the Flemmings therein.

FYNES MORYSON, *Itinerary* 1617

ENGLAND AND THE ENGLISH

The English (a foreign view)

That island of England breeds very valiant creatures: their mastiffs
are of unmatchable courage....And the men do sympathize with the
mastiffs in robustious and rough coming on, leaving their wits with their
wives: and then give them great meals of beef and iron and steel, they
will eat like wolves and fight like devils.

Henry V., III vii. 154—168

The English are grave like the Germans, lovers of shew;
followed wherever they go by whole troops of servants, who
wear their masters' arms in silver fastened to their left arms,
and are not undeservedly ridiculed for wearing tails hanging
down their backs. They excel in dancing and music, for they
are active and lively, though of a thicker make than the French;
they cut their hair close on the middle of the head, letting it grow
on either side; they are good sailors, and better pirates, cunning,
treacherous, and thievish; above 300 are said to be hanged
annually at London. Beheading with them is less infamous
than hanging. They give the wall as the place of honour.
Hawking is the common sport of the gentry. They are more
polite in eating than the French, consuming less bread, but more
meat, which they roast in perfection. They put a great deal of
sugar in their drink. Their beds are covered with tapestry, even
those of farmers. They are often molested with the scurvy, said
to have first crept into England with the Norman conquest.
Their houses are commonly of two stories, except in London,
where they are of three and four, though but seldom of four;
they are built of wood; those of the richer sort with bricks;
their roofs are low, and where the owner has money, covered
with lead. They are powerful in the field, successful against
their enemies, impatient of anything like slavery; vastly fond
of great noises that fill the ear, such as the firing of cannon,
drums, and the ringing of bells, so that in London it is common
for a number of them, that have got a glass in their heads, to
go up into some belfry, and ring the bells for hours together,
for the sake of exercise. If they see a foreigner, very well
made or particularly handsome, they will say, "It is a pity
he is not an Englishman."

PAUL HENTZNER, *Travels in England* 1598 [Rye]

4

Birth and Rank

> How could communities,
> Degrees in schools, and brotherhoods in cities,
> Peaceful commerce from dividable shores,
> The primogenitive and due of birth,
> Prerogative of age, crowns, sceptres, laurels,
> But by degree, stand in authentic place ?
>
> *Troilus and Cressida*, I. iii. 103—108

[Shakespeare's father applies for a coat of arms, Oct. 20, 1596. It is granted in 1599.]

Of Gentlemen

Ordinarily the king doth only make knights and create barons or higher degrees: for as for gentlemen, they be made good cheap in England. For whosoever studieth the laws of the realm, who studieth in the universities, who professeth liberal sciences, and to be short, who can live idly and without manual labour, and will bear the port, charge and countenance of a gentleman, he shall be called master, for that is the title which men give to esquires and other gentlemen, and shall be taken for a gentleman : for true it is with us as is said, *Tanti eris aliis quanti tibi feceris.* And (if need be) a king of heralds shall also give him for money arms, newly made and invented, the title whereof shall pretend to have been found by the said herald in perusing and viewing of old registers, where his ancestors in times past had been recorded to bear the same : or if he will do it more truly and of better faith, he will write that for the merits of that man, and certain qualities which he doth see in him, and for sundry noble acts which he hath performed, he, by the authority which he hath as king of heralds and arms, giveth to him and his heirs these and these arms, which being done I think he may be called a squire, for he beareth ever after those arms. Such men are called sometimes in scorn gentlemen of the first head....

Of Citizens and Burgesses

Next to gentlemen, be appointed citizens and burgesses, such as not only be free and received as officers within the cities, but also be of some substance to bear the charges. But these citizens and burgesses be to serve the commonwealth in their cities and boroughs, or in corporate towns where they

5

dwell. Generally in the shires they be of none accompt, save only in the common assembly of the realm to make laws, which is called the Parliament. The ancient cities appoint four and each borough two to have voices in it, and to give their consent or dissent in the name of the city or borough for which they be appointed.

Of Yeomen

Those whom we call yeomen next unto the nobility, knights and squires, have the greatest charge and doings in the commonwealth, or rather are more travailed to serve in it than all the rest: as shall appear hereafter. I call him a yeoman whom our laws do call *legalem hominem*, a word familiar in writs and inquests, which is a freeman born English, and may dispend of his own free land in yearly revenue to the sum of 40/- sterling: this maketh (if the just value were taken now to the proportion of monies) £6 of our current money at this present. This sort of people confess themselves to be no gentlemen, but give the honour to all which be or take upon them to be gentlemen, and yet they have a certain pre-eminence and more estimation than labourers and artificers, and commonly live wealthily, keep good houses, and do their business, and travail to acquire riches These be (for the most part) farmers unto gentlemen, which with grazing, frequenting of markets, and keeping servants not idle as the gentleman doth, but such as get both their own living and part of their master's: by these means do come to such wealth, that they are able and daily do buy the lands of unthrifty gentlemen, and after setting their sons to the school at the universities, to the law of the realm, or otherwise leaving them sufficient lands whereon they may live without labour, do make their said sons by those means gentlemen. These be not called masters, for that (as I said) pertaineth to gentlemen only: but to their surnames, men add goodman: as if the surname be Luter, Finch, White, Browne, they are called Goodman Luter, Goodman White, Goodman Finch, Goodman Browne, amongst their neighbours I mean, not in matters of importance or in law. But in matters of law and for distinction, if one were a knight they would write him (for example sake) Sir John Finch knight; so if he be an esquire, John Finch esquire or gentleman; if he be no gentleman, John Finch yeoman. For amongst the gentlemen they which claim no higher degree, and yet be to be exempted out of the number of the lowest sort thereof, be written esquires. So amongst the husbandmen, labourers, lowest and rascal sort of the people, such as be exempted out of the number of the rascability of the popular be called and written yeoman, as in the degree next unto gentlemen....

Of the fourth sort of men which do not rule

The fourth sort or class amongst us is of those which the old Romans called *capite censii proletarii* or *operae*, day labourers, poor husbandmen, yea merchants and retailers which have no free land, copyholders, and all artificers, as tailors, shoemakers, carpenters, brickmakers, masons, etc. These have no voice nor authority in our commonwealth, and no account is made of them but only to be ruled, not to rule other, and yet they be not altogether neglected. For in cities and corporate towns for default of yeomen, inquests and juries are impanelled of such manner of people. And in villages they be commonly made churchwardens, aleconners, and many times constables, which office toucheth more the commonwealth and at the first was not employed upon such low and base persons. Wherefore generally to speak of the commonwealth, or policy of England, it is governed, administered, and manured by three sorts of persons, the Prince, Monarch, and head governor, which is called the King, or if the crown fall to a woman, the Queen absolute, as I have heretofore said: in whose name and by whose authority all things are administered. The gentlemen, which be divided into two parts, the barony or estate of lords containing barons and all that be above the degree of a baron, (as I have declared before): and those which be no lords, as knights, esquires, and simply gentlemen. The third and last sort of persons is named the yeomanry : each of these hath his part and administration in judgments, corrections of defaults, in election of offices, in appointing and collecting of tributes and subsidies, or in making laws, as shall appear hereafter.

SIR THOMAS SMITH, *De Republica Anglorum* 1583 (written c. 1551)

English snobbery

In London, the rich disdain the poor. The courtier the citizen. The citizen the country man. One occupation disdaineth another. The merchant the retailer. The retailer the craftsman. The better sort of craftsmen the baser. The shoemaker the cobbler. The cobbler the carman. One nice dame disdains her next neighbour should have that furniture to her house, or dainty dish or device, which she wants. She will not go to church, because she disdains to mix herself with base company, and cannot have her close pew by herself. She disdains to wear that everyone wears, or hear that preacher which everyone hears. So did Jerusalem disdain God's prophets, because they came in the likeness of poor men. She disdained Amos, because he was a keeper of oxen, as also the rest, for they were of the dregs of the people. But their disdain prospered not with them. Their house, for their disdain, was left desolate unto them.

THOMAS NASHE, *Christs Teares over Ierusalem* 1593

The gentlemen disdain traffic, thinking it to abase gentry, but in Italy with graver counsel the very princes disdain not to be merchants by the great, and hardly leave the retailing commodity to men of inferior sort. And by this course they preserve the dignity and patrimony of their progenitors, suffering not the sinew of the commonwealth upon any pretence to be wrested out of their hands. On the contrary, the English and French, perhaps thinking it unjust to leave the common sort no means to be enriched by their industry and judging it equal that gentlemen should live of their revenues, citizens by traffic, and the common sort by the plough and manual arts, as divers members of one body, do in this course daily sell their patrimonies, and the buyers (excepting lawyers) are for the most part citizens and vulgar men. And the daily feeling [? feeding] of this mischief makes the error apparent, whether it be the prodigality of the gentry (greater than in any other nation or age), or their too charitable regard to the inferior sort, or rashness, or slothfulness, which cause them to neglect and despise traffic, which in some commonwealths, and namely in England passeth all other commodities, and is the very sinew of the kingdom.

FYNES MORYSON, *Itinerary* 1617

English women (a foreign view)

Wives in England are entirely in the power of their husbands, their lives only excepted. Therefore, when they marry, they give up the surname of their father and of the family from which they are descended, and take the surname of their husbands, except in the case of duchesses, countesses and baronesses, who, when they marry gentlemen of inferior degree, retain their first name and title, which, for the ambition of the said ladies, is rather allowed than commended. But although the women there are entirely in the power of their husbands, except for their lives, yet they are not kept so strictly as they are in Spain or elsewhere. Nor are they shut up: but they have the free management of the house or housekeeping, after the fashion of those of the Netherlands, and others their neighbours. They go to market to buy what they like best to eat. They are well dressed, fond of taking it easy, and commonly leave the care of household matters and drudgery to their servants. They sit before their doors, decked out in fine clothes, in order to see and be seen by the passers-by. In all banquets and feasts they are shown the greatest honour; they are placed at the upper end of the table, where they are the first served; at the lower end they help the men. All the rest of their time they employ in walking and riding, in playing at cards or otherwise, in visiting their friends and keeping company, conversing with their equals (whom they term gossips) and their neighbours, and making merry with them at child-births, christenings, churchings and funerals; and all this with the permission and knowledge of their husbands, as such is the custom. Although the husbands often recommend to them the pains, industry and care of the German or Dutch women, who do what the men ought to do both in the house and in the shops, for which services in England men are employed, nevertheless the women usually persist in retaining their customs. This is why England is called the Paradise of married women. The girls who are not yet married are kept much more rigorously and strictly than in the Low Countries.

The women are beautiful, fair, well-dressed and modest, which is seen there more than elsewhere, as they go about the streets without any covering either of huke or mantle, hood, veil, or the like. Married women only wear a hat both in the street and in the house; those unmarried go without a hat, although ladies of distinction have lately learnt to cover their faces with silken masks or vizards, and feathers,—for indeed they change very easily, and that every year, to the astonishment of many.

VAN METEREN, *Nederlandtsche Historie* 1575 [Rye]

CHAPTER II

THE COUNTRYSIDE

And this our life exempt from public haunt,
Finds tongues in trees, books in the running brooks,
Sermons in stones, and good in every thing.
I would not change it. *As You Like It*, II. i. 15—18

§ 1. Country-folk

A Country Gentleman

Remember who commended thy yellow stockings.
Twelfth Night, II. v. 160

Is a thing, out of whose corruption the generation of
a justice of peace is produced. He speaks statutes and
husbandry well enough to make his neighbours think him
a wise man; he is well skilled in arithmetic or rates: and
hath eloquence enough to save his twopence. His conversa-
tion amongst his tenants is desperate ; but amongst his equals
full of doubt. His travel is seldom farther than the next
market town, and his inquisition is about the price of corn:
when he travelleth, he will go ten mile out of the way to a
cousin's house of his to save charges; and rewards the servants by
taking them by the hand when he departs. Nothing under
a subpoena can draw him to London: and, when he is there,
he sticks fast upon every object, casts his eyes away upon
gazing, and becomes the prey of every cutpurse. When he
comes home, those wonders serve him for his holiday talk. If
he go to court, it is in yellow stockings; and if it be in winter,
in a slight taffety cloak, and pumps and pantoffles. He is
chained that woes the usher for his coming into the presence,
where he becomes troublesome with the ill managing of his
rapier, and the wearing of his girdle of one fashion and the
hanger of another. By this time he hath learned to kiss his

10

hand, and make a leg both together, and the names of lords and councillors; he hath thus much toward entertainment and courtesy, but of the last he makes more use; for by the recital of "my lord," he conjures his poor countrymen. But this is not his element, he must home again, being like a dor, that ends his flight in a dunghill.

SIR THOMAS OVERBURY, *Characters* 1614—16

A Franklin

And you, good yeomen,
Whose limbs were made in England, shew us here
The mettle of your pasture   *Henry V.*, III. i. 25—27

His outside is an ancient yeoman of England, though his inside may give arms (with the best gentlemen) and ne'er see the herald. There is no truer servant in the house than himself. Though he be master, he says not to his servants, 'Go to field,' but 'Let us go'; and with his own eye doth both fatten his flock, and set forward all manner of husbandry. He is taught by nature to be contented with a little; his own fold yields him both food and raiment: he is pleased with any nourishment God sends, whilst curious gluttony ransacks, as it were, Noah's Ark for food, only to feed the riot of one meal. He is ne'er known to go to law; understanding, to be law-bound among men, is like to be hide-bound among his beasts; they thrive not under it: and that such men sleep as unquietly, as if their pillows were stuffed with lawyers' pen-knives. When he builds, no poor tenant's cottage hinders his prospect: they are indeed his alms-houses, though there be painted on them no such superscription. He never sits up late, but when he hunts the badger, the vowed foe of his lambs: nor uses he any cruelty, but when he hunts the hare; nor subtlety, but when he setteth snares for the snite, or pit-falls for the black-bird; nor oppression, but when in the month of July, he goes to the next river, and shears his sheep. He allows of honest pastime, and thinks not the bones of the dead any thing bruised, or the worse for it, though the country lasses dance in the church-yard after evensong. Rock Monday, and the wake in summer, shrovings, the wakeful ketches on Christmas Eve, the hockey or seed cake, these he yearly keeps, yet holds them no relics of popery*. He is not so inquisitive after news derived from the

* i.e. as the Puritans did.

privy closet, when the finding an aerie of hawks in his own ground, or the foaling of a colt come of a good strain are tidings more pleasant, more profitable. He is lord paramount within himself, though he hold by never so mean a tenure; and dies the more contentedly (though he leave his heir young) in regard he leaves him not liable to a covetous guardian. Lastly, to end him; he cares not when his end comes, he needs not fear his audit, for his quietus is in heaven.

SIR THOMAS OVERBURY, *Characters* 1614—16

A Farmer

Is a concealed commodity. His worth or value is not fully known till he be half rotten: and then he is worth nothing. He hath religion enough to say, God bless his Majesty; God send peace, and fair weather: so that one may glean harvest out of him to be his time of happiness: but the tithe-sheaf goes against his conscience; for he had rather spend the value upon his reapers and ploughmen than bestow any thing to the maintenance of a parson. He is sufficiently book-read, nay a profound doctor, if he can search into the diseases of cattle: and to foretell rain by tokens makes him a miraculous astronomer. To speak good English is more than he much regards; and for him not to contemn all arts and languages, were to condemn his own education. The pride of his housekeeping is a mess of cream, a pig, or a green goose: and if his servants can uncontrolled find the highway to the cupboard, it wins the name of a bountiful yeoman. Doubtless he would murmur against the Tribune's law, by which none might occupy more than five hundred acres, for he murmurs against himself, because he cannot purchase more. To purchase arms (if he emulates gentry) sets upon him like an ague: it breaks his sleep, takes away his stomach, and he can never be quiet till the herald hath given him the harrows, the cuckoo, or some ridiculous emblem for his armoury. The bringing up and marriage of his eldest son, is an ambition which afflicts him so soon as the boy is born, and the hope to see his son superior, or placed above him, drives him to dote upon the boy in his cradle. To peruse the statutes, and prefer them before the Bible makes him purchase the credit of a shrewd fellow; and then he brings all adversaries to composition; and if at length he can discover himself in large legacies beyond expectation, he hath his desire. Meantime, he makes the prevention of a dearth his title to be thought a good commonwealth's man. And therefore he preserves a chandler's treasure of bacon, links and puddings in the chimney corner. He is quickly and contentedly put into the fashion, if his clothes be made against Whitsuntide, or Christmas day: and then outwardly he contemns appearance. He cannot therefore choose but hate a Spaniard likewise, and (he thinks) that hatred only makes him a loyal subject: for benevolence and subsidies be more unseasonable to him, than his quarter's rent. Briefly, being a good housekeeper, he is an honest man: and so, he thinks of no rising higher, but rising early in the morning; and being up, he hath no end of motion, but wanders in his woods and pastures so continually, that when he sleeps, or sits, he wanders also. After this, he turns into his element, by being too venturous hot, and cold: then he is fit for nothing but a chequered grave: howsoever some may think him convenient to make an everlasting bridge; because his best foundation hath been (perhaps) upon wool-packs.

JOHN STEPHENS, *Essayes and Characters* 1615

A Fair and Happy Milkmaid

The queen of curds and cream.
The Winter's Tale, IV. iv. 161

A fair and happy milkmaid is a country wench, that is so far from making herself beautiful by art, that one look of hers is able to put all face-physic out of countenance. She knows a fair look is but a dumb orator to commend virtue, therefore minds it not. All her excellencies stand in her so silently, as if they had stolen upon her without her knowledge. The lining of her apparel (which is herself) is far better than outsides of tissue: for though she be not arrayed in the spoil of the silkworm, she is decked in innocency, a far better wearing. She doth not, with lying long abed, spoil both her complexion and conditions. Nature hath taught her too immoderate sleep is rust to the soul. She rises therefore with chanticleer, her dame's cock, and at night makes the lamb her curfew. In milking a cow, and straining the teats through her fingers, it seems that

13

so sweet a milk-press makes the milk the whiter or sweeter; for never came almond glove or aromatic ointment on her palm to taint it. The golden ears of corn fall and kiss her feet when she reaps them, as if they wished to be bound and led prisoners by the same hand that felled them. Her breath is her own, which scents all the year long of June, like a new-made hay-cock. She makes her hand hard with labour, and her heart soft with pity: and when winter evenings fall early (sitting at her merry wheel) she sings a defiance to the giddy wheel of fortune. She doth all things with so sweet a grace, it seems ignorance will not suffer her to do ill, being her mind is to do well. She bestows her year's wages at next fair; and in choosing her garments, counts no bravery in the world like decency. The garden and bee-hive are all her physic and chirurgery, and she lives the longer for it. She dares go alone and unfold sheep in the night, and fears no manner of ill, because she means none: yet to say truth, she is never alone, for she is still accompanied with old songs, honest thoughts and prayers, but short ones; yet they have their efficacy, in that they are not palled with ensuing idle cogitations. Lastly, her dreams are so chaste, that she dare tell them; only a Friday's dream is all her superstition: that she conceals for fear of anger. Thus lives she, and all her care is she may die in the spring-time, to have store of flowers stuck upon her winding-sheet.

SIR THOMAS OVERBURY, *Characters* 1614—16

A Shepherd

Corin. Sir, I am a true labourer: I earn that I eat, get that I wear, owe no man hate, envy no man's happiness, glad of other men's good, content with my harm; and the greatest of my pride is to see my ewes graze and my lambs suck. *As You Like It*, III. ii. 78—82

An honest shepherd is a man that well verifies the Latin piece, *qui bene latuit bene vixit*: he lives well that lives retired: for he is always thought the most innocent because he is least public: and certainly I cannot well resolve you whether his sheep or he be more innocent. Give him fat lambs and fair weather, and he knows no happiness beyond them. He shows, most fitly among all professions, that nature is contented with a little. For the sweet fountain is his fairest alehouse: the sunny bank his best chamber. Adam had never less need of neighbours' friendship; nor was at any time troubled with neighbours' envy less than he: the next grove or thicket will defend him from a shower: and if they be not so favourable, his homely palace is not far distant. He proves quietness to be best contentment, and that there is no quietness like a certain rest. His flock affords him his whole raiment, outside and linings, cloth and leather: and instead of much costly linen, his little garden yields hemp enough to make his lockram shirts: which do preserve his body sweetened against court-itch and poxes, as a sear-cloth sweetens carcasses. He gives the just epitome of a contented man : for he is neither daunted with lightning and thunder, nor overjoyed with spring-time and harvest. His daily life is a delightful work, whatsoever the work be; whether to mend his garments, cure a diseased sheep, instruct his dog, or change pastures: and these be pleasant actions, because voluntary, patient, not interrupted. He comprehends the true pattern of a moderate wise man : for as a shepherd, so a moderate man hath the supremacy over his thoughts and passions: neither hath he any affection of so wild a nature, but he can bring it into good order, with an easy whistle. The worst temptation of his idleness teaches him no further mischief, than to love entirely some nut-brown milk-maid, or hunt the squirrel, or make his cosset wanton. He may turn many rare esteemed physicians into shame and blushing : for whereas they, with infinite compounds and fair promises, do carry men to death the furthest way about; he with a few simples preserves himself and family to the most lengthened sufferance of nature. Tar and honey be his mithridates and syrups; the which, together with a Christmas carol, defend his desolate life from cares and melancholy. With little knowledge and a simple faith, he purifies his honest soul, in the same manner as he can wash his body in an obscure fountain, better than in the wide ocean. When he seems lazy and void of action, I dare approve his harmless negligence, rather than many approved men's diligence. Briefly he is the perfect allegory of a most blessed governor : and he that will pursue the trope's invention, may make this character a volume.

JOHN STEPHENS, *Essayes and Characters* 1615

THE COUNTRYSIDE

§ 2. Sport

Hunting

Come, shall we go and kill us venison?
And yet it irks me, the poor dappled fools,
Being native burghers of this desert city,
Should in their own confines with forked heads
Have their round haunches gor'd.

As You Like It, II. i. 21—25

I think it not amiss to begin and give that recreation
precedency of place, which in mine opinion (however it may
be esteemed partial) doth many degrees go before and precede
all other, as being most royal for the stateliness thereof, most
artificial for the wisdom and cunning thereof, and most manly
and warlike for the use and endurance thereof. And this I hold
to be the hunting of wild beasts in general : of which, as the
chases are many, so will I speak of them particularly in their
proper places. But before I proceed any farther I will tell
you what hunting is, and from the true definition thereof make
your way more easy and plain into the hidden art of the same.
Hunting is then a curious search or conquest of one beast over
another, pursued by a natural instinct of enmity, and accomplished by the diversities and distinction of smells only, wherein
Nature equally dividing her cunning giveth both to the offender
and offended strange knowledge both of offence and safety.
In this recreation is to be seen the wonderful power of God in
his creatures, and how far rage and policy can prevail against
innocence and wisdom. But to proceed to my main purpose,
you shall understand that as the chases are many which we
daily hunt, as that of the stag, the buck, the roe, the hare, the
fox, the badger, the otter, the boar, the goat and suchlike, so
the pursuers or conquerors of these chases (speaking of hunting
only) are but one kind of creatures, namely hounds.

GERVASE MARKHAM, *Countrey Contentments* 1611

Preparations for the chase

Immediately after supper the huntsman should go to his
master's chamber, and, if he serve a king, then let him go to
the Master of the Games' chamber, to know his pleasure in
what quarter he determineth to hunt the day following, that
he may know his own quarter. That done, he may go to bed,

An Elizabethan Huntsman

to the end he may rise the earlier in the morning, according to the time and season, and according to the place where he must hunt. Then, when he is up and ready, let him drink a good draught and fetch his hound to make him break his fast a little. And let him not forget to fill his bottle with good wine. That done, let him take a little vinegar in the palm of his hand, and put it in the nostrils of his hound, for to make him snuff, to the end his scent may be the perfecter. Then let him to the wood. And if he chance by the way to find any hare, partridge, or any other beast or bird that is fearful, living upon seeds or pasturage, it is an evil sign or presage that he shall have but evil pastime that day. But if he find any beast of ravine, living upon prey, as wolf, fox, raven and such like, that is a token of good luck.

GEORGE TURBERVILE, *The noble arte of venerie or hunting* 1576

The cry of the hounds

My hounds are bred out of the Spartan kind,
So flew'd, so sanded; and their heads are hung
With ears that sweep away the morning dew;
Crook-knee'd, and dew-lapp'd like Thessalian bulls;
Slow in pursuit, but match'd in mouth like bells,
Each under each.
A Midsummer Night's Dream, IV. i. 125—130

If you would have your kennel for sweetness of cry, then you must compound it of some large dogs that have deep solemn mouths and are swift in spending, which must, as it were, bear the bass in the consort, then a double number of roaring and loud ringing mouths which must bear the counter-tenor, then some hollow plain sweet mouths which must bear the mean or middle part: and so with these three parts of music you shall make your cry perfect: and herein you shall observe that these hounds thus mixed do run just and even together, and not hang off loose one from another, which is the vilest sight that may be, and you shall understand that this composition is best to be made of the swiftest and largest deep-mouthed dog, the slowest middle sized dog, and the shortest-legged slender dog; and if amongst these you cast in a couple or two of small singing beagles, which as small trebles may warble amongst them, the cry will be a great deal the sweeter....

If you would have your kennel for depth of mouth, then you shall compound it of the largest dogs, which have the greatest mouths and deepest flews, such as your west-country Cheshire and Lancashire dogs are, and to five or six couple of bass mouths you shall not add above two couple of counter-tenors, as many means, and not above one couple of roarers, which being heard but now and then, as at the opening or hitting of a scent, will give much sweetness to the solemnness and graveness of the cry, and the music thereof will be much more delightful to the ears of every beholder.

Gervase Markham, Countrey Contentments 1611

Football (a puritan view)

> Am I so round with you as you with me,
> That like a football you do spurn me thus?
> You spurn me hence, and he will spurn me hither:
> If I last in this service, you must case me in leather.
>
> The Comedy of Errors, II. i. 82—85

For as concerning football playing, I protest unto you it may rather be called a friendly kind of fight, than a play or recreation; a bloody and murdering practice, than a fellowly sport or pastime. For doth not every one lie in wait for his adversary, seeking to overthrow him and to pick him on his nose, though it be upon hard stones, in ditch or dale, in valley or hill, or what place soever it be he careth not, so he have him down. And he that can serve the most of this fashion, he is counted the only fellow, and who but he? So that by this means, some-times their necks are broken, sometimes their backs, sometimes their legs, sometime their arms, sometime one part thrust out of joint, sometime another, sometime their noses gush out with blood, sometime their eyes start out, and sometimes hurt in one place, sometimes in another. But whosoever scapeth away the best goeth not scot-free, but is either sore wounded, and bruised, so as he dieth of it, or else scapeth very hardly. And no marvel, for they have sleights to meet one betwixt two, to dash him against the heart with their elbows, to hit him under the short ribs with their gripped fists, and with their knees to catch him upon the hip, and to pick him on his neck, with an hundred such murdering devices. And hereof groweth envy, malice, rancour, choler, hatred, displeasure, enmity and what

18

not else: and sometimes fighting, brawling, contention, quarrel picking, murder, homicide and great effusion of blood, as experience daily teacheth.

PHILIP STUBBES, *The Anatomie of Abuses* 1583 (2nd ed.)

Bowling

A bowl-alley is the place where there are three things thrown away besides bowls, to wit, time, money and curses, and the last ten for one. The best sport in it is the gamester's, and he enjoys it that looks on and bets not. It is the school of wrangling, and worse than the schools, for men will cavil here for an hair's breadth, and make a stir where a straw would end the controversy. No antic screws men's bodies into such strange flexures, and you would think them here senseless, to speak sense to their bowl, and put their trust in entreaties for a good cast. The bettors are the factious noise of the alley, or the gamesters' beadsmen that pray for them. They are somewhat like those that are cheated by great men, for they lose their money and must say nothing. It is the best discovery of humours; especially in the losers, where you have fine variety of impatience, whilst some fret, some rail, some swear, and others more ridiculously comfort themselves with philosophy. To give you the moral of it: it is the emblem of the world, or the world's ambition; where most are short, or over, or wide, or wrong-biased, and some few jostle in to the "mistress" fortune. And it is here as in the court, where the nearest are most spited, and all blows aimed at the "toucher."

JOHN EARLE, *Micro-cosmographie* 1628

A Cock-fight

At Stanwick, my son had going with his hens a young cock of a stout and large breed, with very large jollops hanging down on either side of his beak, and a friend of his giving him afterwards a cock and a hen of the game, as they call them (the cockscomb and jollops being finely cut off, close to the head, for advantage in fighting) it fell out that the two cocks, meeting in the yard together, fell close to their fight; where the younger cock fought stoutly a good while, till the old cock, taking advantage of his large jollops hanging so low, took hold thereof, for raising himself to wound the young cock at every blow: which being observed by the spectators, they parted the fray for the present, and caused the young cock's pendant jollops to be cut off, and his head trim'd for the fight, as the old cock's was, who had at first so beaten the young cock, that he durst not stay within his view. But after the sores of his jollops' cut were healed, the young cock coming abroad again, the old cock ran presently upon him to have made him run away as he was wont to do before. But the young cock turning again, and they falling to a new fight, very sharp and eager on both sides, at last the old cock finding his old hold of the young cock's jollops taken from him, was fain to cry creak, and to run away as fast from the young cock, as the young cock did from him before; and ever after the young cock was master of the field.

R. WILLIS, *Mount Tabor* 1639

A Local Play

[The interest of this piece lies in the fact that the author was born in the same year as Shakespeare, 1564. Similar plays were no doubt given at Stratford.]

In the city of Gloucester, the manner is (as I think it is in other like corporations) that when players of interludes come to town, they first attend the mayor, to inform him what nobleman's servants they are, and so to get licence for their public playing; and if the mayor like the actors, or would shew respect to their lord and master, he appoints them to play their first play before himself and the aldermen and common council of the city; and that is called the mayor's play, where everyone that will, comes in without money, the mayor giving the players a reward as he thinks fit to shew respect unto them. At such a play my father took me with him, and made me stand between his legs, as he sat upon one of the benches, where we saw and heard very well. The play was called *The Cradle of Security*, wherein was personated a king or some great prince, with his courtiers of several kinds, amongst which three ladies were in special grace with him; and they keeping him in delights and pleasures, drew him from his graver counsellors, hearing of sermons, and listening to good counsel and admonitions, that in the end they got him to lie

20

down in a cradle upon the stage, where these three ladies joining in a sweet song rocked him asleep, that he snorted again, and in the meantime closely conveyed under the cloths wherewithal he was covered, a vizard like a swine's snout upon his face, with three wire chains fastened thereunto, the other end whereof being holden severally by those three ladies, who fall to singing again, and then discovered his face, that the spectators might see how they had transformed him, going on with their singing. Whilst all this was acting, there came forth of another door at the farthest end of the stage, two old men, the one in blue, with a sergeant at arms, his mace on his shoulder, the other in red, with a drawn sword in his hand, and leaning with the other hand upon the other's shoulder; and so they two went along in a soft pace round about by the skirt of the stage, till at last they came to the cradle, when all the court was in greatest jollity; and then the foremost old man with his mace stroke a fearful blow upon the cradle; whereat all the courtiers, with the three ladies and the vizard, all vanished; and the desolate prince starting up bare-faced, and finding himself thus sent for to judgment, made a lamentable complaint of his miserable case, and so was carried away by wicked spirits. This prince did personate in the moral, the wicked of the world; the three ladies, Pride, Covetousness, and Luxury; the two old men, the end of the world, and the last judgment.

This sight took such impression in me, that when I came towards man's estate it was as fresh in my memory, as if I had seen it newly acted. From whence I observe out of mine own experience, what great care should be had in the education of children, to keep them from seeing of spectacles of ill examples, and hearing of lascivious or scurrilous words; for that their young memories are like fair writing-tables, wherein if the fair sentences or lessons of grace be written, they may (by God's blessing) keep them from many vicious blots of life, wherewithal they may otherwise be tainted...And withal we may observe, how far unlike the plays and harmless morals of former times are to those which have succeeded; many of which (by report of others) may be termed schoolmasters of vice, and provocations to corruptions.

R. WILLIS, *Mount Tabor* 1639

§ 3. Festival

Christmas Day

Some say that ever 'gainst that season comes
Wherein our Saviour's birth is celebrated,
The bird of dawning singeth all night long:
And then, they say, no spirit can walk abroad;
The nights are wholesome; then no planets strike,
No fairy takes, nor witch hath power to charm,
So hallow'd and so gracious is the time.

Hamlet, I. i. 158—164

It is now Christmas, and not a cup of drink must pass without a carol; the beasts, fowl, and fish, come to a general execution; and the corn is ground to dust for the bakehouse, and the pastry. Cards and dice purge many a purse, and the youth shew their agility in shoeing of the wild mare. Now "Good cheer" and "Welcome," and "God be with you," and "I thank you," and "Against the new year," provide for the presents. The Lord of Misrule is no mean man for his time, and the guests of the high table must lack no wine. The lusty bloods must look about them like men, and piping and dancing puts away much melancholy. Stolen venison is sweet, and a fat coney is worth money. Pit-falls are now set for small birds, and a woodcock hangs himself in a gin. A good fire heats all the house, and a full alms-basket makes the beggars prayers. The masquers and mummers make the merry sport: but if they lose their money, their drum goes dead. Swearers and swaggerers are sent away to the ale-house, and unruly wenches go in danger of judgment. Musicians now make their instruments speak out, and a good song is worth the hearing. In sum, it is a holy time, a duty in Christians for the remembrance of Christ, and custom among friends for the maintainance of good fellowship. In brief, I thus conclude of it: I hold it a memory of the Heaven's love and the world's peace, the mirth of the honest, and the meeting of the friendly.

NICHOLAS BRETON, *Fantastickes* 1626

FESTIVAL

Good-Friday

It is now Good Friday, and a general fast must be kept among all Christians, in remembrance of Christ's Passion. Flesh and fish must be banished all stomachs strong or weak. Now begins the farewell to thin fare, and the fishmongers may shut up their shops till the holy-days be past. The butchers now must wash their boards, make clean their aprons, sharpen their knives, and sort their pricks, and cut out their meat for Easter-Eve market. Now must the poulterers make ready their rabbits and their fowl, the cooks have their ovens clean, and all for pies and tarts against the merry feast. Now the maids bestir them about their houses, the launders about their linen, the tailors about apparel, and all for this holy time. Now young lambs, young rabbits, and young chickens die for fine appetites, and now the minstrel tunes his instruments, to have them ready for the young people. But with the aged and the religious, there is nothing but sorrow and mourning, confession, contrition, and absolution, and I know not what. Few that are merry, but children that break up school, and wenches that are upon the marriage. In sum, it is such an odd day by itself, that I will only make this conclusion of it: it is the bridle of nature, and the examiner of reason.

Nicholas Breton, Fantastickes 1626

Easter-Day

It is now Easter, and Jack of Lent is turned out of doors. The fishermen now hang up their nets to dry, while the calf and the lamb walk toward the kitchen and the pastry. The velvet heads of the forests fall at the loose of the cross-bow. The salmon-trout plays with the fly, and the March rabbit runs dead into the dish. The Indian commodities pay the merchant's adventure: and Barbary sugar puts honey out of countenance. The holy feast is kept for the faithful, and a known Jew hath no place among Christians. The earth now begins to paint her upper garment, and the trees put out their young buds. The little kids chew their cuds, and the swallow feeds on the flies in the air. The stork cleanseth the brooks of the frogs, and the spar-hawk prepares her wing for the partridge. The little fawn is stolen from the doe, and the male deer begin to herd. The spirit of youth is inclined to mirth, and the conscionable scholar will

23

not break a holy-day. The minstrel calls the maid from her dinner, and the lover's eyes do troll like tennis balls. There is mirth and joy, when there is health and liberty: and he that hath money will be no mean man in his mansion. The air is wholesome and the sky comfortable, the flowers odoriferous and the fruits pleasant. I conclude, it is a day of much delightfulness: the sun's dancing day, and the earth's holy-day.

NICHOLAS BRETON, Fantastickes 1626

May-day (a puritan view)

They rose up early to observe
The rite of May.
A Midsummer Night's Dream, IV. i. 138—139

Against May, Whitsunday, or some other time of the year, every parish, town and village assemble themselves together, both men, women and children, old and young, even all indifferently; and either going all together or dividing themselves into companies, they go some to the woods and groves, some to the hills and mountains, some to one place and some to another, where they spend all the night in pleasant pastimes; and in the morning they return, bringing with them birch boughs and branches of trees, to deck their assemblies withal. And no marvel, for there is a great lord present amongst them, as superintendent and lord over their pastimes and sports, namely Sathan, prince of hell. But their chiefest jewel they bring from thence is their May-pole, which they bring home with great veneration, as thus. They have twenty or forty yoke of oxen, every ox having a sweet nose-gay of flowers placed on the tip of his horns; and these oxen draw home this May-pole (this stinking idol, rather) which is covered all over with flowers and herbs, bound round about with strings from the top to the bottom, and sometime painted with variable colours, with two or three hundred men, women and children following it with great devotion. And thus being reared up with handkerchiefs and flags streaming on the top, they straw the ground about, bind green boughs about it, set up summer-halls, bowers, and arbours hard by it; and then they fall to banquet and feast, to leap and dance about it, as the heathen people did at the dedication of their idols, whereof this is a perfect pattern, or rather the thing itself.

PHILIP STUBBES, The Anatomie of Abuses 1583 (2nd ed.)

Robin Hood

I came once myself to a place, riding on a journey homeward from London, and I sent word over night into the town that I would preach there in the morning because it was holy day, and methought it was an holy day's work. The church stood in my way, and I took my horse, and my company, and went thither. I thought I should have found a great company in the church, and when I came there, the church door was fast locked.

I tarried there half an hour and more, at last the key was found, and one of the parish comes to me and says: "Sir this is a busy day with us, we cannot hear you, it is Robin Hood's day. The parish are gone abroad to gather for Robin Hood. I pray you let them not." I was fain there to give place to Robin Hood; I thought my rochet should have been regarded, though I were not, but it would not serve, it was fain to give place to Robin Hood's men.

It is no laughing matter my friends, it is a weeping matter, a heavy matter, under the pretence for gathering for Robin Hood, a traitor, and a thief, to put out a preacher, to have his office less esteemed, to prefer Robin Hood before the ministration of God's word, and all this hath come of unpreaching prelates. This realm hath been ill provided for, that it hath had such corrupt judgments in it, to prefer Robin Hood to God's word

BISHOP HUGH LATIMER, *Sermon preached before Edward VI*,
April 12, 1549

The Lord of Misrule (a puritan view)

The name, indeed, is odious both to God and good men, and such as the very heathen people would have blushed at, once to have named amongst them. And if the name importeth some evil, then what may the thing itself be, judge you? But because you desire to know the manner of them, I will show you as I have seen them practised myself. First, all the wildheads of the parish, conventing together, choose them a Grand-Captain (of all mischief) whom they ennoble with the title of my Lord of Misrule, and him they crown with great solemnity, and adopt for their king. This king annointed, chooseth forth twenty, forty, threescore or a hundred lusty guts, like to himself, to wait upon his lordly majesty, and to guard his noble person. Then, every one of these his men, he investeth with his liveries of green, yellow, or some other light wanton colour; and as though they were not (bawdy) gaudy enough I should say, they bedeck themselves with scarfs, ribbons and laces hanged all over with gold rings, precious stones, and other jewels: this done, they tie about either leg twenty or forty bells, with rich handkerchiefs in their hands, and sometimes laid across over their shoulders and necks, borrowed for the most part of their pretty Mopsies and loving Bessies, for bussing them in the dark. Thus all things set in order, then have they their hobby-horses, dragons and other antics, together with their bawdy pipers and thundering drummers to strike up the devil's dance withal. Then march these heathen company towards the church and church-yard, their pipers piping, their drummers thundering, their stumps dancing, their bells jingling, their handkerchiefs swinging about their heads like madmen, their hobby-horses and other monsters skirmishing amongst the throng: and in this sort they go to the church (I say) and into the church, (though the minister be at prayer or preaching), dancing and swinging their handkerchiefs, over their heads in the church, like devils incarnate, with such a confused noise, that no man can hear his own voice. Then, the foolish people they look, they stare, they laugh, they fleer, and mount upon forms and pews to see these goodly pageants solemnized in this sort. Then, after this, about the church they go again and again, and so forth into the church-yard, where they have commonly their summer-halls, their bowers, arbours, and banquetting houses set up, wherein they feast, banquet and dance all that day and (peradventure) all the night too. And thus these terrestrial furies spend the Sabbath day.

They have also certain papers, wherein is painted some babblery or other of imagery work, and these they call 'my Lord of Misrule's badges': these they give to every one that will give money for them to maintain them in their heathenry, devilry, whoredom, drunkenness, pride, and what not. And who will not show himself buxom to them, and give them money for these the devil's cognizances, they shall be mocked and flouted at shamefully. And so assotted are some, that they not only give them money to maintain their abomination withal, but also wear their badges and cognizances in their hats or caps openly. But let them take heed; for these are the badges, seals, brands, and cognizances of the devil, whereby he knoweth his servants and clients from the children of God, and so long as they wear them, *Sub vexillo diaboli militant contra Dominum et legem suam*: they fight under the banner and standard of the devil against Christ Jesus, and all his laws. Another sort of fantastical fools bring to these hell-hounds (the Lord of Misrule and his complices) some bread, some good ale, some new cheese, some old cheese, some custards, and cakes, some flawns, some tarts, some cream, some meat, some one thing, some another; but if they knew that as often as they bring anything to the maintainance of these execrable pastimes, they offer sacrifice to the devil and Sathanas, they would repent and withdraw their hands; which God grant they may!

PHILIP STUBBES, *The Anatomie of Abuses*, 1583 (2nd ed.)

The Country in Spring

I

When daisies pied and violets blue
And lady-smocks all silver-white
And cuckoo-buds of yellow hue
Do paint the meadows with delight,
The cuckoo then, on every tree,
Mocks married men; for thus sings he,
Cuckoo;
Cuckoo, cuckoo: O word of fear,
Unpleasing to a married ear!

II

When shepherds pipe on oaten straws,
And merry larks are ploughmen's clocks,
When turtles tread, and rooks, and daws,
And maidens bleach their summer smocks,
The cuckoo then, on every tree,
Mocks married men; for thus sings he,
Cuckoo;
Cuckoo, cuckoo: O word of fear,
Unpleasing to a married ear!

THE COUNTRYSIDE

The Country in Winter

I

When icicles hang by the wall,
  And Dick the shepherd blows his nail,
And Tom bears logs into the hall,
  And milk comes frozen home in pail,
When blood is nipp'd, and ways be foul,
Then nightly sings the staring owl,
                    Tu-who;
  Tu-whit, tu-who—a merry note,
  While greasy Joan doth keel the pot.

II

When all aloud the wind doth blow,
  And coughing drowns the parson's saw,
And birds sit brooding in the snow,
  And Marian's nose looks red and raw,
When roasted crabs hiss in the bowl,
Then nightly sings the staring owl,
                    Tu-who;
  Tu-whit, tu-who—a merry note,
  While greasy Joan doth keel the pot.

Love's Labour's Lost, **v.** ii. 902—937

CHAPTER III

SUPERSTITION

Horatio. O day and night, but this is wondrous strange!
Hamlet. And therefore as a stranger give it welcome.
There are more things in heaven and earth, Horatio,
Than are dreamt of in your philosophy.

Hamlet, I. v. 164—167

O ! these flaws and starts—
Impostors to true fear—would well become
A woman's story at a winter's fire,
Authoriz'd by her grandam. *Macbeth*, III. iv. 63—66

§ 1. The nature of superstition

Superstition is godless religion, devout impiety. The superstitious is fond in observation, servile in fear: he worships God, but as he lists: he gives God what he asks not, more than he asks, and all but what he should give; and makes more sins than the ten commandments. This man dares not stir forth, till his breast be crossed and his face sprinkled. If but a hare cross him the way, he returns; or, if his journey began unawares on the dismal day ; or, if he stumbled at the threshold. If he see a snake unkilled, he fears a mischief: if the salt fall towards him, he looks pale and red, and is not quiet, till one of the waiters have poured wine on his lap: and when he sneezeth, thinks them not his friends that uncover not. In the morning, he listens whether the crow crieth even or odd; and, by that token, presages of the weather. If he hear but a raven croak from the next roof, he makes his will; or, if a bittour fly over his head by night: but, if his troubled fancy shall second his thoughts with the dream of a fair garden, or green rushes, or the salutation of a dead friend, he takes leave of the world, and says he cannot live. He will never set to sea but on a Sunday; neither ever goes without an *Erra Pater* in his pocket. St. Paul's day, and St. Swithin's, with the Twelve, are his oracles; which he dares believe against the almanac. When he lies sick on his death-bed, no sin troubles him so much, as that he did once eat flesh on a Friday: no repentance can expiate that; the rest need none. There is no dream of his, without an interpretation, without a prediction; and, if the event answer not his exposition, he expounds it according to the event. Every dark grove and pictured wall strikes him with an awful, but carnal devotion. Old wives and stars are his counsellors: his nightspell is his guard; and charms, his physicians. He wears Paracelsian characters for the toothache : and a little hallowed wax is his antidote for all evils. This man is strangely credulous; and calls impossible things, miraculous. If he hear that some sacred block speaks, moves, weeps, smiles, his bare feet carry him thither with an offering; and, if a danger miss him in the way, his saint hath the thanks. Some ways he will not go; and some he dares not: either there are bugs, or he feigneth them: every lantern is a ghost, and every noise is of chains. He knows not why, but his custom is to go a little about, and to leave the cross still on the right-hand. One event is enough to make a rule: out of these rules he concludes fashions, proper to himself; and nothing can turn him out of his own course. If he have done his task, he is safe: it matters not, with what affection. Finally, if God would let him be the carver of his own obedience, he could not have a better subject: as he is, he cannot have a worse.

JOSEPH HALL, *Characters of Vertues and Vices* 1608

> The spirit that I have seen
> May be the devil : and the devil hath power
> To assume a pleasing shape ; yea, and perhaps
> Out of my weakness and my melancholy—
> As he is very potent with such spirits—
> Abuses me to damn me.   *Hamlet,* II. ii. 635—640

Many through melancholy do imagine, that they see or hear visions, spirits, ghosts, strange noises, &c.: as I have already proved before, at large. Many again through fear proceeding from a cowardly nature and complexion, or from an effeminate and fond bringing up, are timorous and afraid of spirits, and bugs, &c. Some through imperfection of sight also are afraid of their own shadows, and (as Aristotle saith) see themselves sometimes as it were in a glass. And some through weakness of body have such imperfect imaginations. Drunken men also sometimes suppose they see trees walk, &c.: according to that which Solomon saith to the drunkards: "Thine eyes shall see strange visions, and marvellous appearances."

REGINALD SCOT, *The Discoverie of Witchcraft* 1584

§ 2. Ghosts and Spirits

> Ghosts, wandering here and there,
> Troop home to churchyards: damned spirits all,
> That in cross-ways and floods have burial,
> Already to their wormy beds are gone;
> For fear lest day should look their shames upon,
> They wilfully themselves exile from light,
> And must for aye consort with black-brow'd night.
>
> *A Midsummer Night's Dream,* III. ii. 381—387

How many stories and books are written of walking spirits and souls of men, contrary to the word of God, a reasonable volume cannot contain. How common an opinion was it among the papists, that all souls walked on the earth, after they departed from their bodies? In so much as it was in the time of popery a usual matter to desire sick people in their death beds, to appear to them after their death, and to reveal their estate. The fathers and ancient doctors of the church were too credulous herein, &c. Therefore no marvel, though the common simple sort of men, and least of all that women be deceived herein. God in times past did send down visible angels and appearances to men; but now he doth not so. Through ignorance of late in religion, it was thought that every churchyard swarmed with souls and spirits: but now the word of God being more free, open, and known, those conceits and illusions are made more manifest and apparent....

And first you shall understand, that they hold that all the souls in heaven may come down and appear to us when they list, and assume any body saving their own: otherwise (say they)

31

such souls should not be perfectly happy. They say that you may know the good souls from the bad very easily. For a damned hath a very heavy and sour look; but a saint's soul hath a cheerful and a merry countenance: these also are white and shining, the other coal black. And these damned souls also may come up out of hell at their pleasure; although Abraham made Dives believe the contrary. They affirm that damned souls walk oftenest: next unto them the souls of purgatory; and most seldom the souls of saints. Also they say that in the old law souls did appear seldom; and after doomsday they shall never be seen more: in the time of grace they shall be most frequent. The walking of these souls (saith Michael Andreas) is a most excellent argument for the proof of purgatory: for (saith he) those souls have testified that which the popes have affirmed in that behalf; to wit, that there is not only such a place of punishment, but that they are released from thence by masses, and such other satisfactory works; whereby the goodness of the mass is also ratified and confirmed.

These heavenly and purgatory souls (say they) appear most commonly to them that are born upon ember days, and they also walk most usually on those ember days: because we are in best state at that time to pray for the one, and to keep company with the other. Also they say, that souls appear oftenest by night; because men may then be at best leisure, and most quiet. Also they never appear to the whole multitude, seldom to a few, and most commonly to one alone: for so one may tell a lie without controlment. Also they are oftenest seen by them that are ready to die.

REGINALD SCOT, The Discoverie of Witchcraft 1584

Exorcism

> I charge thee, Satan, hous'd within this man,
> To yield possession to my holy prayers.
> And to thy state of darkness hie thee straight:
> I conjure thee by all the saints in heaven.

The Comedy of Errors, IV. iv. 56—59

If a soul wander in the likeness of a man or woman by night, molesting men, with bewailing their torments in purgatory, by reason of tithes forgotten, &c.: and neither masses nor conjurations can help; the exorcist in his ceremonial apparel must go to the tomb of that body, and spurn thereat with his foot, saying: *"Vade ad gehennam,* Get thee packing to hell": and by and by the soul goeth thither, and there remaineth for ever.

REGINALD SCOT, *The Discoverie of Witchcraft* 1584

§ 3. Witchcraft

What are these,
So wither'd and so wild in their attire,
That look not like th' inhabitants o' the earth,
And yet are on 't? Live you? or are you aught
That man may question? You seem to understand me,
By each at once her choppy finger laying
Upon her skinny lips: you should be women,
And yet your beards forbid me to interpret
That you are so. *Macbeth,* I. iii. 39—47

King James and Witches in Scotland

First Witch. ...In a sieve I'll thither sail,
And, like a rat without a tail,
I'll do, I'll do, and I'll do.
Second Witch. I'll give thee a wind.
First Witch. Thou'rt kind.
Third Witch. And I another.
First Witch. I myself have all the other;

* * * *

Though his bark cannot be lost,
Yet it shall be tempest-tost. *Macbeth,* I. iii. 8—25

[It is well-known that *Macbeth* was written for the eye of King James. The following account of actual doings in Scotland seems to throw light upon Shakespeare's description of the witches.]

Within the town of Trenent, in the kingdom of Scotland, there dwelleth one David Seaton, who, being deputy bailiff in the said town, had a maid called Geillis Duncane, who used secretly to absent and lie forth of her master's house every other night. This Geillis Duncane took in hand to help all such as were troubled or grieved with any kind of sickness or infirmity, and in short space did perform many matters most miraculous; which things, for as much as she began to do them upon a sudden, having never done the like before, made her master and others to be in great admiration, and wondered thereat: by means whereof, the said David Seaton had his

W. c 33

maid in great suspicion that she did not those things by natural and lawful ways, but rather supposed it to be done by some extraordinary and unlawful means. Whereupon, her master began to grow very inquisitive, and examined her which way and by what means she was able to perform matters of so great importance; whereat she gave him no answer. Nevertheless, her master, to the intent that he might the better try and find out the truth of the same, did with the help of others torment her with the torture of the pilliwinks upon her fingers, which is a grievous torture; and binding or wrenching her head with a cord or rope, which is a most cruel torment also; yet would she not confess anything; whereupon, they suspecting that she had been marked by the devil, (as commonly witches are,) made diligent search about her, and found the enemy's mark to be in her fore crag, or fore part of her throat; which being found, she confessed that all her doings were done by the wicked allurements and enticements of the devil, and that she did them by witchcraft. After this her confession, she was committed to prison, where she continued a season, where immediately she accused these persons following to be notorious witches, and caused them forthwith to be apprehended, one after another, viz. Agnes Sampson, the eldest witch of them all, dwelling in Haddington; Agnes Tompson of Edinburgh; Doctor Fian alias John Cuningham, master of the school at Saltpans in Lothian....

The said Agnes Sampson was after brought again before the King's Majesty and his Council, and being examined of the meetings and detestable dealings of those witches, she confessed, that upon the night of All-hallow Even last, she was accompanied, as well with the persons aforesaid, as also with a great many other witches, to the number of two hundred, and that all they together went to sea, each one in a riddle or sieve, and went into the same very substantially, with flagons of wine, making merry and drinking by the way in the same riddles or sieves, to the kirk of North Berwick in Lothian; and that after they had landed, took hands on the land, and danced this reel or short dance, singing all with one voice,

> Commer go ye before, commer go ye,
> Gif ye will not go before, commer let me.

At which time she confessed, that this Geillis Duncane did go before them, playing this reel or dance, upon a small trump, called a Jew's trump, until they entered into the kirk of North Berwick.

These confessions made the King in a wonderful admiration, and he sent for the said Geillis Duncane, who upon the like trump did play the said dance before the King's Majesty, who in respect of the strangeness of these matters, took great delight to be present at their examinations.

The said Agnes Sampson confessed that the devil, being then at North Berwick kirk attending their coming, in the habit or likeness of a man, and seeing that they tarried over long, he at their coming enjoined them all to a penance, which was, that they should kiss his buttocks, in sign of duty to him; which being put over the pulpit bare, everyone did as he had enjoined them. And having made his ungodly exhortations, wherein he did greatly inveigh against the King of Scotland, he received their oaths for their good and true service towards him, and departed; which done, they returned to sea, and so home again. At which time, the witches demanded of the devil, 'Why he did bear such hatred to the King?' Who answered, 'By reason the King is the greatest enemy he hath in the world.' All which their confessions and depositions are still extant upon record.

The said Agnes Sampson confessed before the King's Majesty sundry things, which were so miraculous and strange, as that his Majesty said 'they were all extreme liars'; whereat she answered, 'she would not wish his Majesty to suppose her words to be false, but rather to believe them, in that she would discover such matter unto him as his Majesty should not anyway doubt of.' And thereupon taking his Majesty a little aside, she declared unto him the very words which passed between the King's Majesty and his Queen at Upslo in Norway, the first night of marriage, with the answer each to other; whereat the King's Majesty wondered greatly, and swore 'by the living God, that he believed all the devils in hell could not have discovered the same,' acknowledging her words to be most true; and therefore gave the more credit to the rest that is before declared.

Touching this Agnes Sampson, she is the only woman who, by the devil's persuasion, should have intended and put in execution the King's Majesty's death in this manner. She confessed that she took a black toad, and did hang the same up by the heels three days, and collected and gathered the venom as it dropped and fell from it in an oyster shell, and kept the same venom close covered, until she should obtain any part or piece of foul linen cloth that had appertained to the King's Majesty, as shirt, handkercher, napkin or any other thing, which she practised to obtain by means of one John Kers, who being attendant in his Majesty's chamber, desired him for old acquaintance between them, to help her to one, or a piece of such a cloth as is aforesaid; which thing the said John Kers denied to help her to saying he could not help her unto it. And the said Agnes Sampson, by her depositions since her apprehension, saith, that if she had obtained any one piece of linen cloth which the King had worn and fouled, she had bewitched him to death, and put him to such extraordinary pains, as if he had been lying upon sharp thorns and ends of needles. Moreover she confessed, that at the time when his Majesty was in Denmark, she being accompanied by the parties before specially named, took a cat and christened it, and afterward bound to each part of that cat, the chiefest part of a dead man, and several joints of his body: and that in the night following, the said cat was conveyed into the midst of the sea by all these witches, sailing in their riddles or sieves, as is aforesaid, and so left the said cat right before the town of Leith in Scotland. This done, there did arise such a tempest in the sea, as a greater hath not been seen; which tempest was the cause of the perishing of a boat or vessel coming from the town of Brunt Island to the town of Leith, wherein was sundry jewels and rich gifts, which should have been presented to the now Queen of Scotland, at her Majesty's coming to Leith. Again, it is confessed, that the said christened cat was the cause that the King's Majesty's ship, at his coming forth of Denmark, had a contrary wind to the rest of his ships then being in his company; which thing was most strange and true, as the King's Majesty acknowledgeth, for when the rest of the ships had a fair and good wind, then was the wind contrary and altogether against his Majesty; and further, the said witch declared, that his Majesty had never come safely from the sea, if his faith had not prevailed above their intentions.

WITCHCRAFT

The Witches' Cauldron

Double, double toil and trouble;
Fire burn and cauldron bubble.

Macbeth, IV. i. 10—11

Then he (the Devil) teacheth them to make ointments of the bowels and members of children, whereby they ride in the air, and accomplish all their desires. So as, if there be any children unbaptised, or not guarded with the sign of the cross, or orisons; then the witches may and do catch them from their mothers' sides in the night, or out of their cradles, or otherwise kill them with their ceremonies; and after burial steal them out of their graves, and seethe them in a cauldron, until their flesh be made potable. Of the thickest whereof they make ointments, whereby they ride in the air; but the thinner potion they put into flagons, whereof whosoever drinketh, observing certain ceremonies, immediately becometh a master or rather a mistress in that practice and faculty....

It shall not be amiss here in this place to repeat an ointment greatly to this purpose....The receipt is as followeth. R. The fat of young children, and seethe it with water in a brazen vessel, reserving the thickest of that which remaineth boiled in the bottom, which they lay up and keep, until occasion serveth to use it. They put hereunto *eleoselinum, aconitum, frondes populeas*, and soot. Another receipt to the same purpose. R. *Sium, acarum vulgare, pentaphyllon*, the blood of a flitter-mouse, *solanum somniferum, et oleum*. They stamp all these together, and then they rub all parts of their bodies exceedingly, till they look red, and be very hot, so as the pores may be opened, and their flesh soluble and loose. They join herewithal either fat, or oil instead thereof, that the force of the ointment may the rather pierce inwardly, and so be more effectual. By this means in a moonlight night they seem to be carried in the air, to feasting, singing, dancing, kissing, culling, and other acts of venery, with such youths as they love and desire most: for the force of their imagination is so vehement, that almost all that part of the brain, wherein the memory consisteth, is full of such conceits.

37

SUPERSTITION

And whereas they are naturally prone to believe any thing; so do they receive such impressions and steadfast imaginations into their minds, as even their spirits are altered thereby; not thinking upon any thing else, either by day or by night. And this helpeth them forward in their imaginations, that their usual food is none other commonly but beets, roots, nuts, beans, peas, &c.

REGINALD SCOT, *The Discoverie of Witchcraft* 1584

Transformation

Snout. O Bottom, thou art changed! what do I see on thee?
Bottom. What do you see? you see an ass-head of your own, do you?
Quince. Bless thee, Bottom! bless thee! thou art translated.

A Midsummer Night's Dream, III. i. 120—125

It happened in the city of Salamin, in the kingdom of Cyprus (wherein is a good haven) that a ship loaden with merchandize stayed there for a short space. In the mean time many of the soldiers and mariners went to shore, to provide fresh victuals. Among which number, a certain Englishman, being a sturdy young fellow, went to a woman's house, a little way out of the city, and not far from the sea side, to see whether she had any eggs to sell. Who perceiving him to be a lusty young fellow, a stranger, and far from his country (so as upon the loss of him there would be the less miss or inquiry) she considered with herself how to destroy him; and willed him to stay there awhile, whilst she went to fetch a few eggs for him. But she tarried long, so as the young man called unto her, desiring her to make haste: for he told her that the tide would be spent, and by that means his ship would be gone, and leave him behind. Howbeit, after some detracting of time, she brought him a few eggs, willing him to return to her, if his ship were gone when he came. The young fellow returned towards his ship: but before he went aboard, he would needs eat an egg or twain to satisfy his hunger, and within short space he became dumb and out of his wits (as he afterwards said). When he would have entered into the ship, the mariners beat him back with a cudgel, saying: "What a murrain lacks the ass? Whither the devil will this ass?" The ass or young man (I cannot tell by which name I should term him) being many

38

times repelled, and understanding their words that called him ass, considering that he could speak never a word, and yet could understand every body ; he thought that he was bewitched by the woman, at whose house he was. And therefore, when by no means he could get into the boat, but was driven to tarry and see her departure, being also beaten from place to place as an ass, he remembered the witch's words, and the words of his own fellows that called him ass, and returned to the witch's house, in whose service he remained by the space of three years, doing nothing with his hands all that while, but carried such burdens as she laid on his back; having only this comfort, that although he were reputed an ass among strangers and beasts, yet that both this witch, and all other witches knew him to be a man.

After three years were passed over, in a morning betimes he went to town before his dame, who upon some occasion (of like to make water) stayed a little behind. In the mean time being near to a church, he heard a little sacring bell ring to the elevation of a morrow mass, and not daring to go into the church, lest he should have been beaten and driven out with cudgels, in great devotion he fell down in the churchyard upon the knees of his hinder legs, and did lift his forefeet over his head, as the priest doth hold the sacrament at the elevation. Which prodigious sight when certain merchants of Genoa espied and with wonder beheld, anon cometh the witch with a cudgel in her hand, beating forth the ass. And because (as it hath been said) such kinds of witchcrafts are very usual in those parts, the merchants aforesaid made such means, as both the ass and the witch were attached by the judge. And she being examined and set upon the rack, confessed the whole matter, and promised, that if she might have liberty to go home, she would restore him to his old shape : and being dismissed, she did accordingly. So as notwithstanding, they apprehended again, and burned her : and the young man returned into his country with a joyful and merry heart.

REGINALD SCOT, *The Discoverie of Witchcraft* 1584

§ 4. Fairy-land

> But we are spirits of another sort.
> *A Midsummer Night's Dream*, III. ii. 388

> Either I mistake your shape and making quite
> Or else you are that shrewd and knavish sprite
> Call'd Robin Goodfellow : are you not he
> That frights the maidens of the villagery ;
> Skim milk, and sometimes labour in the quern
> And bootless make the breathless housewife churn ;
> And sometime make the drink to bear no barm ;
> Mislead night-wanderers, laughing at their harm ?
> Those that Hobgoblin call you and sweet Puck,
> You do their work, and they shall have good luck :
> Are not you he ? *ibid.* II. i. 32—42

[The little book from which the following extracts are taken, has been described as the most valuable and important contemporary illustration of *A Midsummer Night's Dream*. Though the first edition extant is dated 1628, it was probably written far earlier, and Shakespeare's masterpiece may owe something to it.]

How King Oberon called Robin Good-fellow to dance

King Oberon, seeing Robin Good-fellow do so many honest and merry tricks, called him one night out of his bed with these words, saying :

> *Robin, my son, come quickly rise :*
> *First stretch, then yawn, and rub your eyes ;*
> *For thou must go with me to-night,*
> *To see, and taste of my delight.*
> *Quickly come, my wanton son ;*
> *'Twere time our sports were now begun.*

Robin, hearing this, rose and went to him. There were with King Oberon a many fairies, all attired in green silk : all these, with King Oberon, did welcome Robin Good-fellow into their company. Oberon took Robin by the hand and led him a dance. Their musician was little Tom Thumb, for he had an excellent bag-pipe made of a wren's quill and the skin of a Greenland louse. This pipe was so shrill, and so sweet, that a Scottish pipe, compared to it, it would no more come near it, than a Jew's-trump doth to an Irish harp. After they had danced, King Oberon spake to his son, Robin Good-fellow, in this manner :

> *Whene'er thou hear my piper blow,*
> *From thy bed see that thou go;*
> *For nightly you must with us dance,*
> *When we in circles round do prance.*
> *I love thee, son, and by the hand*
> *I carry thee to Fairy Land,*
> *Where thou shalt see what no man knows:*
> *Such love to thee King Oberon owes.*

So marched they in good manner, with their piper before, to the Fairy Land : there did King Oberon shew Robin Good-fellow many secrets, which he never did open to the world.

How the fairies called Robin Good-fellow to dance with them, and how they shewed to him their several conditions

> Come unto these yellow sands,
>   And then take hands :
> Curtsied when you have, and kiss'd,—
>   The wild waves whist,—
> Foot it featly here and there ;
> And, sweet sprites, the burden bear.
>
> *The Tempest,* i. ii. 375—380

Robin Good-fellow, being walking one night, heard the excellent music of Tom Thumb's brave bag-pipe : he, remembering the sound, according to the command of King Oberon went toward them. They, for joy that he was come, did circle him in, and in a ring did dance round about him. Robin Good-fellow, seeing their love to him, danced in the midst of them, and sung them this song to the tune of *To him Bun.*

> *Round about, little ones, quick, quick and nimble,*
> *In and out, wheel about, run, hop, or amble.*
> *Join your hands lovingly : well done musician!*
> *Mirth keepeth man in health like a phisician.*
> *Elves, urchins, goblins all, and little fairies*
> *That do filch, black, and pinch maids of the dairies;*
> *Make a ring on the grass with your quick measures,*
> *Tom shall play, and I'll sing for all your pleasures.*

SUPERSTITION

Pinch and Patch, Gull and Grim,
Go you together,
For you can change your shapes
Like to the weather.
Sib and Tib, Lick and Lull,
You all have tricks, too;
Little Tom Thumb that pipes
Shall go betwixt you.
Tom, tickle up thy pipes
Till they be weary:
I will laugh, ho, ho, hoh!
And make me merry.
Make a ring on this grass
With your quick measures:
Tom shall play, I will sing
For all your pleasures.

The moon shines fair and bright,
And the owl holloas,
Mortals now take their rests
Upon their pillows:
The bats abroad likewise,
And the night raven,
Which doth use for to call
Men to Death's haven.
Now the mice peep abroad,
And the cats take them,
Now do young wenches sleep,
Till their dreams wake them.
Make a ring on the grass
With your quick measures:
Tom shall play, I will sing
For all your pleasures.

Thus danced they a good space. At last they left and sat down upon the grass, and to requite Robin Good-fellow's kindness, they promised to tell to him all the exploits that they were accustomed to do : Robin thanked them and listened to them, and one begun to tell his tricks in this manner.

FAIRY-LAND

The tricks of the fairy called Pinch

Pinch him, fairies, mutually;
Pinch him for his villany;
Pinch him, and burn him and turn him about,
Till candles and starlight and moonshine be out.
The Merry Wives of Windsor, v. v. 105—108

I am sent with broom before,
To sweep the dust behind the door.
A Midsummer Night's Dream, v. ii. 19—20

After that we have danced in this manner as you have beheld, I, that am called Pinch, do go about from house to house. Sometimes I find the doors of the house open. That negligent servant that left them so, I do so nip him or her, that with my pinches their bodies are as many colours as a mackerel's back. Then take I them, and lay them in the door, naked or unnaked I care not whether: there they lie, many times till broad day, ere they waken; and many times, against their wills, they shew some parts about them, that they would not have openly seen.

Sometimes I find a slut sleeping in the chimney corner, when she should be washing of her dishes, or doing something else which she hath left undone: her I pinch about the arms, for not laying her arms to her labour. Some I find in their bed snorting and sleeping, and their houses lying as clean as a nasty dog's kennel; in one corner bones, in another egg-shells, behind the door a heap of dust, the dishes under feet, and the cat in the cupboard: all these sluttish tricks I do reward with blue legs, and blue arms. I find some slovens too, as well as sluts: they pay for their beastliness too, as well as the women-kind; for if they uncase a sloven and not untie their points, I so pay their arms that they cannot sometimes untie them, if they would. Those that leave foul shoes, or go into their beds with their stockings on, I use them as I did the former, and never leave them till they have left their beastliness.

But to the good I do no harm,
But cover them, and keep them warm:
Sluts and slovens I do pinch,
And make them in their beds to wince.
This is my practice, and my trade.
Many have I cleanly made.

SUPERSTITION

The tricks of the fairy called Gull

She is the fairies' midwife, and she comes
In shape no bigger than an agate-stone
On the fore-finger of an alderman,
Drawn with a team of little atomies
Athwart men's noses as they lie asleep.

Romeo and Juliet, I. iv. 55—59

She as her attendant hath
A lovely boy, stol'n from an Indian king;
She never had so sweet a changeling.

A Midsummer Night's Dream, II. i. 21—23

When mortals keep their beds I walk abroad, and for my pranks am called by the name of Gull. I with a feigned voice do often deceive many men, to their great amazement. Many times I get on men and women, and so lie on their stomachs, that I cause them great pain, for which they call me by the name of Hag, or Night-mare. 'Tis I that do steal children, and in the place of them leave changelings. Sometimes I also steal milk and cream, and then with my brothers Patch, Pinch, and Grim, and sisters Sib, Tib, Lick, and Lull, I feast with my stolen goods. Our little piper hath his share in all our spoils, but he nor our women fairies do ever put themselves in danger to do any great exploit.

> *What Gull can do, I have you shown;*
> *I am inferior unto none.*
> *Command me, Robin, thou shalt know,*
> *That I for thee will ride or go:*
> *I can do greater things than these*
> *Upon the land, and on the seas.*

FAIRY-LAND

The tricks of the fairy called Grim

I'll follow you, I'll lead you about a round,
Through bog, through bush, through brake, through brier:
Sometime a horse I'll be, sometime a hound,
A hog, a headless bear, sometime a fire;
And neigh, and bark, and grunt, and roar, and burn,
Like horse, hound, hog, bear, fire, at every turn.

A Midsummer Night's Dream, III. i. 112—117

Where the bee sucks, there suck I:
In a cowslip's bell I lie;
There I couch when owls do cry.
On the bat's back do I fly
After summer merrily:
Merrily, merrily shall I live now
Under the blossom that hangs on the bough.

The Tempest, v. i. 88—94

I walk with the owl, and make many to cry as loud as she doth holloa. Sometimes I do affright many simple people, for which some have termed me the Black Dog of Newgate. At the meeting of young men and maids I many times am, and when they are in the midst of all their good cheer, I come in, in some fearful shape, and affright them, and then carry away their good cheer, and eat it with my fellow fairies. 'Tis I that do, like a screech-owl, cry at sick men's windows, which makes the hearers so fearful, that they say, that the sick person cannot live. Many other ways have I to fright the simple, but the understanding man I cannot move to fear, because he knows I have no power to do hurt.

My nightly business I have told,
To play these tricks I use of old:
When candles burn both blue and dim,
Old folks will say, Here's fairy Grim.
More tricks than these I use to do:
Hereat cry'd Robin, Ho, ho, hoh!

Robin Good-fellow; his mad prankes and merry jests 1628

SUPERSTITION

§ 5. Astrology

Soothsayer. Beware the ides of March.
Caesar. He is a dreamer; let us leave him: pass.

Julius Caesar, I. ii. 23—24

Edgar. How now, brother Edmund! What serious contemplation
are you in?
Edmund. I am thinking, brother, of a prediction I read this other
day, what should follow these eclipses.
Edgar. Do you busy yourself with that?
Edmund. I promise you the effects he writes of succeed unhappily;
as of unnaturalness between the child and the parent; death, dearth,
dissolutions of ancient amities; divisions in state; menaces and maledic-
tions against king and nobles; needless diffidences, banishment of friends,
dissipation of cohorts, nuptial breaches, and I know not what.
Edgar. How long have you been a sectary astronomical?

King Lear, I. ii. 155—170

A Mock Prognostication

The eclipse of the sun according to Proclus' opinion is
like to produce many hot and pestilent infirmities, especially
amongst summoners and pettifoggers, whose faces being combust
with many fiery inflamatives shall show ye dearth that by
their devout drinking is like to ensue of barley, if violent
death take not away such consuming maltworms....And Mars
being placed near unto the sun sheweth that there shall be
a great death among people. Old women that can live no
longer shall die for age: and young men that have usurers to
their father shall this year have great cause to laugh, for the
devil hath made a decree, that after they are once in hell, they
shall never rise again to trouble their executors. Beside that by
all conjectural arguments the influence of Mars shall be so
violent, that divers soldiers in parts beyond the seas, shall fall
out for want of their pay, and here in our meridional clime,
great quarrels shall be raised between man and man, especially
in cases of law. Gentry shall go check-mate with justice, and
coin out countenance ofttimes equity*. The poor sitting on
penniless bench, shall sell their coats to strive for a straw, and

* See Glossary under "Checkmate."

46

lawyers laugh such fools to scorn as cannot keep their crowns in their purses....

It is further to be feared, that because the eclipse happeneth in July, there will through the extreme heat grow such abundance of fleas, that women shall not go to bed before twelve o'clock at night, for the great murders and stratagems they are like to commit upon those little animals.

And whereas this eclipse falleth out at three of the clock in the afternoon, it foresheweth that many shall go soberer into taverns than they shall come out: and that he which drinks hard and lies cold, shall never die of the sweat; although Gemini, combust and retrograde, sheweth that some shall have so sore a sweating, that they may sell their hair by the pound to stuff tennis balls. But if the beadles of Bridewell be careful this summer, it may be hoped that Petticoat Lane may be less pestered with ill airs than it was wont: and the houses there so clear cleansed, that honest women may dwell there without any dread of the whip and the cart....

But here by the way, gentle reader, note that this eclipse sheweth that this year shall be some strange births of children produced in some monstrous form, to the great grief of the parents, and fearful spectacle of the beholders: but because the eclipse chanceth southerly, it is little to be feared that the effects shall fall in England: yet somewhat it is to be doubted, that divers children shall be born, that when they come to age shall not know their own fathers. Some shall be born with feet like unto hares, that they shall run so swift, that they shall never tarry with master, but trudge from post to pillar, till they take up Beggars' Bush for their lodging. Others shall have noses like swine, that there shall not be a feast within a mile, but they shall smell it out. But especially it is to be doubted, that divers women this year shall be born with two tongues, to the terrible grief of such as shall marry them, uttering in their fury such rough-cast eloquence, that 'knave' and 'slave' shall be but holiday words to their husbands. And whereas this fearful eclipse doth continue but an hour and a half, it signifieth that this year women's love to their husbands shall be very short, sometimes so momentary, that it shall scarce continue from the church door to the wedding house: and that hens, capons, geese, and other pullin shall little haunt poor men's tables, but

47

fly away with spits in their bellies to fat churls' houses, that pamper themselves up with delicates and dainties. Although very few other effects are to be prognosticated, yet let me give this caveat to my countrymen, as a clause to this wonderful eclipse. Let such as have clothes enow, keep themselves warm from taking cold: and I would wish rich men all this winter to sit by a good fire, and hardly to go to bed without a cup of sack, and that so qualified with sugar, that they prove not rheumatic: let them feed daintily and take ease enough, and no doubt according to the judgment of Albumazar, they are like to live as long as they can, and not to die one hour before their time.

THOMAS NASHE? *A wonderful astrological prognostication* 1591

CHAPTER IV

EDUCATION

> At first the infant,
> Mewling and puking in the nurse's arms.
> And then the whining schoolboy, with his satchel
> And shining morning face, creeping like snail
> Unwillingly to school.
>
> *As You Like It*, II. vii. 143—147

§ 1. Child and parent

Two views of childhood
(a) *A humourist's*

A child is a man in a small letter, yet the best copy of Adam before he tasted of Eve or the apple; and he is happy, whose small practice in the world can only write his character. He is nature's fresh picture newly drawn in oil, which time and much handling dims and defaces. His soul is yet a white paper unscribbled with observations of the world, wherewith at length it becomes a blurred note-book. He is purely happy because he knows no evil, nor hath made means by sin to be acquainted with misery. He arrives not at the mischief of being wise, nor endures evils to come by foreseeing them. He kisses and loves all, and when the smart of the rod is past, smiles on his beater. Nature and his parents alike dandle him, and tice him on with a bait of sugar to a draught of worm-wood. He plays yet, like a young prentice the first day, and is not come to his task of melancholy. All the language he speaks yet is tears, and they serve him well enough to express his necessity. His hardest labour is his tongue, as if he were loth to use so deceitful an organ; and he is best company with it when he can but prattle. We laugh at his foolish sports, but his game is our earnest: and his drums, rattles, and hobby-horses but the emblems and mocking of men's business. His father hath writ him as his own little story, wherein he reads those days of his life that he cannot remember; and sighs to see what innocence he has out-lived. The elder he grows, he is a stair lower from God, and like his first father much worse in his breeches. He is the Christian's example, and the old man's relapse. The one imitates his pureness, and the other falls into his simplicity. Could he put off his body with his little coat, he had got eternity without a burden, and exchanged but one heaven for another.

JOHN EARLE, *Micro-cosmographie* 1628

(b) A puritan's
Meditations of the misery of infancy

What wast thou being an infant but a brute, having the shape of a man? Was not thy body conceived in the heat of lust, the secret of shame, and stain of original sin? And thus wast thou cast naked upon the earth, all imbrued in the blood of filthiness, (filthy indeed when the Son of God, who disdained not to take on him man's nature and the infirmities thereof, yet thought it unbeseeming his Holiness to be conceived after the sinful manner of man's conception): so that thy mother was ashamed to let thee know the manner thereof. What cause then hast thou to boast of thy birth, which was a cursed pain to thy mother, and to thyself the entrance into a troublesome life? The greatness of which miseries, because thou couldest not utter in words, thou diddest express (as well as thou couldest) in weeping tears.

Meditations of the miseries of youth

What is youth, but an untamed beast? All whose actions are rash, and rude, not capable of good counsel when it is given; and ape-like, delighting in nothing but in toys and baubles? Therefore thou no sooner begannest to have a little strength and discretion, but forthwith thou wast kept under the rod and fear of parents and masters: as if thou hadst been born to live under the discipline of others, rather than at the disposition of thine own will. No tired horse was ever more willing to be rid of his burden, than thou wast to get out of the servile state of this bondage—a state not worth the description.

LEWES BAYLY, *Practice of Pietie* 1612

CHILD AND PARENT

Of parents and children

The joys of parents are secret, and so are their griefs and fears. They cannot utter the one, nor they will not utter the other. Children sweeten labours, but they make misfortunes more bitter. They increase the cares of life, but they mitigate the remembrance of death. The perpetuity by generation is common to beasts, but memory, merit and noble works are proper to men; and surely a man shall see the noblest works and foundations have proceeded from childless men, which have sought to express the images of their minds, when those of their body have failed. So the care of posterity is most in them that have no posterity. They that are the first raisers of their houses are most indulgent towards their children; beholding them as the continuance, not only of their kind, but of their work; and so both children and creatures.

The difference in affection of parents towards their several children is many times unequal, and sometimes unworthy, especially in the mother; as Solomon saith, 'A wise son rejoiceth the father, but an ungracious son shames the mother.' A man shall see, where there is a house full of children, one or two of the eldest respected and the youngest made wantons; but, in the middest, some there are, as it were forgotten, who many times nevertheless prove the best. The illiberality of parents, in allowance towards their children, is an harmful error, makes them base, acquaints them with shifts, makes them sort with mean company, and makes them surfeit more when they come to plenty. And therefore the proof is best, where men keep their authority towards their children, but not their purse. Men have a foolish manner (both parents, and school-masters, and servants) in creating and breeding an emulation between brothers during childhood which many times sorteth to discord when they are men, and disturbeth families. The Italians make little difference between children and nephews or near kinsfolks. But, so they be of the lump, they care not though they pass not through their own body. And to say truth, in Nature it is much a like matter. In so much that we see a nephew sometimes resembleth an uncle, or a kinsman, more than his own parent, as the blood happens.

Let parents choose betimes the vocations and courses they mean their children should take; for then they are most flexible. And let them not too much apply themselves to the disposition of their children, as thinking they will take best to that, which they have most mind to. It is true that if the affection or aptness of the children be extraordinary, then it is good not to cross it. But generally the precept is good : *optimum elige, suave et facile illud faciet consuetudo.* Younger brothers are commonly fortunate, but seldom or never where the elder are disinherited.

FRANCIS BACON, Essays 1597—1625

§ 2. The Grammar school

Mrs Quickly. Mistress Ford desires you to come suddenly.

Mrs Page. I'll be with her by and by : I'll but bring my young man here to school. Look, where his master comes ; 'tis playing-day, I see. How now, Sir Hugh ! no school to-day ?

Evans. No ; Master Slender is get the boys leave to play.

Mrs Quick. Blessing of his heart !

Mrs Page. Sir Hugh, my husband says my son profits nothing in the world at his book : I pray you ask him some questions in his accidence.

Evans. Come hither, William ; hold up your head ; come.

Mrs Page. Come on, sirrah ; hold up your head ; answer your master, be not afraid.

Evans. William, how many numbers is in nouns ?

William. Two.

* * * * * * *

Evans. Show me now, William, some declensions of your pronouns.

William. Forsooth, I have forgot.

Evans. It is *qui, quae, quod*; if you forget your *quis*, your *quaes*, and your *quods*, you must be preeches. Go your ways and play ; go.

Mrs Page. He is a better scholar than I thought he was.

Evans. He is a good sprag memory. Farewell, Mistress Page.

The Merry Wives of Windsor, IV. i.

An interesting parallel

[Shakespeare was an exact contemporary of Willis. Like him, he is supposed to have received no education save that provided by a free grammar school. Like him, too, he found it quite sufficient for his needs in later life.]

It was not my happiness to be bred up at the university, but all the learning I had was in the free grammar school, called Christ's school in the city of Gloucester; yet even there it pleased God to give me an extraordinary help by a new schoolmaster brought thither, one Master Gregory Downhale of Pembroke Hall in Cambridge, after I had lost some time under his predecessor. This Master Downhale having very convenient lodgings over the school, took such liking to me, as he made me his bedfellow (my father's house being next of all to the school). This bedfellowship begat in him familiarity and gentleness towards me; and in me towards him reverence and love; which made me also love my book, love being the most prevalent affection in nature to further our studies and endeavours in any profession. He came thither but bachelor of arts, a good scholar, and who wrote both the secretary and the Italian hands exquisitely well. But after a few years that he had proceeded master of arts, finding the school's entertainment not worthy of him, he left it, and betook himself to another course of being secretary to some nobleman, and at last became secretary to the worthy Lord Chancellor Ellesmere, and in that service (as I think) died. And myself, his scholar, following his steps, as near as I could, (though furnished with no more learning than he taught me in that grammar school) came at last to be secretary to the Lord Brooke, Chancellor of the Exchequer; and after that to my much honoured Lord, the Earl of Middlesex, Lord high Treasurer of England; and lastly to the most worthy, my most noble Lord, the Lord Coventry, Lord-keeper of the great seal, in whose service I expect to end my days. And this I note, that though I were no graduate of the university, yet (by God's blessing) I had so much learning as fitted me for the places whereunto the Lord advanced me, and (which I think to be very rare) had one that was after a Lord Chancellor's secretary to be my schoolmaster, whom (by God's blessing) I followed so close, that I became a successor to his successors in the like place of eminent service and employment.

R. WILLIS (b. 1564), *Mount Tabor* 1639

The School Day

Philoponus. The school-time should begin at six....

Spoudeus. Would you then have the master and usher present so early?

Philoponus. The usher should necessarily be there to be present amongst them, though he follow his own private study that hour, yet to see that all the scholars do their duties appointed, and that there be no disorder: which will be, unless he or some other of authority be amongst them. For otherwise the best children, left to their own liberty, will shew themselves children. If the master be present at seven it may suffice, where there is any in his place, whose presence they stand in awe of.

Spoudeus. But it is hard for the little children to rise so early, and in some families all lie long: how would you have have them come so soon then? You would not have them beaten every time they come over-late, as the custom is in some schools.

Philoponus. That I take far too great severity and whereby many a poor child is driven into wonderful fear, and either to play the truant, or make some device to leave the school; at least to come with a marvellous ill will, and oft to be dragged to school, to the reproach of the master and the school. The best means that ever I could find to make them to rise early, to prevent all this fear of whipping, is this: by letting the little ones to have their places in their forms daily, according to their coming after six of the clock. So many as are there at six, to have their places as they had them by election on the day before. All who come after six, every one to sit as he cometh, and so to continue that day and until he recover his place again by the election of the form or otherwise. Thus deal with them at all times, after every intermission, when they are to be in their places again and you shall have them ever attending who to be first in his place. So greatly even children are provoked by the credit of their places. If any cannot be brought by this, then to be noted in the black bill by a special mark, and feel the punishment thereof: and sometimes present correction to be used for terror; though this (as I said) to be more seldom, for making them to fear coming to the school.

The higher scholars must of necessity rest to do their exercises, if their exercises be strictly called for. Thus they are to continue until nine, signified by monitors, subdoctor, or otherwise. Then at nine I find that order which is in Westminster to be far the best; to let them to have a quarter of an hour at least, or more for intermission, either for breakfast, for all who are near unto the school, that can be there within the time limited, or else for the necessity of everyone, or their honest recreation, or to prepare their exercises against the master's coming in.

After, each of them to be in his place in an instant upon the knocking of the door or some other sign given by the subdoctor or monitors, in pain of loss of his place, or further punishment, as was noted before; so to continue until eleven of the clock; or somewhat after, to countervail the time of the intermission at nine.

To be again all ready and in their places at one, in an instant; to continue until three or half an hour after: then to have another quarter of an hour or more, as at nine, for drinking and necessities. So to continue till half an hour after five, thereby in that half hour to countervail the time at three. Then to end so as was showed, with reading a piece of a chapter and with singing two staves of a psalm: lastly with prayer to be used by the master. For the psalms, every scholar should begin to give the psalm and the time in order, and to read every verse before them; or every one to have his book (if it can be) and read it as they do sing it. Where anyone cannot begin the time, his next fellow beneath is to help him and take his place. By this they will all learn to give the tunes sweetly which is a thing very commendable; and also it will help reading, voice and audacity in the younger.

Spoudeus. But these intermissions at nine and three may be offensive. They who know not the manner of them may reproach the school, thinking that they do nothing but play.

Philoponus. We are, so much as may be, in all things to avoid offence. But when by long custom the order is once made known, it will be no more offensive than it is at Westminster, or than it is at noon and night; so that it be done in a decent order.

The benefits of such intermissions will be found very great and to prevent many inconveniences.

1. By this means neither masters nor scholars shall be over-toiled, but have fit times of refreshing. For there is none (no not almost of the least) but being used to it a while, they will sit very well in their places for two hours together, or two hours and a half, without any weariness or necessity, observing duly those times.

2. By this means also the scholars may be kept ever in their places, and hard to their labours, without that running out to the campo (as they term it) at school times, and the manifold

disorders thereof; as watching and striving for the club and loitering then in the fields, some hindered that they cannot go forth at all. But hereby all may have their free liberty in due time; and none can abuse their liberty in that sort, nor have their minds drawn away, nor stir abroad all the day at school times, except upon some urgent necessity, to be signified to the master or usher; and so leave to be gotten privately, to return presently again. And also in those cases to loose their places for that day, unless the case be approved very necessary and sure; to the end to cut off occasions from such as will pretend necessities. If any one be catched abusing his master or his liberty, without necessity only, upon desire of idleness or play, he is to be corrected sharply for ensample. By this means you shall bring them to that order and obedience in a short time, as they will not think of stirring all the day, but at their times appointed, or upon very urgent and almost extraordinary necessity.

3. Besides these benefits, this will also gain so so much time every day, as is lost in those intermissions; because there is no day but they will all look for so much time or more to the campo: especially as the shrewdest boys, who use to wait for the club, and watch their times, these will be sure to have much more than that. Besides all the time which they lose in waiting for that idle fit and that, they will, if they can, be away at lectures, and shewing exercises: and likewise they will exceedingly trouble the master in asking three or four sometimes together, what business soever he be about.

Spoudeus. I have been well acquainted with these disorders of the campo, and vexed with them many a time. I shall be most glad, if I may thus reform them and find these benefits instead thereof. But what say you for their recreations? Let me also hear your judgment in them: for I see that you would have in like manner a special regard to be kept thereof.

Philoponus. I would indeed have their recreations as well looked unto, as their learning; as you may perceive plainly by their intermissions at nine and at three. Besides those and all other their intermissions, it is very requisite also, that they should have weekly one part of an afternoon for recreation, as a reward of their diligence, obedience and profiting: and that to be appointed at the master's discretion, either the Thursday after the usual custom, or according to the best opportunity of the place. That also to be procured by some verses made by the victors, as was shewed: and then only when there hath been already no play-day in the week before nor holy day in all the week...

All recreations and sports of scholars would be meet for gentlemen. Clownish sports, or perilous, or yet playing for money are no way to be admitted. The recreations of the studious are as well to be looked unto, as the study of the rest: that none take hurt by his study, either for mind or body, or any way else.

Yet here of the other side, very great care is to be had in the moderating of their recreation. For schools, generally, do not take more hindrance by any one thing, than by over-often leave to play. Experience teacheth, that this draweth their minds utterly away from their books, that they cannot take pains, for longing after play and talking of it; as also devising means to procure others to get leave to play: so that ordinarily when they are but in hope thereof, they will do things very negligently; and after the most play they are evermore far the worst.

JOHN BRINSLEY, *Ludus Literarius or the Grammar Schoole* 1612

Punishment

Philoponus. For inflicting punishments we ought to come thereunto unwillingly, and even enforced; and therefore to proceed by degrees: that who cannot be moved by any of the former means of preferments nor encouragements nor any gentle exhortation nor admonition, may be brought into order and obedience by punishment. And therefore, first to begin with the lesser kinds of punishments; and so by degrees to the highest and severest, after this manner observing carefully the natures of everyone, as was said:

1. To use reproofs; and those sometimes more sharp according to the nature of the offender and his fault.

2. To punish by loss of place to him who doth better according to our discretion.

3. To punish by a note, which may be called the black bill. This I would have the principal punishment, I mean most of use. For you shall find by experience, that it being rightly used, it is more available than all other, to keep all in

obedience; and specially for any notoriously idle or stubborn, or which are of evil behaviour any way. The manner of it may be thus. To keep a note in writing, or, which may more easily be done, to keep a remembrance of all whom you observe very negligent, stubborn, lewd, or any way disobedient, to restrain them from all liberty of play. And therefore to give them all to know so much beforehand, that whosoever asketh leave to play, or upon what occasion soever, yet we intend always to except all such; and that liberty is granted only for the painful and obedient which are worthy to have the privileges of scholars and of the school, because they are such, and are an ornament to the school: not for them who are a disgrace unto it.

So always at such playing times before the exeats, the master and ushers to view every form through; and then to cause them all to sit still whom they remember to have been negligent or faulty in any special sort worthy of punishment, and to do some exercises in writing besides; either those which they have omitted before or such as wherein they cannot be idle. But herein there must be a special care when they are thus restrained from play, that either master or usher, if it can be conveniently, have an eye to them, that they cannot loiter; or some one specially appointed, to see that they do their tasks. Also that they be called to an account the next morning whether they have done the tasks enjoined, under pain of six jerks to be surely paid.

Moreover for all those who are notoriously stubborn or negligent or have done any gross fault, to cause them to sit thus, not only one day but every play-day continually, until they shew themselves truly sorry for their faults, and to amend; becoming as dutiful and submiss as any other; and until they do declare by good signs their desire and purpose to please and obey their master; unless they be released at very great suit or upon sufficient sureties of their fellows to incur otherwise their penalty if they amend not. This course straitly observed, partly through the shame of being noted in the rank of disordered fellows and also lest their parents should know it; and partly through depriving them of play and more also through this strict account to be given of their tasks, and severity of correction otherwise, will more tame the stubbornest and proudest, through God's blessing, than any correction by rod: and this without danger to the scholar, or offence to their friends. And therefore, when rod and all other means fail, let us look carefully to this, not to leave one stubborn boy, until he be brought as submiss and dutiful as any of the rest. For, those being brought into obedience, the rest may easily be kept in order, with very little correction: whereas one stubborn boy suffered will spoil, or at leastwise endanger all the rest.

4. Sometimes in greater faults, to give three or four jerks with a birch, or with a small red willow where birch cannot be had. Or for terror in some notorious fault, half a dozen stripes or more, soundly laid on, according to the discretion of the master. Some do only keep a bill, and note carefully their several principal disorders; and now and then, shew them their names and faults mildly, how oft they have been admonished, and when they take them in hand pay them soundly and by this policy keep them in great obedience.

In this correction with the rod, special provision must be had for sundry things.

I. That when you are to correct any stubborn or unbroken boy, you may be sure with him to hold him fast; as they are enforced to do, who are to shoe or to tame an unbroken colt. To this end appoint three or four of your scholars, whom you know to be honest, and strong enough, or more if need be, to lay hands upon him together, to hold him fast, over some form, so that he cannot stir hand nor foot; or else if no other remedy will serve, to hold him to some post (which is far the safest and free from inconvenience) so as he cannot anyway hurt himself or others, be he never so peevish. Neither that he can have hope by any device or turning, or by his apparel, or any other means to escape. Nor yet that any one be left in his stubbornness to go away murmuring, pouting, or blowing and puffing, until he shew as much submission as any, and that he will lie still of himself without any holding; yet so as ever a wise moderation be kept. Although this must of necessity be looked unto; because besides the evil example to others, there is no hope to do any good to count of with any, till their stomachs be first broken: and then they once thoroughly brought under, you may have great hope to work all good according to their capacity; so that it may be, you shall have little occasion to correct them after. Moreover every child suffered in his stubbornness to escape for his struggling, will in a short time come to trouble two or three men to take him up and to correct him without danger of hurting himself, or others.

II. To be wary for smiting them over the backs, in any case, or in such sort as in any way to hurt or endanger them. To the end to prevent all mischiefs, for our own comfort; and to cut off all occasions from quarrelling parents or evil reports of the school. And withal, to avoid for these causes, all smiting them upon the head, with hand, rod or ferula. Also to the end that we may avoid all danger and fear for desperate boys hurting themselves, not to use to threaten them afore, and when they have done any notorious fault, nor to let them know when they shall be beaten; but when they commit a new fault, or that we see the school most full or opportunity most fit, to take them of a sudden.

III. That the master do not in any case abase himself to strive or struggle with any boy to take him up: but to appoint other of the strongest to do it, where such need is, in such sort as was shewed before; and the rather for fear of hurting them in his anger, and for the evils which may come thereof and which some schoolmasters have lamented after.

IV. That the masters and ushers also do by all means avoid all furious anger, threatening, chasing, fretting, reviling: for these things will diminish authority and may do much hurt, and much endanger many ways. And therefore on the contrary, that all their correction be done with authority, and with a wise and sober moderation, in a demonstration of duty to God and love to the children, for their amendment, and the reformation of their evil manners.

Finally, as God hath sanctified the rod and correction, to cure the evils of their conditions, to drive out that folly which is bound up in their hearts, to save their souls from hell, to give them wisdom; so it is to be used as God's instrument to these purposes. To spare them in these cases is to hate them. To love them is to correct them betime. Do it under God, and for Him to these ends and with these cautions, and you shall never hurt them: you have the Lord for your warrant.

Correction in such manner, for stubbornness, negligence and carelessness, is not to be accounted over-great severity, much less cruelty...

Spoudeus. I like your advice wonderful well herein: but when would you have the time of common punishment to be inflicted; as namely that for their misdemeanors in the church, or other gross faults noted by the monitors?

Philoponus. I would have this done commonly at the giving up of the monitors' bills, some day before prayer; sometimes one day sometimes another: and when the master finds the greatest company present, then to call for the monitors of that week; lest keeping a set time, any absent themselves by feigned excuses or otherwise, or cry unto their parents, that they dare not go to the school, because they must be beaten. But for extreme negligence, or other faults in the school, the very fittest time is immediately before the breaking up, upon the play-days; then if needs so require, first to whip all the stubborn and notoriously negligent, as also those who have done any gross fault: and after to cause them to sit, and do some exercises, whereof they are to give a strict account, as I said. This will surely by God's blessing tame the proudest of them in time and bring them to be as submiss as the least child; as experience will manifest.

Spoudeus. But what if you have any, whom you cannot yet reform of their ungraciousness or loitering and whom you can do no good withal, no not by all these means? As some there are ever in all schools extremely untoward.

Philoponus. These I would have some way removed from the school; at least by giving the parents notice and entreating them to employ them some other way; that neither other be hurt by their example, nor they be a reproach to the school, nor yet we be enforced to use that severity with them which they will deserve. But keep these courses strictly, and you shall see that they will either amend, or get away of themselves, by one means or other; I mean by some device to their parents to leave the school, and to go to some other employment.

JOHN BRINSLEY, *Ludus Literarius or the Grammar Schoole* 1612

EDUCATION

Country Schoolmasters

Sir, I praise the Lord for you, and so may my parishioners; for their sons are well tutored by you, and their daughters profit very greatly under you: you are a good member of the commonwealth.

Love's Labour's Lost, IV. ii. 75—79

If they be well gowned and bearded, they have two good apologies ready made; but they are beholden to the tailor and barber for both: if they can provide for two pottles of wine against the next lecture-day, the school being void, there are great hopes of preferment: if he gets the place, his care next must be for the demeanour of his countenance: he looks over his scholars with as great and grave a countenance, as the emperor over his army. He will not at first be over busy to examine his usher, for fear he should prove, as many curates, better scholars than the chief master. As he sits in his seat, he must with a grace turn his mustachios up; his sceptre lies not far from him, the rod: he uses martial law most, and the day of execution ordinarily is the Friday: at six o'clock his army all begin to march; at eleven they keep rendezvous, and at five or six at night, they take up their quarters. There are many set in authority to teach youth, which never had much learning themselves; therefore if he cannot teach them, yet his looks and correction shall affright them. But there are some who deserve the place by their worth and wisdom, who stayed with their mother the university, until learning, discretion and judgment had ripened them for the well-managing of a school. These I love, respect, and wish that they may have good means either here, or somewhere else. These come from the sea of learning, well furnished with rich prizes of knowledge and excellent qualities, ballasted they are well with gravity and judgment, well steered by religion and a good conscience. And these abilities make them the only fit men to govern and instruct tender age; he learns the cradle to speak several languages and fits them for places of public note: being thus qualified, 'tis pity he should either want means or employment.

DONALD LUPTON, *London and the Countrey carbonadoed* 1632

THE UNIVERSITY

§ 3. The University

Some to the studious universities.
The Two Gentlemen of Verona, I. iii. 10

Study is like the heaven's glorious sun,
That will not be deep-search'd with saucy looks;
Small have continual plodders ever won,
Save base authority from others' books.
Love's Labour's Lost, I. i. 84—87

The Universities of England

In my time there are three noble universities in England, to wit, one at Oxford, the second at Cambridge and the third in London, of which the first two are the most famous, I mean Cambridge and Oxford, for that in them the use of the tongues, philosophy and the liberal sciences, beside the profound studies of the civil law, physic and theology are daily taught and had: whereas in the latter the laws of the realm are only read and learned by such as give their minds unto the knowledge of the same. In the first also there are not only divers goodly houses builded four square for the most part of hard freestone or brick, with great numbers of lodgings and chambers in the same for students, after a sumptuous manner, through the exceeding liberality of kings, queens, bishops, noblemen and ladies of the land; but also large livings and great revenues bestowed upon them (the like whereof is not to be seen in any other region, as Peter Martyr did oft affirm) to the maintainance only of such convenient numbers of poor men's sons as the several stipends bestowed upon the said houses are able to support....

The manner to live in these universities is not as in some other of foreign countries we see daily to happen, where the students are enforced for want of such houses to dwell in common inns and taverns, without all order or discipline. But in these our colleges we live in such exact order, and under so precise rules of government, as that the famous learned man Erasmus of Rotterdam, being here among us fifty years past, did not let to compare the trades in living of students in these two places even with the very rules and orders of the

63

ancient monks, affirming moreover, in flat words, our orders to be such as not only came near unto, but rather far exceeded, all the monastical institutions that ever were devised.

In most of our colleges there are also great numbers of students, of which many are found by the revenues of the houses and other by the purveyances and help of their rich friends, whereby in some one college you shall have two hundred scholars, in others an hundred and fifty, in divers a hundred and forty, and in the rest less numbers, as the capacity of the said houses is able to receive: so that at this present, of one sort and other, there are about three thousand students nourished in them both (as by a late survey it manifestly appeared). They were erected by their founders at the first only for poor men's sons, whose parents were not able to bring them up unto learning; but now they have the least benefit of them, by reason the rich do so encroach upon them. And so far hath this inconvenience spread itself that it is in my time an hard matter for a poor man's child to come by a fellowship (though he be never so good a scholar and worthy of that room). Such packing also is used at elections that not he which best deserveth, but he that hath most friends, though he be the worst scholar, is always surest to speed; which will turn in the end to the overthrow of learning. That some gentlemen also, whose friends have been in times past benefactors to certain of those houses, do intrude into the disposition of their estates without all respect of order or statutes devised by the founders, only thereby to place whom they think good (and not without some hope of gain), the case is too too evident: and their attempt would soon take place if their superiors did not provide to bridle their endeavours. In some grammar schools likewise which send scholars to these universities, it is lamentable to see what bribery is used; for, ere the scholar can be preferred, such bribage is made that poor men's children are commonly shut out, and the richer sort received (who in time past thought it dishonour to live as it were upon alms), and yet, being placed, most of them study little other than histories, tables, dice, and trifles, as men that make not living by their study the end of their purposes, which is a lamentable hearing. Beside this, being for the most part either gentlemen or rich men's sons, they oft bring the universities into much slander. For, standing upon their reputation and liberty, they ruffle and roist it out, exceeding in apparel and haunting riotous company (which draweth them from their books unto another trade) ; and for excuse, when they are charged with breach of all good order, think it sufficient to say that they be gentlemen, which grieveth many not a little.

WILLIAM HARRISON, *Description of England* 1587 (2nd ed.)

The life at Oxford

The students lead a life almost monastic ; for as the monks had nothing in the world to do but, when they had said their prayers at stated hours, to employ themselves in instructive studies, no more have these. They are divided into three tables. The first is called the fellows' table, to which are admitted earls, barons, gentlemen, doctors and masters of arts, but very few of the latter ; this is more plentifully and expensively served than the others. The second is for masters of arts, bachelors, some gentlemen, and eminent citizens. The third for people of low condition. While the rest are at dinner or supper in a great hall, where they are all assembled, one of the students reads aloud the Bible, which is placed on a desk in the middle of the hall, and this office everyone of them takes upon himself in his turn. As soon as grace is said after each meal, everyone is at liberty, either to retire to his own chambers, or to walk in the college garden, there being none that has not a delightful one. Their habit is almost the same as that of the Jesuits, their gowns reaching down to their ankles, sometimes lined with fur ; they wear square caps ; the doctors, masters of arts and professors have another kind of gown that distinguishes them : every student of any considerable standing has a key to the college library, for no college is without one.

PAUL HENTZNER, *Travels in England* 1598 [Rye]

A young gentleman of the University

Sir Andrew Aguecheek. I would I had bestowed that time in the tongues that I have in fencing, dancing and bear-baiting. O ! had I but followed the arts ! *Twelfth-Night*, I. iii. 99—101

A young gentleman of the university is one that comes there to wear a gown, and to say hereafter he has been at the university. His father sent him thither, because he heard there were the best fencing and dancing schools; from these he has his education, from his tutor the over-sight. The first element of his knowledge is to be shewn the colleges, and initiated in a tavern by the way, which hereafter he will learn of himself. The two marks of his seniority is the bare velvet of his gown and his proficiency at tennis, where when he can once play a set, he is a fresh-man no more. His study has commonly handsome shelves, his books neat silk strings, which he shews to his father's man, and is loth to untie or take down, for fear of misplacing. Upon foul days, for recreation, he retires thither, and looks over the pretty book his tutor reads to him, which is commonly some short history, or a piece of *Euphormio*; for which his tutor gives him money to spend next day. His main loitering is at the library, where he studies arms and books of honour, and turns a gentlemen-critic in pedigrees. Of all things he endures not to be mistaken for a scholar, and hates a black suit though it be of satin. His companion is ordinarily some stale fellow, that has been notorious for an ingle to gold hat-bands, whom he admires at first, afterward scorns. If he have spirit or wit, he may light of better company and may learn some flashes of wit, which may do him knight's service in the country hereafter. But he is now gone to the Inns of Court, where he studies to forget what he learned before,—his acquaintance and the fashion.

JOHN EARLE, Micro-cosmographie 1628

A mere scholar

They have been at a great feast of languages and stolen the scraps.

Love's Labour's Lost, v. i. 40

A mere scholar is an intelligible ass, or a silly fellow in black, that speaks sentences more familiarly than sense. The antiquity of his university is his creed, and the excellency of his college (though but for a match at football) an article of his faith. He speaks Latin better than his mother-tongue; and is a stranger in no part of the world but his own country. He does usually tell great stories of himself to small purpose, for they are commonly ridiculous, be they true or false. His

66

ambition is, that he either is or shall be a graduate: but if ever he get a fellowship, he has then no fellow. In spite of all logic he dare swear and maintain it, that a cuckold and a townsman are *termini convertibiles*, though his mother's husband be an alderman. He was never begotten (as it seems) without much wrangling ; for his whole life is spent in *pro* and *contra*. His tongue goes always before his wit, like gentleman-usher, but somewhat faster. That he is a complete gallant in all points, *cap à pie*, witness his horsemanship and the wearing of his weapons. He is commonly longwinded, able to speak more with ease, than any man can endure to hear with patience. University jests are his universal discourse, and his news the demeanour of the proctors. His phrase, the apparel of his mind, is made of divers shreds like a cushion, and when it goes plainest, it hath a rash outside, and fustian linings. The current of his speech is closed with an *ergo* ; and whatever be the question, the truth is on his side. 'Tis a wrong to his reputation to be ignorant of any thing ; and yet he knows not that he knows nothing. He gives directions for husbandry from Virgil's *Georgics* ; for cattle from his *Bucolics* ; for warlike stratagems from his *Aeneid*, or Caesar's *Commentaries*. He orders all things by the book, is skilful in all trades, and thrives in none. He is led more by his ears than his understanding, taking the sound of words for their true sense : and does therefore confidently believe, that Erra Pater was the father of heretics ; Rodulphus Agricola a substantial farmer ; and will not stick to aver that Systema's *Logic* doth excel Keckerman's. His ill luck is not so much in being a fool, as in being put to such pains to express it to the world : for what in others is natural, in him (with much-a-do) is artificial. His poverty is his happiness, for it makes some men believe, that he is none of fortune's favourites. That learning which he hath, was in his nonage put in backward like a clyster, and 'tis now like ware mislaid in a pedlar's pack ; 'a has it, but knows not where it is. In a word, he is the index of a man, and the title-page of a scholar ; or a puritan in morality : much in profession, nothing in practice.

SIR THOMAS OVERBURY, Characters 1614—16

EDUCATION

§ 4. Travel

> Home-keeping youth have ever homely wits.
> > *The Two Gentlemen of Verona*, I. i. 2

> *Hortensio.* And tell me now, sweet friend, what happy gale
> Blows you to Padua here from old Verona?
> *Petruchio.* Such wind as scatters young men through the world
> To seek their fortunes farther than at home,
> Where small experience grows.
> > *The Taming of the Shrew*, I. ii. 48—52

> My tablets—meet it is I set it down.
> > *Hamlet*, I. v. 107

Travel, in the younger sort, is a part of education; in the elder, a part of experience. He that travelleth into a country, before he hath some entrance into the language, goeth to school and not to travel. That young men travel under some tutor or grave servant, I allow well; so that he be such a one that hath the language and hath been in the country before; whereby he may be able to tell them what things are worthy to be seen in the country where they go, what acquaintances they are to seek, what exercises or discipline the place yieldeth. For else young men shall go hooded and look abroad little. It is a strange thing that in sea voyages, where there is nothing to be seen but sky and sea, men should make diaries; but in land travel, wherein so much is to be observed, for the most part they omit it; as if chance were fitter to be registered than observation. Let diaries, therefore, be brought in use. The things to be seen and observed are :—the courts of princes, specially when they give audience to ambassadors; the courts of justice, while they sit and hear causes, and so of consistories ecclesiastic; the churches and monasteries, with the monuments which are therein extant; the walls and fortifications of cities and towns, and so the havens and harbours; antiquities and ruins : libraries, colleges, disputations and lectures, where any are; shipping and navies; houses and gardens of state and pleasure near great cities; armories; arsenals; magazines; exchanges; burses; warehouses; exercises of horsemanship; fencing; training of soldiers and the like; comedies, such whereunto the better sort of persons do resort; treasuries of jewels and robes; cabinets and rarities; and, to conclude, whatsoever is memorable in the places where they go. After

68

all which the tutors or servants ought to make diligent enquiry. As for triumphs, masques, feasts, weddings, funerals, capital executions and such shews, men need not to be put in mind of them ; yet are they not to be neglected. If you will have a young man to put his travel into a little room, and in short time to gather much, this you must do. First, as was said, he must have some entrance into the language before he goeth. Then he must have such a servant or tutor, as knoweth the country, as was likewise said. Let him carry with him also some card or book describing the country where he travelleth ; which will be a good key to his enquiry. Let him keep also a diary. Let him not stay long in one city or town ; more or less as the place deserveth, but not long : nay, when he stayeth in one city or town, let him change his lodging from one end and part of the town to another; which is a great adamant of acquaintance. Let him sequester himself from the company of his countrymen, and diet in such places where there is good company of the nation where he travelleth. Let him upon his removes from one place to another procure recommendation to some person of quality residing in the place whither he removeth, that he may use his favour in those things he desireth to see or know. Thus he may abridge his travel, with much profit. As for the acquaintance which is to be sought in travel, that which is most of all profitable is acquaintance with the secretaries and employed men of ambassadors ; for so in travelling in one country he shall suck the experience of many. Let him also see and visit eminent persons in all kinds which are of great name abroad, that he may be able to tell how the life agreeth with the fame. For quarrels, they are with care and discretion to be avoided : they are commonly for mistresses, healths, place and words. And let a man beware how he keepeth company with choleric and quarrelsome persons, for they will engage him into their own quarrels. When a traveller returneth home, let him not leave the countries where he hath travelled altogether behind him, but maintain a correspondence, by letters, with those of his acquaintance which are of most worth. And let his travel appear rather in his discourse than in his apparel or gesture : and in his discourse, let him be rather advised in his answers than forward to tell stories : and let it appear, that he doth not

EDUCATION

change his country manners for those of foreign parts, but only prick in some flowers of that he hath learned abroad into the customs of his own country.

FRANCIS BACON, Essays 1597—1625

The abuse of foreign travel

Farewell, Monsieur Traveller: look you lisp, and wear strange suits, disable all the benefits of your own country, be out of love with your nativity, and almost chide God for making you that countenance you are; or I will scarce think you have swam in a gondola.

As You Like It, IV. i. 35—40

Foreign travel oftentimes makes many to wander from themselves as well as from their country, and to come back mere mimics; and so in going far to fare worse, and bring back less wit than they carried forth. They go out figures (according to the Italian proverb) and return ciphers. They retain the vice of a country, and will discourse learnedly thereon, but pass by and forget the good, their memories being herein like hair-sieves, that keep up the bran and let go the fine flour. They strive to degenerate as much as they can from Englishmen, and all their talk is still foreign, or at least will bring it to be so, though it be by head and shoulders, magnifying other nations, and derogating from their own. Nor can one hardly exchange three words with them at an ordinary (or elsewhere) but presently they are th' other side of the sea, commending either the wines of France, the fruits of Italy, or the oil and salads of Spain.

Some also there are who by their countenance more than by their carriage, by their diseases more than by their discourses, discover themselves to have been abroad under hot climates.

Others have a custom to be always relating strange things and wonders (of the humour of Sir John Mandeville), and they usually present them to the hearers through multiplying glasses, and thereby cause the thing to appear far greater than it is in itself. They make mountains of mole-hills, like Charenton bridge echo, which doubles the sound nine times. Such a traveller was he, that reported the Indian fly to be as big as a fox, China birds to be as big as some horses, and their mice to be as big as monkeys. But they have the wit to fetch this far enough off, because the hearer may rather believe it than make a voyage so far to disprove it.

70

THE ITALIANATE ENGLISHMAN

Everyone knows the tale of him who reported he had seen a cabbage under whose leaves a regiment of soldiers were sheltered from a shower of rain. Another who was no traveller (yet the wiser man) said, he had passed by a place where there were four hundred braziers making of a cauldron, two hundred within and two hundred without, beating the nails in. The traveller asking for what use that huge cauldron was, he told him, "Sir it was to boil your cabbage."...

Furthermore, there is amongst many others (which were too long to recite here) an odd kind of anglicism, wherein some do frequently express themselves, as to say "Your boors of Holland, sir; your Jesuits of Spain, sir; your courtezans of Venice, sir:" whereunto one answered (not impertinently) "My courtezans sir? Pox on them all for me, they are none of my courtezans."

Lastly, some kind of travellers there are, whom their gait and strutting, their bending in the hams and shoulders, and looking upon their legs, with frisking and singing do speak them travellers.

Others by a fantastic kind of ribanding themselves, by their modes of habit and clothing...do make themselves known to have breathed foreign air.

JAMES HOWELL, *Instructions for forreine travell* 1642

The Italianate Englishman

Fashions in proud Italy,
Whose manners still our tardy apish nation
Limps after in base imitation.

Richard II., II. i. 21—23

Sir Richard Sackville, that worthy gentleman of worthy memory, as I said in the beginning, in the queen's privy chamber at Windsor, after he had talked with me for the right choice of a good wit in a child for learning, and of the true difference betwixt quick and hard wits, of alluring young children by gentleness to love learning, and of the special care that was to be had to keep young men from licentious living, he was most earnest with me, to have me say my mind also, what I thought concerning the fancy that many young gentlemen of England have to travel abroad, and namely to lead a long life in Italy. His request, both for his authority and good will toward me, was a sufficient commandment unto me to

71

satisfy his pleasure with uttering plainly my opinion in that matter. "Sir," quoth I, "I take going thither and living there for a young gentleman that doth not go under the keep and guard of such a man, as both by wisdom can, and authority dare rule him, to be marvellous dangerous." And why I said so then, I will declare at large now : which I said then privately and write now openly, not because I do contemn either the knowledge of strange and diverse tongues, and namely the Italian tongue, which next to the Greek and Latin tongue I like and love above all other; or else because I do despise the learning that is gotten, or the experience that is gathered in strange countries; or for any private malice that I bear to Italy, which country, and in it namely Rome I have always specially honoured. Because, time was, when Italy and Rome have been, to the great good of us that now live, the best breeders and bringers up of the worthiest men, not only for wise speaking, but also for well doing in all civil affairs, that ever was in the world. But now, that time is gone, and though the place remain, yet the old and present manners do differ as far as black and white, as virtue and vice. Virtue once made that country mistress over all the world. Vice now maketh that country slave to them that before were glad to serve it. All men seeth it : they themselves confess it, namely such as be best and wisest amongst them. For sin, by lust and vanity, hath and doth breed up everywhere common contempt of God's word, private contention in many families, open factions in every city : and so, making themselves bond to vanity and vice at home, they are content to bear the yoke of serving strangers abroad. Italy now is not that Italy, that it was wont to be : and therefore now not so fit a place, as some do count it, for young men to fetch either wisdom or honesty from thence. For surely, they will make other but bad scholars, that be so ill masters to themselves....

But I am afraid that over many of our travellers into Italy do not eschew the way to Circe's court, but go, and ride, and run, and fly thither. They make great haste to come to her : they make great suit to serve her : yea, I could point out some with my finger, that never had gone out of England, but only to serve Circes in Italy. Vanity and vice, and any licence to ill living in England was counted stale and rude unto them.

And so, being mules and horses before they went, returned very swine and asses home again, yet everywhere very foxes with subtle and busy heads, and, where they may, very wolves with cruel malicious hearts. A marvellous monster, which for filthiness of living, for dullness to learning himself, for wiliness in dealing with others, for malice in hurting without cause, should carry at once in one body the belly of a swine, the head of an ass, the brain of a fox, the womb of a wolf. If you think we judge amiss, and write too sore against you, hear what the Italian saith of the Englishman, what the master reporteth of the scholar: who uttereth plainly, what is taught by him, and what learned by you, saying, *Englese italianato, è un diavolo incarnato,* that is to say, you remain men in shape and fashion, but become devils in life and condition. This is not the opinion of one for some private spite, but the judgment of all in a common proverb, which riseth of that learning and those manners which you gather in Italy: a good schoolhouse of wholesome doctrine and worthy masters of commendable scholars, where the master had rather defame himself for his teaching, than not shame his scholar for his learning. A good nature of the master and fair conditions of the scholars. And now choose you, you Italian Englishmen, whether you will be angry with us for calling you monsters, or with the Italians for calling you devils, or else with your own selves, that take so much pains and go so far to make your selves both. If some yet do not well understand what is an Englishman Italianated, I will plainly tell him. He, that by living and travelling in Italy, bringeth home into England out of Italy the religion, the learning, the policy, the experience, the manners of Italy. That is to say, for religion papistry or worse: for learning less commonly than they carried out with them: for policy a factious heart, a discoursing head, a mind to meddle in all men's matters: for experience plenty of new mischiefs never known in England before: for manners variety of vanities, and change of filthy living. These be the enchantments of Circes, brought out of Italy to mar men's manners in England; much by example of ill life, but more by precepts of fond books, of late translated out of Italian into English, sold in every shop in London, commended by honest titles the sooner to corrupt honest manners, dedicated over boldly to virtuous and

honourable personages, the easier to beguile simple and innocent wits. It is pity that those which have authority and
charge to allow and disallow books to be printed, be no more
circumspect herein than they are. Ten sermons at Paul's
Cross do not so much good for moving men to true doctrine, as
one of those books do harm with enticing men to ill living.
Yea, I say farther, those books tend not so much to corrupt
honest living, as they do to subvert true religion. More
papists be made, by your merry books of Italy, than by your
earnest books of Louvain. And because our great physicians
do wink at the matter, and make no count of this sore, I,
though not admitted one of their fellowship, yet having been
many years a prentice to God's true religion, and trust to
continue a poor journey-man therein all days of my life, for
the duty I owe and love I bear both to true doctrine and
honest living, though I have no authority to amend the sore
myself, yet I will declare my good will to discover the sore to
others.

Roger Ascham, *The Scholemaster* 1570

The South Bank of the Thames 1647
showing the Globe Theatre and a bear-garden

CHAPTER V

LONDON

Shallow. I'll drink to Master Bardolph and to all the cavaleiroes about London.

Davy. I hope to see London once ere I die.

2 Henry IV., v. iii. 60—61

Shallow. O, Sir John, do you remember since we lay all night in the windmill in Saint George's fields?...

Silence That's fifty-five year ago.

Shallow. Ha! cousin Silence, that thou hadst seen that that this knight and I have seen. Ha! Sir John, said I well?

Falstaff. We have heard the chimes at midnight, Master Shallow.

Shallow. That we have, that we have, that we have; in faith, Sir John, we have. Our watchword was, "Hem, boys!" Come, let's to dinner; come, let's to dinner. Jesus, the days that we have seen! come, come.

ibid. III. ii. 208—237

§ 1. The road to London

Jog on, jog on the foot-path way,
And merrily hent the stile-a:
A merry heart goes all the day,
Your sad tires in a mile-a.

The Winter's Tale, IV. ii. 133—136

The State of the Roads

Now to speak generally of our common highways through the English part of the isle (for of the rest I can say nothing), you shall understand that in the clay or cledgy soil they are often very deep and troublesome in the winter half. Wherefore by authority of parliament an order is taken for their yearly amendment, whereby all sorts of the common people do employ their travail for six days in summer upon the same. And albeit that the intent of the statute is very profitable for the reparations of the decayed places, yet the rich do so cancel their portions, and the poor so loiter in their labours, that of all the six, scarcely two good days' work are well performed and accomplished in a parish on these so necessary affairs. Besides this, such as have land lying upon the sides of the ways do utterly neglect to ditch and scour their drains and water-courses for better avoidance of the winter waters (except it may be set off or cut from the meaning of the statute), whereby the streets do grow to be much more gulled than before, and thereby very noisome for such as travel by the same. Sometimes also, and that very often, these days' works are not employed upon those ways that lead from market to market, but each surveyor amendeth such by-plots and lanes as seem best for his own commodity and more easy passage unto his fields and pastures. And whereas in some places there is such want of stones, as thereby the inhabitants are driven to seek them far off in other soils, the owners of the lands wherein those stones are to be had, and which hitherto have given money to have them borne away, do now reap no small commodity by raising the same to excessive prices, whereby their neighbours are driven to grievous charges, which is another cause wherefore the meaning of that good law is very much defrauded. Finally, this is another thing likewise to be considered of, that the trees and bushes growing by the streets' sides do not a little keep off the force of the sun in summer for drying up of the lanes. Wherefore if order were taken that their boughs should continually be kept short, and the bushes not suffered to spread so far into the narrow paths, that inconvenience would also be remedied, and many a slough prove hard ground that yet is deep and hollow. Of the daily encroaching of the covetous upon the highways I speak not. But this I know by experience, that whereas some streets within these five and twenty years have been in most places fifty foot broad according to the law, whereby the traveller might either escape the thief, or shift the mire, or pass by the loaden cart without danger of himself and his horse; now they are brought unto twelve, or twenty, or six and twenty at the most, which is another cause also whereby the ways be the worse, and many an honest man encumbered in his journey. But what speak I of these things whereof I do not think to hear a just redress, because the error is so common, and the benefit thereby so sweet and profitable to many by such houses and cottages as are raised upon the same.

WILLIAM HARRISON, Description of England 1587 (2nd ed.)

The Cambridge to London road

On the road we passed through a villainous boggy and wild country and several times missed our way because the country thereabouts is very little inhabited and is nearly a waste ; and there is one spot in particular where the mud is so deep that in my opinion it would scarcely be possible to pass with a coach in winter or in rainy weather.

Visit of Frederick, Duke of Würtemberg, 1592 [Rye]

Means of Communication

SCENE. Rochester. An Inn-yard

Gadshill. Good morrow, carriers. What's o'clock ?

First Carrier. I think it be two o'clock.

Gadshill. I prithee, lend me thy lanthorn, to see my gelding in the stable.

Second Carrier. ...Lend me thy lanthorn, quoth a' ? marry, I'll see thee hanged first.

Gadshill. Sirrah carrier, what time do you mean to come to London ?

Second Carrier. Time enough to go to bed with a candle, I warrant thee. Come, neighbour Mugs, we'll call up the gentlemen : they will along with company, for they have great charge.

1 Henry IV., II. i. 36—51

The Post

In England towards the south, and in the west parts, and from London to Berwick upon the confines of Scotland, post-horses are established at every ten miles or thereabouts, which they ride a false gallop after some ten miles an hour sometimes, and that makes their hire the greater : for with a commission from the chief post-master, or chief lords of the Council (given either upon public business, or at least pretence thereof) a passenger shall pay twopence halfpenny each mile for his horse, and as much for his guide's horse : but one guide will serve the whole company, though many ride together, who

77

may easily bring back the horses, driving them before him, who know the way as well as a beggar knows his dish. They which have no such commission pay threepence for each mile. This extraordinary charge of horses' hire may well be recompensed with the speed of the journey, whereby greater expenses in the inns are avoided. All the difficulty is to have a body able to endure the toil. For these horses the passenger is at no charge to give them meat, only at the ten miles' end the boy that carries them back will expect some few pence in gift. Some nobleman hath the office of chief post-master, being a place of such account as commonly he is one of the King's Council. And not only he, but other lords of the Council, according to the qualities of their offices, use to give the foresaid commissions signed with their hands jointly or severally : but their hands are less regarded than the post-master's, except they be favourites, and of the highest offices, or the business be important.

Inn-charges

In the inns men of inferior condition use to eat at the host's table, and pay some sixpence a meal : but gentlemen have their chambers, and eat alone, except perhaps they have consorts and friends in their company and of their acquaintance. If they be accompanied, perhaps their reckoning may commonly come to some two shillings a man, and one that eats alone in his own chamber with one or two servants attending him, perhaps upon reckoning may spend some five or six shillings for supper and breakfast. But in the northern parts, when I passed towards Scotland, gentlemen themselves did not use to keep their chambers, but to eat at an ordinary table together, where they had great plenty of good meat and especially of choice kinds of fish, and each man paid no more than sixpence and sometimes but fourpence a meal. One horse's meat will come to twelve pence, or eighteen pence the night for hay, oats and straw, and in summer time commonly they put the horses to grass, after the rate of threepence each horse, though some who ride long journeys will either keep them in the stable at hard meat as they do in winter, or else give them a little oats in the morning when they are brought up from grass. English passengers taking any journey seldom dine, especially not in winter, and withal ride long journeys. But there is no place in the world where passengers may so freely command as in the English inns, and are attended for themselves and their horses as well as if they were at home, and perhaps better, each servant being ready at call, in hope of a small reward in the morning. Neither did I ever see inns so well furnished with household stuff.

Coaches and hackneys

Coaches are not to be hired anywhere but only at London; and howsoever England is for the most part plain, or consisting of pleasant hills, yet the ways far from London are so dirty as hired coachmen do not ordinarily take any long journeys, but only for one or two days any way from London, the ways so far being sandy and very fair and continually kept so by labour of hands. And for a day's journey, a coach with two horses used to be let for some ten shillings the day (or the way being short for some eight shillings, so as the passengers paid for the horses' meat) or some fifteen shillings a day for three horses, the coachman paying for his horses' meat. Sixty or seventy years ago coaches were very rare in England, but at this day pride is so far increased, as there be few gentlemen of any account (I mean elder brothers) who have not their coaches, so as the streets of London are almost stopped up with them. Yea, they who only respect comeliness and profit, and are thought free from pride, yet have coaches; because they find the keeping thereof more commodious and profitable than of horses, since two or three coach-horses will draw four or five persons, besides the commodity of carrying many necessaries in a coach. For the most part Englishmen, especially in long journeys, use to ride upon their own horses. But if any will hire a horse, at London they use to pay two shillings the first day, and twelve or perhaps eighteen pence a day for as many days as they keep him, till the horse be brought home to the owner, and the passenger must either bring him back, or pay for the sending of him, and find him meat both going and coming. In other parts of England a man may hire a horse for twelve pence a day, finding him meat and bringing or sending him back; and if the journey be long, he may hire him at a convenient rate for a month or two.

LONDON

Carriers

Likewise carriers let horses from city to city, with caution that the passenger must lodge in their inn, that they may look to the feeding of their horses, and so they will for some five or six days' journey let him a horse, and find the horse meat themselves for some twenty shillings. Lastly, these carriers have long covered waggons, in which they carry passengers from city to city : but this kind of journeying is so tedious, by reason they must take waggon very early, and come very late to their inns, as none but women and people of inferior condition, or strangers (as Flemings with their wives and servants) use to travel in this sort.

FYNES MORYSON, Itinerary 1617

A carrier is his own hackneyman, for he lets himself out to travel as well as his horses. He is the ordinary ambassador between friend and friend, the father and the son, and brings rich presents to the one, but never returns any back again. He is no unlettered man, though in shew simple, for question-less he has much in his budget which he can utter too in fit time and place. He is like the vault in Gloucester church, that conveys whispers at a distance ; for he takes the sound out of your mouth at York, and makes it be heard as far as London. He is the young students' joy and expectation, and the most accepted guest, to whom they lend a willing hand to discharge him of his burden. His first greeting is, " Your friends are well " ; then in a piece of gold delivers their blessing. You would think him a churlish blunt fellow, but they find in him many tokens of humanity. He is a great afflicter of the highways, and beats them out of measure ; which injury is sometimes revenged by the purse-taker, and then the voyage miscarries. No man domineers more in his inn, nor calls his host unreverently with more presumption, and this arrogance proceeds out of the strength of his horses. He forgets not his load where he takes his ease, for he is drunk commonly before he goes to bed. He is like the prodigal child still packing away, and still returning again. But let him pass.

JOHN EARLE, Micro-cosmographie 1628

THE ROAD TO LONDON

English Inns

Servants in league with highwaymen

Chamberlain. Good morrow, Master Gadshill. It holds current that I told you yesternight : there's a franklin in the wild of Kent hath brought three hundred marks with him in gold : I heard him tell it to one of his company last night at supper ; a kind of auditor ; one that hath abundance of charge too, God knows what. They are up already and call for eggs and butter : they will away presently.

*   *   *   *   *   *

Gadshill. Give me thy hand : thou shalt have a share in our purchase, as I am a true man.

Chamberlain. Nay, rather let me have it, as you are a false thief.

1 *Henry IV.,* II. i. 58—103

Those towns that we call thoroughfares have great and sumptuous inns builded in them for the receiving of such travellers and strangers as pass to and fro. The manner of harbouring wherein is not like to that of some other countries in which the host or goodman of the house doth challenge a lordly authority over his guests, but clean otherwise, sith every man may use his inn as his own house in England and have for his money how great or little variety of victuals, and what other service himself shall think expedient to call for. Our inns are also very well furnished with napery, bedding and tapestry, especially with napery : for beside the linen used at the tables, which is commonly washed daily, is such and so much as belongeth unto the estate and calling of the guest. Each comer is sure to lie in clean sheets, wherein no man hath been lodged since they came from the laundress or out of the water wherein they were last washed. If the traveller have an horse, his bed doth cost him nothing, but if he go on foot he is sure to pay a penny for the same : but whether he be horseman or footman if his chamber be once appointed he may carry the key with him, as of his own house, so long as he lodgeth there. If he lose ought whilst he abideth in the inn, the host is bound by a general custom to restore the damage, so that there is no greater security anywhere for travellers than in the greatest inns of England. Their horses in like sort are walked, dressed and looked unto by certain hostlers or hired servants, appointed at the charges of the goodman of the house, who in hope of extraordinary reward will deal very diligently, after outward appearance, in this their function and calling. Herein nevertheless are many of them blameworthy, in that they do not only deceive the beast oftentimes of his allowance by sundry means, except their owners look well to them; but also make such packs with slipper merchants which hunt after prey (for what place is sure from evil and wicked persons?) that many an honest man is spoiled of his goods as he travelleth to and fro, in which feat also the counsel of the tapsters or drawers of drink, and chamberlains is not seldom behind or wanting. Certes I believe that not a chapman or traveller in England is robbed by the way without the knowledge of some of them; for when he cometh into the inn, and alighteth from his horse, the hostler forthwith is very busy to take down his budget or capcase in the yard from his saddle-bow, which he peiseth slyly in his hand to feel the weight thereof: or if he miss of this pitch, when the guest hath taken up his chamber, the chamberlain that looketh to the making of the beds will be sure to remove it from the place where the owner hath set it, as if it were to set it more conveniently somewhere else, whereby he getteth an inkling whether it be money or other sort wares, and thereof giveth warning to such odd guests as haunt the house and are of his confederacy, to the utter undoing of many an honest yeoman as he journeyeth by the way. The tapster in like sort for his part doth mark his behaviour, and what plenty of money he draweth when he payeth the shot, to the like end: so that it shall be an hard matter to escape all their subtle practices. Some think it a gay matter to commit their budgets at their coming to the goodman of the house: but thereby they oft bewray themselves. For albeit their money be safe for the time that it is in his hands (for you shall not hear that a man is robbed in his inn) yet after their departure the host can make no warrantise of the same, sith his protection extendeth no further than the gate of his own house: and there cannot be a surer token unto such as pry and watch for those booties, than to see any guest deliver his capcase in such manner.

In all our inns we have plenty of ale, beer and sundry kinds of wine, and such is the capacity of some of them that they are able to lodge two hundred or three hundred persons and their horses at ease, and thereto with a very short warning make such provision for their diet, as to him that is unacquainted withal may seem to be incredible. Howbeit of all in England there are no worse inns than in London, and yet many are there far better than the best that I have heard of in any foreign country, if all circumstances be duly considered...And it is a world to see how each owner of them contendeth with other for goodness of entertainment of their guests, as about fineness and change of linen, furniture of bedding, beauty of rooms, service at the table, costliness of plate, strength of drink, variety of wines, or well using of horses. Finally there is not so much omitted among them as the gorgeousness of their very signs at their doors, wherein some do consume thirty or forty pounds, a mere vanity in mine opinion; but so vain will they needs be, and that not only to give some outward token of the inn-keeper's wealth, but also to procure good guests to the frequenting of their houses in hope there to be well used.

WILLIAM HARRISON, *Description of England* 1587 (2nd ed.)

Highwaymen on Gadshill

First Traveller. Come, neighbour; the boy shall lead our horses down the hill; we'll walk afoot awhile, and ease our legs.

Thieves. Stand!

Travellers. Jesu bless us!

Falstaff. Strike; down with them; cut the villains' throats: ah! whoreson caterpillars! bacon-fed knaves! they hate us youth: down with them; fleece them.   *1 Henry IV.*, II. ii. 86—95

Afterwards his Highness rode back again [from Rochester] to Gravesend, the night being as dark as pitch and the wind high and boisterous; he slept there that night. On the road, however, an Englishman, with a drawn sword in his hand, came upon us unawares and ran after us as fast as he could; perhaps he expected to find other persons, for it is very probable that he had an ambush, as that particular part of the road is not the most safe.

Visit of Frederick, Duke of Würtemberg, 1592 [Rye]

LONDON

§ 2. First impressions of London

> But now behold,
> In the quick forge and working-house of thought,
> How London doth pour out her citizens.
>
> *Henry V.*, v. chor. 22—24

A foreigner's opinion

London is a large, excellent and mighty city of business, and the most important in the whole kingdom ; most of the inhabitants are employed in buying and selling merchandize, and trading in almost every corner of the world, since the river is most useful and convenient for this purpose, considering that ships from France, the Netherlands, Sweden, Denmark, Hamburg and other kingdoms, come almost up to the city, to which they convey goods and receive and take away others in exchange.

It is a very populous city, so that one can scarcely pass along the streets, on account of the throng.

The inhabitants are magnificently apparelled, and are extremely proud and overbearing ; and because the greater part, especially the tradespeople, seldom go into other countries, but always remain in their houses in the city attending to their business, they care little for foreigners, but scoff and laugh at them ; and moreover one dare not oppose them, else the street-boys and apprentices collect together in immense crowds and strike to the right and left unmercifully without regard to person ; and because they are the strongest, one is obliged to put up with the insult as well as the injury.

The women have much more liberty than perhaps in any other place ; they also know well how to make use of it, for they go dressed out in exceedingly fine clothes, and give all their attention to their ruffs and stuffs, to such a degree indeed, that, as I am informed, many a one does not hesitate to wear velvet in the streets, which is common with them, whilst at home perhaps they have not a piece of dry bread. All the English women are accustomed to wear hats upon their heads, and gowns cut after the old German fashion—for indeed their descent is from the Saxons.

Visit of Frederick, Duke of Würtemberg, 1592 [Rye]

FIRST IMPRESSIONS

The Buildings

Now at London the houses of the citizens (especially in the chief streets) are very narrow in the front towards the street, but are built five or six roofs high, commonly of timber and clay with plaster, and are very neat and commodious within : and the building of citizens' houses in other cities is not much unlike this. But withal understand, that in London many stately palaces, built by noblemen upon the river Thames, do make a very great shew to them that pass by water ; and that there be many more like palaces, also built towards land, but scattered and great part of them in back lanes and streets, which if they were joined to the first in good order, as other cities are built uniformly, they would make not only fair streets, but even a beautiful city, to which few might justly be preferred for the magnificence of the building. Besides that, the aldermen's and chief citizens' houses, howsoever they are stately for building, yet being built all inward, that the whole room towards the streets may be reserved for shops of tradesmen, make no shew outwardly, so as in truth all the magnificence of London building is hidden from the view of strangers at the first sight, till they have more particular view thereof by long abode there, and then they will prefer the buildings of this famous city to many that appear more stately at the first sight. Great part of the towns and villages are built like the citizens' houses in London, save that they are not so many stories high nor so narrow in the front towards the street. Others of them are built in like sort of unpolished small stones, and some of the villages in Lincolnshire and some other countries are of mere clay, and covered with thatch ; yet even these houses are more commodious within for cleanliness, lodging and diet, than any stranger would think them to be. Most of the houses in cities and towns have cellars under them, where for coolness they lay beer and wine. Gentlemen's houses for the most part are built like those in the cities, but very many of gentlemen's and noblemen's palaces, as well near London as in other countries, are stately built of brick and freestone, whereof many yield not in magnificence to like buildings of other kingdoms, as Homby, built by Sir Christopher Hatton ; Tybals lately belonging to the Earl of Salisbury, seated near London ; and the Earl of Exeter his house near Stamford : by which palaces lying near the highway a stranger may judge of many other like stately buildings in other parts. The King's palaces are of such magnificent building, so curious art, and such pleasure and beauty for gardens and fountains, and are so many in number, as England need not envy any other kingdom therein. Among them being many a stranger may see near London : the King's palaces of Hampton Court, of Richmond, of Greenwich, of Nonsuch, of Oatlands, of Sheen, of Windsor, and in London the palace of Whitehall.

FYNES MORYSON, *Itinerary* 1617

The Thames

This is a long, broad, slippery fellow ; rest he affects not, for he is always in motion : he seems something like a carrier, for he is still either going or coming, and once in six or eight hours, salutes the sea his mother and then brings tidings from her. He follows the disposition of the wind, if that be rough, so is the water ; if that calm, so is this : and he loves it, because when the wind is at highest, then the water will best show her strength and anger : it is altogether unsteady, for it commonly is sliding away. Man's unconstant state, and uncertain frail condition is truly resembled by this, always either ebbing or flowing, being in a trice high and low. He will not be a martyr, for he will turn but never burn. Resolution is absolutely his guide and counsellor, for he will run his course. He cannot be said to be a well or spring without water, for he is *puteus inexhaustus.*

Merchandise he likes and loves ; and therefore sends forth ships of traffic to most parts of the earth : his subjects and inhabitants live by oppression like hard landlords at land, the greater rule, and many times devour the less : the city is wondrously beholden to it, for she is furnished with almost all necessaries by it. He is wondrously crossed, he is the maintainer of a great company of watermen. He is a great labourer, for he works as much in the night as the day. He is led by an unconstant guide, the moon : he is clean contrary to Smithfield, because that is all for flesh, but this for fish : his inhabitants are different from those upon land, for they are most without legs : fishermen seem to offer him much wrong, for they rob him of many of his subjects : he is seldom without company, but in the night or rough weather. He meets the sun but follows the moon: he seems to complain at the bridge, because it hath intruded into his bowels, and that makes him roar at that place. To speak truth of him, he is the privileged place for fish and ships, the glory and wealth of the city, the highway to the sea, the bringer in of wealth and strangers, and his business is all for water, yet he deals much with the land too: he is a little sea, and a great river.

DONALD LUPTON, *London and the Countrey carbonadoed* 1632

A Water-man

Is one that hath learnt to speak well of himself; for always he names himself, "the first man." If he had betaken himself to some richer trade, he could not have choosed but done well: for in this (though it be a mean one) he is still plying it, and putting himself forward. He is evermore telling strange news, most commonly lies. If he be a sculler, ask him if he be married, he'll equivocate and swear he's a single man. Little trust is to be given to him, for he thinks that day he does best, when he fetches most men over. His daily labour teaches him the art of dissembling: for like a fellow that rides to the pillory, he goes not that way he looks. He keeps such a bawling at Westminster, that if the lawyers were not acquainted with it, an order would be taken with him. When he is upon the water, he is fare-company: when he comes ashore, he mutinies, and contrary to all other trades is most surly to gentlemen, when they tender payment. The play-houses* only keep him sober; and, as it doth many other gallants, make him an afternoon's man. London-bridge is the most terrible eye-sore to him that can be. And to conclude, nothing but a great press makes him fly from the river; nor any thing, but a great frost, can teach him any good manners.

SIR THOMAS OVERBURY, *Characters* 1614—16

London Bridge

The bridge at London is worthily to be numbered among the miracles of the world, if men respect the building and foundation laid artificially and stately over an ebbing and flowing water upon 21 piles of stone, with 20 arches, under which barks may pass, the lowest foundation being (as they say) packs of wool, most durable against the force of water, and not

* On the South bank of the river, cp. p. 170.

to be repaired but upon great fall of the waters and by artificial turning or stopping the recourse of them ; or if men respect the houses built upon the bridge, as great and high as those of the firm land, so as a man cannot know that he passeth a bridge, but would judge himself to be in the street, save that the houses on both sides are combined in the top, making the passage somewhat dark, and that in some few open places the river of Thames may be seen on both sides.

Fynes Moryson, Itinerary 1617

It is almost art's wonder for strength, length, beauty, wideness, height : it may be said to be polypus, because it is so well furnished with legs : every mouth is four times filled in eight and forty hours, and then as a child it is still, but as soon as they be empty, like a lion it roars, and is wondrous impatient : it is made of iron, wood and stone, and therefore it is a wondrous hardy fellow. It hath changed the form, but as few do now-a-days, from worse to better : certainly it is full of patience, because it bears so much and continually. It's no prison, for any one goes through it : it is something addicted to pride, for many a great man goes under it, and yet it seems something humble too, for the poorest peasant treads upon it : it hath more wonders than arches ; the houses here built are wondrous strong, yet they neither stand on land or water. It is some prejudice to the waterman's gains; many go over here which otherwise should row or sail : it helps many a penniless purse to pass the water without danger or charges. Nothing affrights it more than spring tides or violent innundations. It is chargeable to keep, for it must be continually repaired. It is the only chief crosser of the water. His arches out-face the water, and like judges in the parliament are placed upon wool-sacks. One that lives here need not buy strong water, for here is enough for nothing ; it seems to hinder the water-bearers' profit for the inhabitants easily supply their wants by buckets. He is a settled fellow, and a main upholder of houses ; he is meanly placed, for there are divers above him, and many under him, and his houses may well be called Nonsuch, for there is none like them. And to conclude, he partakes of two elements, his nether parts are all for water, his upper for land ; in a word, it is without compare, being a dainty street, and a strong and most stately bridge.

Donald Lupton, London and the Countrey carbonadoed 1632

Cheapside

My lord, when shall we go to Cheapside and take up commodities upon
our bills? *2 Henry VI., iv. vii.* 133

Tis thought the way through this street is not good, because
so broad and so many go in it; yet though it be broad, it's
very straight, because without any turnings. It is suspected here
are not many sufficent able men, because they would sell all:
and but little honesty, for they show all, and, some think, more
sometime than their own: they are very affable, for they'll
speak to most that pass by: they care not how few be in the
streets, so their shops be full: they that bring them money,
seem to be used worst, for they are sure to pay soundly: their
books of accounts are not like to their estates, for the latter are
best without, but the other with, long crosses. There are a great
company of honest men in this place, if all be gold that glisters:
their parcel-gilt plate is thought to resemble themselves, most
of them have better faces than heart; their monies and coins
are used as prisoners at sea, kept under hatches. One would
think them to be good men, for they deal with the purest and
best metals and every one strives to work best, and stout too,
for they get much by knocking and especially by leaning on
their elbows. Puritans do hold it for a fine street but something
addicted to popery, for adorning [adoring?] the cross too much.
The inhabitants seem not to affect the standard; the kings and
queens would be offended with, and punish them, knew they
how these batter their faces on their coins. Some of their wives
would be ill prisoners, for they cannot endure to be shut up; and
as bad nuns, the life is so solitary. There are many virtuous and
honest women, some truly so, others are so for want of
opportunity. They hold that a harsh place of scripture: That
women must be no goers or gadders abroad. In going to a
lecture many use to visit a tavern: the young attendant must
want his eyes, and change his tongue, according as his mistress
shall direct, though many times they do mistake the
place, yet they will remember the time an hour and half, to
avoid suspicion. Some of the men are cunning launders of
plate, and get much by washing that plate they handle, and it
hath come from some of them, like a man from the broker's
that hath cashiered his cloak, a great deal the lighter. Well, if

all the men be rich and true, and the women all fair and honest, then Cheapside shall stand by Charing Cross for a wonder, and I will make no more characters. But I proceed.

DONALD LUPTON, *London and the Countrey carbonadoed* 1632

A Shop-keeper

His shop is his well-stuffed book, and himself the title-page of it or index. He utters much to all men, though he sells but to a few, and intreats for his own necessities by asking others what they lack. No man speaks more and no more, for his words are like his wares, twenty of one sort, and he goes over them alike to all comers. He is an arrogant commender of his own things; for whatsoever he shews you, is the best in the town, though the worst in his shop. His conscience was a thing that would have laid upon his hands, and he was forced to put it off, and makes great use of honesty to profess upon. He tells you lies by rote, and not minding, as the phrase to sell in and the language he spent most of his years to learn. He never speaks so truly, as when he says he would use you as his brother, for he would abuse his brother; and in his shop thinks it lawful. His religion is much in the nature of his customers, and indeed the pander to it: and by a misinterpreted sense of scripture makes a gain of his godliness. He is your slave while you pay him ready money, but if he once befriend you, your tyrant, and you had better deserve his hate than his trust.

JOHN EARLE, *Micro-cosmographie* 1628

Paul's Walk

Falstaff. Where's Bardolph?
Page. He's gone into Smithfield to buy your worship a horse.
Falstaff. I bought him in Paul's, and he'll buy me a horse in Smithfield.
2 *Henry IV.,* I. ii. 54—58

Paul's Walk is the land's epitome, or you may call it the lesser isle of Great Britain. It is more than this the whole world's map, which you may here discern in its perfectest motion, jostling and turning. It is a heap of stones and men, with a vast confusion of languages, and were the steeple not sanctified, nothing liker Babel. The noise in it is like that of bees, a strange humming or buzz, mixed of walking, tongues and feet. It is a kind of still roar or loud whisper. It is the great exchange of all discourse, and no business whatsoever but is here stirring and afoot. It is the synod of all pates politic, jointed and laid together in most serious posture, and they are not half so busy at the parliament. It is the antic of tails to tails, and backs to backs, and for vizards you need go no further than faces. It is the market of young lecturers, whom you may cheapen here at all rates and sizes. It is the general mint of all famous lies, which are here, like the legends of popery, first coined and stamped in the church. All inventions are emptied here, and not few pockets. The best sign of a temple in it is that it is the thieves' sanctuary, which rob more safely in the crowd than a wilderness, whilst every searcher is a bush to hide them. It is the other expense of the day, after plays, tavern, and a bawdy-house ; and men have still some oaths left to swear here. It is the ears' brothel and satisfies their lust and itch. The visitants are all men without exceptions, but the principal inhabitants and possessors are stale knights, and captains out of service, men of long rapiers and breeches, which after all turn merchants here, and traffic for news. Some make it a preface to their dinner, and travel for a stomach : but thriftier men make it their ordinary, and board here very cheap. Of all such places it is least haunted with hobgoblins, for if a ghost would walk more, he could not.

JOHN EARLE, *Micro-cosmographie* 1628

The Noise and Bustle of the Streets
Why sweat they under burdens?
The Merchant of Venice, IV. i. 94

In every street, carts and coaches make such a thundering as if the world ran upon wheels : at every corner, men, women and children meet in such shoals, that posts are set up of purpose to strengthen the houses, lest with jostling one another they should shoulder them down. Besides, hammers are beating in one place, tubs hooping in another, pots clinking in a third, water-tankards running at tilt in a fourth. Here are porters sweating under burdens, their merchant's men bearing bags of money. Chapmen (as if they were at leap frog) skip out of one shop into another. Tradesmen (as if they were dancing galliards) are lusty at legs and never stand still. All are as busy as country attorneys at an assizes.

THOMAS DEKKER, *The Seuen Deadly Sinnes of London* 1606

LONDON

§ 3. Disorders

> What work's, my countrymen, in hand? where go you
> With bats and clubs?   *Coriolanus,* I. i. 57

> Up Fish Street! down St Magnus Corner! kill and knock down!
> throw them into Thames!   2 *Henry VI.,* IV. viii. 1—3

A busy week for the authorities
Riots outside the theatres

Right honourable and my very good Lord. Upon Whit-sunday there was a very good sermon preached at the new churchyard near Bethlehem, whereat my Lord Mayor was with his brethren, and, by reason no plays were the same day, all the city was quiet. Upon Monday I was at the court and went to Kingston to bed and upon Tuesday I kept the law-day for the whole liberty of Kingston and found all quiet and in good order. There lieth in Kingston Sir John Savage of Cheshire with his lady at Mr Le Grises his house, the which is at vicarage.

That night I returned to London and found all the wards full of watchers, the cause thereof was for that very near the Theater or Curtain at the time of the plays there lay a prentice sleeping upon the grass and one Challes at Grostock did turn upon the toe upon the belly of the same prentice, whereupon the apprentice start up and after words they fell to plain blows. The company increased of both sides to the number of five hundred at the least. This Challes exclaimed and said that he was a gentleman and that the apprentice was but a rascal, and some there were little better than rogues that took upon them the name of gentlemen, and said the prentices were but the scum of the world. Upon these troubles the prentices began the next day being Tuesday to make mutinies and assemblies, and did conspire to have broken the prisons and to have taken forth the prentices that were imprisoned, but my lord and I having intelligence thereof apprehended four or five of the chief conspirators, who are in Newgate and stand indicted of their lewd demeanours.

Upon Wednesday one Browne a serving-man in a blue coat, a shifting fellow, having a perilous wit of his own, in-tending a spoie [?] if he could have brought it to pass, did at Theater door quarrel with certain poor boys, handicraft prentices, and struck some of them and lastly he with his

92

sword wounded and maimed one of the boys upon the left hand, whereupon there assembled near a thousand people. This Browne did very cunningly convey himself away, but by chance he was taken after and brought to Mr Humphrey Smith, and because no man was able to charge him he dismissed him. And after this Browne was brought before Mr Young, where he used himself so cunningly and subtly, no man being there to charge him, that there also he was dismissed. And after I sent a warrant for him, and the constables with the deputy at the Bell in Holborn found him in a parlour fast locked in ; and he would not obey the warrant, but by the mean of the host he was conveyed away ; and then I sent for the host and caused him to appear at Newgate at the sessions oyer and determiner, where he was committed until he brought forth his guest. The next day after he brought him forth and so we indicted him for his misdemeanor. This Browne is a common cozener, a thief and a horse stealer, and coloured all his doings here about this town with a suit that he hath in the law against a brother of his in Staffordshire. He resteth now in Newgate.

Upon the same Wednesday at night two companions, one being a tailor and the other a clerk of the common pleas, both of the duchy and both very lewd fellows, fell out about an harlot, and the tailor raised the prentices and other light persons and, thinking that the clerk was run into Lyon's Inn, came to the house with three hundred at the least, brake down the windows of the house, and struck at the gentlemen, during which broil one Randolds a baker's son came into Fleet street and there made solemn proclamation for " clubs." The street rose and took and brought him unto me and the next day we indicted him also for this misdemeanour with many other more.

Upon Wednesday, Thursday, Friday and Saturday we did nothing else but sit in commission and examine these misdemeanours : we had good help of my lord Anderson and Mr Sackforth.

Upon Sunday my lord sent two aldermen to the court for the suppressing and pulling down of the Theater and Curtain. All the lords agreed thereunto saving my Lord Chamberlain and Mr Vizch, but we obtained a letter to suppress them all. Upon the same night I sent for the Queen's players and my lord of Arundel his players, and they all willingly obeyed the lords' letters. The chiefest of her highness' players advised me to send for the owner of the Theater who was a stubborn fellow and to bind him. I did so. He sent me word that he was my lord of Hunsdon's man and that he would not come at me but he would in the morning ride to my lord. Then I sent the undersheriff for him and he brought him to me, and at his coming he stouted me out very hasty, and in the end I shewed him my lord his master's hand and then he was more quiet, but to die for it he would not be bound. And then I minding to send him to prison, he made suit that he might be bound to appear at the oyer and determiner the which is to-morrow, where he said that he was sure the court would not bind him being a councillor's man. And so I have granted his request, where he shall be sure to be bound or else is like to do worse.

William Fleetwood, City Recorder, to Lord Burghley, June 18, 1584

Duelling and street brawling

Tybalt. What wouldst thou have with me?

Mercutio. Good king of cats, nothing but one of your nine lives, that I mean to make bold withal, and, as you shall use me hereafter, dry-beat the rest of the eight. Will you pluck your sword out of his pilcher by the ears? make haste, lest mine be about your ears ere it be out.

Tybalt (drawing). I am for you.

Romeo. Gentle Mercutio, put thy rapier up.

Mercutio. Come, sir, your passado. [*They fight.*]

Romeo and Juliet, III. i. 81—90

Englishmen, especially being young and unexperienced, are apt to take all things in snuff. Of old, when they were fenced with bucklers, as with a rampier, nothing was more common with them, than to fight about taking the right or left hand, or the wall, or upon any unpleasing countenance. Clashing of swords was then daily music in every street, and they did not only fight combats, but cared not to set upon their enemy upon advantages and unequal terms. But at this day when no nation labours more than the English (as well by travelling into foreign kingdoms, as by the study of good letters, and by other means) to enrich their minds with all virtues, I say in these days, they scorn such men, and esteem them of an idle brain who for ridiculous or trifling causes run the trial of single fight, and howsoever they behave themselves stoutly therein, yet they repute them to have lost as much opinion of wisdom, as they have gained of daring. Much more do they despise them who quarrel and fight in the streets publicly, and do not rather make private trial of their difference, as also those who make quarrels with men of base condition, yea they think them infamous who with disparity of number do many assail one man, and for this beastly quality, comparing them to hogs, whereof, when one grunts, all the herd comes to help him, they think them worthy of any punishment : besides that upon killing any man mercy is seldom or never shewed them, howsoever in other fair combats the prince's mercy hath many times given life to the man-slayer. And the cause why single fights are more rare in England in these times is the dangerous fight at single rapier, together with the confiscation of man-slayers' goods. So as I am of opinion, contrary to the vulgar, and think them worthy of praise who invented dangerous weapons, as rapiers, pistols, guns and gunpowder, since the invention whereof much smaller number of men hath perished by single fights or open war than in former times : and conquests and such inundations of barbarous people, as were those of the Goths, Huns and Longbards, are much less to be feared. Nothing did in old time more animate strong tyrants and giants to oppress weaker men than the huge weight of their clubs and of their arms, wherewith Goliath had easily quelled David, if God had not put in his mind to fight against him with a new kind of weapon more suitable to his strength. I return to the purpose, and do freely profess, that in case of single fights in England, the magistrate doth favour a wronged stranger more than one of the same nation, howsoever the law favours neither, and that a stranger, so fighting, need fear no treason by any disparity or otherwise. But in the mean time, here and in all places happy are the peaceable. Let me add one thing of corrupt custom in England, that those who are not grown men, never have the opinion of valour, till in their youth they have gained it with some single fight, which done, they shall after live more free from quarrels : but it were to be wished that a better way were found to preserve reputation than this of single fights, as well contrary to the law of God, as a capital crime by the laws of men. FYNES MORYSON, *Itinerary* 1617

95

Constables and Watchmen

Dogberry. This is your charge: you shall comprehend all vagrom men; you are to bid any man stand, in the prince's name.

Watchman How, if a' will not stand?

Dogberry. Why, then take no note of him, but let him go; and presently call the rest of the watch together, and thank God you are rid of a knave.

Verges. If he will not stand when he is bidden, he is none of the prince's subjects.

Dogberry. True, and they are to meddle with none but the prince's subjects. You shall also make no noise in the streets: for, for the watch to babble and to talk is most tolerable and not to be endured.

Second Watchman. We will rather sleep than talk: we know what belongs to a watch.

Dogberry. Why, you speak like an ancient and most quiet watchman, for I cannot see how sleeping should offend; only have a care that your bills be not stolen. *Much Ado About Nothing*, III. iii. 25—45

Uxor. What number of men in harness are these? Some sleeping, and many of them seemeth to go whispering together, and behind them there appeareth other men putting forth their heads out of corners, wearing no harness.

Civis. These are not only the constables with the watchmen in London, but also almost through this realm, most falsely abusing the time, coming very late to the watch, sitting down in some common place of watching, wherein some falleth on sleep by the reason of labour or much drinking before, or else nature requireth rest in the night. These fellows think every hour a thousand until they go home, home, home, every man to bed. Good night, good night! God save the Queen! sayeth the constables, farewell, neighbours. Eftsoons after their departing creepeth forth the wild rogue and his fellows, having two or three other harlots for their turn, with picklocks, handsaws, long hooks, ladders, &c., to break into houses, rob, murder, steal, and do all mischief in the houses of true men, utterly undoing honest people to maintain their harlots. Great hoses, lined cloaks, long daggers, and feathers, these must be paid for, &c. This cometh for want of punishment by the day, and idle watch in the night. God grant that some of the watch be not the scouts to the thieves. Yes; God grant that some men have not conspirators of thieves in their own houses, which, like Judases, deceive their masters. If this watch be not better looked unto, good wife, in every place in this realm, and all the night long searching every suspected corner, no man shall be able to keep a penny, no, scant his own life in a while. For they that dare attempt such matters in the city of London, what will they do in houses smally guarded, or by the highway? Yet there is much execution, but it helpeth not. It is the excess of apparel. Hose, hose, great hose! too little wages, too many serving-men, too many tippling-houses, too many drabs, too many knaves, too little labour, too much idleness.

WILLIAM BULLEIN, *A Dialogue against the Pestilence* 1573 (1st ed. 1564)

London at Night

When the searching eye of heaven is hid
Behind the globe, and lights the lower world,
Then thieves and robbers range abroad unseen,
In murders, and in outrage bloody here.
Richard II., III. ii. 37—40

How far that little candle throws his beams!
So shines a good deed in a naughty world.
The Merchant of Venice, V. i. 90—91

An arraignment of candle-light

O Candle-light! and art thou one of the cursed crew? hast thou been set at the table of princes, and noblemen? have all sorts of people done reverence unto thee, and stood bare so soon as ever they have seen thee? have thieves, traitors, and murderers been afraid to come in thy presence, because they knew thee just, and that thou wouldest discover them? and art thou now a harbourer of all kinds of vices? nay, dost thou play the capital Vice thyself?

Hast thou had so many learned lectures read before thee, and is the light of thy understanding now clean put out? And have so many profound scholars profited by thee? hast thou done such good to universities, been such a guide to the lame, and seen the doing of so many good works, yet dost thou now look dimly and with a dull eye upon all goodness? What comfort have sick men taken (in weary and irksome nights) but only in thee? Thou hast been their physician and apothecary, and when the relish of nothing could please them, the very shadow of thee hath been to them a restorative consolation. The nurse hath stilled her wayward infant, shewing it but to thee. What gladness hast thou put into mariners' bosoms, when thou hast met them on the sea? What joy into the faint and benighted traveller when he has met thee on the land? How many poor handicraftsmen by thee have earned the best part of their living? And art thou now become a companion for drunkards, for lechers, and for prodigals? Art thou turned reprobate? Thou wilt burn for it in hell. And so odious is this thy apostacy, and hiding thyself from the light of the truth, that at thy death and going out of the world, even they that love thee best will tread thee under their feet: yea I that have thus played the herald, and proclaimed thy good parts, will now play the crier and call thee into open court, to arraign thee for thy misdemeanours.

Let the world therefore understand, that this tallow-faced gentleman (called Candle-light) so soon as ever the sun was gone out of sight, and that darkness like a thief out of a hedge crept upon the earth, sweat till he dropped again with bustling to come into the city. For having no more but one only eye (and that fiery red with drinking and sitting up late) he was ashamed to be seen by day, knowing he should be laughed to scorn and hooted at. He makes his entrance therefore at Aldersgate of set purpose, for though the street be fair and spacious, yet, few lights in misty evenings using there to thrust out their golden heads, he thought that the aptest circle for him to be raised in, because there his glittering would make greatest show.

What expectation was there of his coming? Setting aside the bonfires, there is not more triumphing on midsummer night. No sooner was he advanced up into the most famous streets, but a number of shops for joy began to shut in: mercers rolled up their silks and velvets: the goldsmiths drew back their plate, and all the city looked like a private play-house, when the windows are clapped down, as if some nocturnal, or dismal tragedy were presently to be acted before all the tradesmen. But Cavaleiro Candle-light came for no such solemnity: no, he had other crackers in hand to which he watched but his hour to give fire. Scarce was his entrance blown abroad, but the bankrupt, the felon, and all that owed any money, and for fear of arrests or justices' warrants had, like so many snails, kept their houses over their heads all the day before, began now to creep out of their shells, and to stalk up and down the streets as uprightly, and with as proud a gait as if they meant to knock against the stars with the crowns of their heads.

The damask-coated citizen, that sat in his shop both forenoon and afternoon, and looked more sourly on his poor neighbours than if he had drunk a quart of vinegar at a draught, sneaks out of his own doors and slips into a tavern, where either alone, or with some other that battles their money together, they so ply themselves with penny pots, which (like small-shot) go off, pouring into their fat paunches, that at length they have not an eye to see withal, nor a good leg to stand upon. In which pickle if any of them happen to be jostled down by a post (that in spite of them will take the wall) and so reels them into the kennel, who takes them up or leads them home? who has them to bed, and with a pillow smooths this stealing so of good liquor, but that brazen-face Candle-light? Nay more, he entices their very prentices to make their desperate sallies out and quick retires in (contrary to the oath of their indentures which are seven years a-swearing) only for their pints, and away.

Tush, this is nothing! young shopkeepers that have but newly ventured upon the pikes of marriage, who are every hour shewing their wares to their customers, plying their business harder all day than Vulcan does his anvil, and seem better husbands than fiddlers that scrape for a poor living both day and night, yet even these if they can but get Candle-light to sit up all night with them in any house of reckoning (that's to say in a tavern) they fall roundly to play the London prize, and that's at three several weapons, drinking, dancing, and dicing; their wives lying all that time in their beds sighing like widows, which is lamentable: the giddy-brained husbands wasting the portions they had with them, which lost once, they are (like maiden-heads) never recoverable. Or which is worse, this going a-bat-fowling a-nights being noted by some wise young man or other that knows how to handle such cases, the bush is beaten for them at home, whilst they catch the bird abroad. But what bird is it? the woodcock.

LONDON

Never did any city pocket up such wrong at the hands of one over whom she is so jealous and so tender, that in winter nights if he be but missing and hide himself in the dark, I know not how many beadles are sent up and down the streets to cry him: yet you see, there is more cause she should send out to curse him. For what villanies are not abroad so long as Candle-light is stirring? The serving-man dare then walk with his wench: the private punk (otherwise called one that boards in London) who like a pigeon sits billing all day within doors and fears to step over the threshold, does then walk the round till midnight, after she hath been swaggering amongst pottle-pots and vintners' boys. Nay, the sober perpetuana-suited puritan, that dares not (so much as by moonlight) come near the suburb-shadow of a house where they set stewed prunes before you, raps as boldly at the hatch, when he knows Candle-light is within, as if he were a new chosen constable. When all doors are locked up, when no eyes are open, when birds sit silent in bushes, and beasts lie sleeping under hedges, when no creature can be smelt to be up but they that may be smelt every night a street's length ere you come at them, even then doth this *ignis fatuus* (Candle-light) walk like a fire-drake into sundry corners. If you will not believe this, shoot but your eye through the iron grates into the cellars of vintners, there you shall see him hold his neck in a gin, made of a cleft hoop-stick, to throttle him from telling tales, whilst they most abominably jumble together all the papistical drinks that are brought from beyond-sea: the poor wines are racked and made to confess any thing: the Spanish and the French meeting both in the bottom of the cellar, conspire together in their cups, to lay the Englishman (if he ever come into their company) under the board. To be short, such strange mad music do they play upon their sack-butts, that if Candle-light being overcome with the steam of new sweet wines, when they are at work, should not tell them 'tis time to go to bed, they would make all the hogsheads that use to come to the house to dance the canaries till they reel again. When the grape-mongers and he are parted, he walks up and down the streets squireing old midwives to any house (very secretly) where any bastards are to be brought into the world. From them (about the hour when spirits walk and cats go a-gossiping) he visits the watch, where creeping into the beadle's cothouse (which stands between his legs, that are lapped about with pieces of rug, as if he had new struck off shackles) and seeing the watchmen to nod at him, he hides himself presently (knowing the token) under the flap of a gown, and teaches them (by instinct) how to steal naps into their heads, because he sees all their cloaks have not one good nap upon them: and upon his warrant snort they so loud, that to those night-walkers (whose wits are up so late) it serves as a watch-word to keep out of the reach of their brown bills: by which means they never come to answer the matter before master constable, and the bench upon which his men (that should watch) do sit: so that the counters are cheated of prisoners, to the great damage of those that should have their morning's draught out of the garnish.

O Candle-light, Candle-light! to how many costly sack-possets, and rear-banquets hast thou been invited by prentices and kitchen-maidens? When the bell-man for anger to spite [spy?] such a purloiner of so many citizens' goods, hath bounced at the door like a madman; at which (as if Robin Good-fellow had been conjured up amongst them) the wenches have fallen into the hands of the green-sickness, and the young fellows into cold agues, with very fear lest their master (like old Jeronimo and Isabella his wife after him) starting out of his naked bed should come down with a weapon in his hand and this in his mouth: "What out-cries pull us from our naked bed? Who calls? &c." as the players can tell you. O Candle-light, how hast thou stunk then, when they have popped thee out of their company; how hast thou taken it in snuff, when thou hast been smelt out, especially the master of the house exclaiming, that by day that deed of darkness had not been. One veney more with thee, and then I have done.

How many lips have been worn out with kissing at the street door or in the entry, in a winking blind evening? How many odd matches and uneven marriages have been made there between young prentices and their masters' daughters, whilst thou (O Candle-light) hast stood watching at the stair's head, that none could come stealing down by thee, but they must be seen?

It appears by these articles put in against thee, that thou art partly a bawd to diverse loose sins, and partly a cozener. For if any in the city have bad wares lying dead upon their

hands, thou art better than *aqua vitae* to fetch life into them,
and to send them packing. Thou shalt therefore be taken out
of thy proud chariot, and be carted. Yet first will we see what
workmanship and what stuff it is made of, to the intent that if
it be not dangerous for a city to keep any relic belonging to
such a crooked saint, it may be hung up as a monument to
shew with what dishonour thou wert driven out of so noble
a lodging, to deface whose buildings thou hast been so envious,
that when thou hast been left alone by any thing that would
take fire, thou hast burnt to the ground many of her goodliest
houses.

Candle-light's coach is made all of horn, shaven as thin as
changelings are. It is drawn (with ease) by two rats : the
coachman is a chandler, who so sweats with yerking them,
that he drops tallow, and that feeds them as provender : yet
are the lashes that he gives the squeaking vermin more deadly
to them than all the ratsbane in Bucklersbury. Painfulness
and Study are his two lackeys and run by him : Darkness, Conspiracy, Opportunity, Stratagems and Fear, are his attendants :
he's sued unto by diggers in mines, gravers, scholars, mariners,
nurses, drunkards, unthrifts and shrode husbands : he destroys
that which feeds him, and therefore Ingratitude comes behind
all this, driving them before her.

THOMAS DEKKER, *The Seuen Deadly Sinnes of London* 1606

§ 4. Temptations

Polonius.   Such wanton, wild and usual slips
              As are companions noted and most known
              To youth and liberty.
Reynaldo.   As gaming, my lord?
Polonius. Ay, or drinking, fencing, swearing, quarrelling,
              Drabbing.   *Hamlet*, II. i. 22—26

A. Drink
Its effects. (a) Falstaff's opinion

A good sherris-sack hath a two-fold operation in it. It
ascends me into the brain ; dries me there all the foolish and dull
and crudy vapours which environ it ; makes it apprehensive,
quick, forgetive, full of nimble fiery and delectable shapes ;
which, deliver'd o'er to the voice, the tongue, which is the

102

The Southwark Gate of London Bridge 1616

birth, becomes excellent wit. The second property of your excellent sherris is, the warming of the blood; which, before cold and settled, left the liver white and pale, which is the badge of pusillanimity and cowardice : but the sherris warms it and makes it course from the inwards to the parts extreme. It illumineth the face, which, as a beacon, gives warning to all the rest of this little kingdom, man, to arm ; and then the vital commoners and inland petty spirits muster me all to their captain, the heart, who, great and puffed up with this retinue, doth any deed of courage ; and this valour comes of sherris. So that skill in the weapon is nothing without sack, for that sets it a-work ; and learning, a mere hoard of gold kept by a devil till sack commences it and sets it in act and use. Hereof comes it that Prince Harry is valiant; for the cold blood he did naturally inherit of his father, he hath, like lean, sterile, and bare land, manured, husbanded, and tilled, with excellent endeavour of drinking good and good store of fertile sherris, that he is become very hot and valiant. If I had a thousand sons, the first human principle I would teach them should be, to forswear thin potations and to addict themselves to sack.

2 Henry IV., IV. iii. 103—136

(b) *A puritan's opinion*

Dost thou think, because thou art virtuous, there shall be no more cakes and ale ?   *Twelfth Night*, II. iii. 123

Spudeus. You spake of drunkenness, what say you of that ? *Philoponus.* I say that it is a horrible vice, and too too much used in Ailgna [England]. Every country, city, town, village and other places hath abundance of alehouses, taverns and inns, which are so fraught with malt-worms, night and day, that you would wonder to see them. You shall have them there sitting at the wine and good-ale all the day long, yea, all the night too, peradventure a whole week together, so long as any money is left ; swilling, gulling and carousing from one to another, till never a one can speak a ready word. Then, when with the spirit of the buttery they are thus possessed, a world it is to consider their gestures and demeanours, one towards another and towards every one else. How they stut and stammer, stagger and reel to and fro like madmen....and which is most horrible, some fall to swearing, cursing and banning, interlacing their speeches with curious terms of blasphemy, to the great dishonour of God, and offence of the godly ears present.

Sp. But they will say that God ordained wines and strong drinks to cheer the heart and to sustain the body withal, therefore it is lawful to use them to that end.

Philo. Meats (moderately taken) corroborate the body, refresh the arteries and revive the spirits, making them apter, every member, to do his office as God hath appointed; but being immoderately taken (as commonly they be), they are instruments of damnation to the abusers of the same, and nourish not the body, but corrupt it rather, casting it into a world of diseases. And a man once drunk with wine or strong drink rather resembleth a brute beast than a Christian man. For do not his eyes begin to stare and to be red, fiery and bleared, blubbering forth seas of tears? Doth he not froth and foam at the mouth like a boar? Doth not his tongue falter and stammer in his mouth? Doth not his head seem as heavy as a millstone, he not being able to bear it up? Are not his wits and spirits, as it were, drowned? Is not his understanding altogether decayed? Do not his hands, and all his body vibrate, quaver and shake, as it were, with a quotidian fever? Besides these, it casteth him into a dropsy or pleurisy, nothing so soon; it enfeebleth the sinews, it weakeneth the natural strength, it corrupteth the blood, it dissolveth the whole man at the length, and finally maketh him forgetful of himself altogether, so that what he doth being drunk, he remembreth not being sober. The drunkard, in his drunkenness, killeth his friend, revileth his lover, discloseth secrets, and regardeth no man. He either expelleth all fear of God out of his mind, all love of his friends and kinsfolks, all remembrance of honesty, civility, and humanity; so that I will not fear to call drunkards beasts, and no men; and much worse than beasts, for beasts never exceed in any such kind of excess or superfluity, but alway *modum adhibent appetitui*, they measure their appetites by the rule of necessity, which, would God, we would do.

PHILIP STUBBES, *The Anatomie of Abuses* 1583 (2nd ed.)

DRINK

A fearful example

If all that hath been said hitherto, be not sufficient to withdraw us from this beastly vice of drunkenness: yet let us set before our eyes this most fearful judgment of God, executed upon a sort of drunkards, the story whereof is this. The eighth day of February 1578 in the country of Swaben, there were dwelling eight men, citizens, and citizens' sons, very riotously and prodigally inclined, the names of whom, for the better credit of the story, I have set down, viz. Adam Giebens, George Kepell, John Keisell, Peter Hersdorse, John Waganaer, Simon Henrickes, Herman Fron, Jacob Hermans, all which would needs go to the tavern upon the Sabbath day in the morning very early, in contempt of the Lord and his Sabbath. And coming to the house of one Anthony Hage, an honest, godly man, who kept a tavern in the same town, called for burnt wine, sack, malmsey, hippocras and what not. The host told them, that they should have none of all these, before the divine service and the sermon time were past, and counselled them to go hear the sacred word of God preached. But they (save Adam Giebens, who advised them to hear the sermon, for fear of God's wrath) denied, saying : That they loathed that kind of exercise. The good host, neither giving them any wine himself, nor suffering any other, went to the sermon, as duty did bind him, who being gone, they fell to cursing, banning, and swearing, wishing that he might break his neck, or ever he came again from the sermon ; and bursting forth into these intemperate speeches, " The Devil break our necks, if we depart hence this day, either quick or dead, till we have had some wine! " Straightway, the Devil appeared unto them, in the likeness of a young man, bringing in his hand a flagon of wine, and demanding of them why they caroused not, he drank unto them, saying: "Good fellows, be merry, for ye shall have wine enough, for you seem lusty lads, and I hope you will pay me well," who inconsiderately answered, that they would pay him, or else they would gage their necks, yea their bodies and souls, rather than to fail. Thus they continued swilling, gulling, and carousing so long, as till one could not see another. At the last the Devil their host, told them, that they must needs pay the shot, whereat their hearts waxed cold. But the Devil comforting them, said : "Be of good cheer, for now must you drink boiling lead, pitch and brimstone with me in the pit of hell for evermore." Hereupon immediately he made their eyes like flames of fire, and in breadth as broad as saucers. Then began they to call for mercy, but it was too late. And ere they could call again for mercy and grace, the Devil prevented them, and break their necks asunder, and threw most horrible flames of fire, flashing out of their mouths. And thus ended these seven drunkards their miserable days, whose judgment I leave to the Lord. The other Adam Giebens, who counselled them before to go to hear the sermon, having some sparks of faith in him, was preserved from death, by the great mercy of God, and greatly repented his former life, yielding praise unto God for his deliverance. Thus have I *in sempiternam rei memoriam*, faithfully recorded the story of these eight drunkards, and of their fearful end, taken out of the Dutch copy printed at Amsterdam, and at Strasbourg, for a caveat to all drunkards, gluttons, and riotous persons throughout the whole world, that they offend not the Lord in the like kind of offence.

PHILIP STUBBES, *The Anatomie of Abuses* 1583 (2nd ed.)

Ale-houses

Here's a pot of good double beer, neighbour.
                    2 *Henry VI.*, II. iii. 63

Mistress Quickly. By this heavenly ground I tread on, I must be fain to pawn both my plate and the tapestry of my dining-chambers.
Falstaff. Glasses, glasses, is the only drinking : and for thy walls, a pretty slight drollery, or the story of the Prodigal, or the German hunting in water-work, is worth a thousand of these bed-hangings and these fly-bitten tapestries.   2 *Henry IV.*, II. i. 156—163

If these houses have a box-bush, or an old post, it is enough to show their profession. But if they be graced with a sign complete, it's a sign of good custom. In these houses you shall see the history of Judith, Susanna, Daniel in the lions' den, or Dives and Lazarus painted upon the wall. It may be reckoned a wonder to see or find the house empty, for either the parson, churchwarden, or clerk, or all are doing some church or court business usually in this place. They thrive best where there are fewest : it is the host's chiefest pride to be speaking of such

a gentleman, or such a gallant that was here, and will be again
ere long. Hot weather and thunder, and want of company are
the hostess's grief, for then her ale sours. Your drink usually
is very young, two days old : her chiefest wealth is seen, if she
can have one brewing under another : if either the hostess, or
her daughter, or maid will kiss handsomely at parting, it is a
good shoeing-horn or birdlime to draw the company thither
again the sooner. She must be courteous to all, though not by
nature, yet by her profession ; for she must entertain all, good
and bad, tag and rag, cut and long-tail. She suspects tinkers
and poor soldiers most, not that they will not drink soundly,
but that they will not pay lustily. She must keep touch with
three sorts of men ; that is, the malt-man, the baker, and the
justice's clerks. She is merry, and half mad, upon Shrove
Tuesday, May days, feast days, and morris-dances : a good ring
of bells in the parish helps her to many a tester ; she prays the
parson may not be a puritan : a bagpiper, and a puppet-play
brings her in birds that are flush, she defies a wine tavern as an
upstart outlandish fellow, and suspects the wine to be poisoned.
Her ale, if new, looks like a misty morning, all thick ; well, if
her ale be strong, her reckoning right, her house clean, her fire
good, her face fair, and the town great or rich, she shall seldom
or never sit without chirping birds to bear her company, and at
the next churching or christening, she is sure to be rid of two
or three dozen of cakes and ale by gossiping neighbours.

DONALD LUPTON, *London and the Countrey carbonadoed* 1632

A Tavern

Falstaff's reckoning.

Item, A capon	...	...	...	2*s*. 2*d*.
Item, Sauce	...	...	...	4*d*.
Item, Sack, two gallons		...	...	5*s*. 8*d*.
Item, Anchovies and sack after supper				2*s*. 6*d*.
Item, Bread	...	...	...	ob.

1 *Henry IV.*, II. iv. 593—598

A tavern is a degree, or (if you will) a pair of stairs above an
alehouse, where men are drunk with more credit and apology.
If the vintner's nose be at door, it is a sign sufficient, but the
absence of this is supplied by the ivy bush. The rooms are ill
breathed, like the drinkers that have been washed well over-

night, and are smelt too fasting next morning....It is a broacher of more news than hogsheads, and more jests than news, which are sucked up here by some spongy brain, and from thence squeezed into a comedy. Men come here to make merry, but indeed make a noise, and this music above is answered with the clinking below. The drawers are the civilest people in it, men of good bringing up, and howsoever we esteem of them, none can boast more justly of their high calling. 'Tis the best theatre of natures, where they are truly acted, not played, and the business, as in the rest of the world, up and down, to wit, from the bottom of the cellar to the great chamber. A melancholy man would find here matter to work upon, to see heads as brittle as glasses, and often broken. Men come hither to quarrel, and come hither to be made friends; and if Plutarch will lend me his simile, it is even Telephus his sword that makes wounds and cures them. It is the common consumption of the afternoon, and the murderer or maker away of a rainy day. It is the Torrid Zone that scorches the face, and tobacco the gun-powder that blows it up. Much harm would be done, if the charitable vintner had not water ready for these flames. A house of sin you may call it, but not a house of darkness, for the candles are never out, and it is like those countries far in the north, where it is as clear at mid-night as at mid-day....To give you the total reckoning of it: it is the busy man's recreation, the idle man's business, the melancholy man's sanctuary, the stranger's welcome, the Inns of Court man's entertainment, the scholar's kindness, and the citizen's courtesy. It is the study of sparkling wits, and a cup of canary their book, where we leave them.

John Earle, Micro-cosmographie 1628

Shakespeare and Ben Jonson at the Mermaid Tavern

Many were the wit-combats betwixt him and Ben Jonson; which two I behold like a Spanish great galleon and an English man-of-war. Master Jonson (like the former) was built far higher in learning; solid, but slow, in his performances. Shakespeare, with the English man-of-war, lesser in bulk, but lighter in sailing, could turn with all tides, tack about, and take advantage of all winds, by the quickness of his wit and invention.

Thomas Fuller, English Worthies 1662

TOBACCO

The Sobriety of the English (two views)

Iago. Some wine, ho !
    And let me the canakin clink, clink;
    And let me the canakin clink:
    A soldier's a man;
    A life's but a span;
    Why then let a soldier drink.
Some wine, boys!
Cassio. 'Fore God, an excellent song.
Iago. I learned it in England, where indeed they are most potent in potting; your Dane, your German, and your swag-bellied Hollander,—drink, ho!—are nothing to your English.   *Othello*, II. iii. 71—82

For the point of drinking, the English at the feast will drink two or three healths in remembrance of special friends, or respected honourable persons, and in our time some gentlemen and commanders from the wars of Netherland brought in the custom of the Germans' large carousing, but this custom is in our time also in good measure left. Likewise in some private gentlemen's houses, and with some captains and soldiers, and with the vulgar sort of citizens and artisans, large and intemperate drinking is used; but in general the greater and better part of the English, hold all excess blameworthy, and drunkenness a reproachful vice.

            FYNES MORYSON, *Itinerary* 1617

B. Tobacco

A tobacco-seller

Is the only man that finds the good in it which others brag of, but do not; for it is meat, drink, and clothes to him. No man opens his ware with greater seriousness, or challenges your judgment more in the approbation. His shop is the rendezvous of spitting, where men dialogue with their noses, and their communication is smoke. It is the place only where Spain is commended and preferred before England itself. He should be well experienced in the world; for he has daily trial of men's nostrils, and none is better acquainted with humours. He is the piecing, commonly, of some other trade, which is bawd to his tobacco, and that to his wife, which is the flame that follows this smoke.

            JOHN EARLE, *Micro-cosmographie* 1628

Royal disapprobation of tobacco

How you are by this custom disabled in your goods, let the gentry of this land bear witness, some of them bestowing three, some four hundred pounds a year upon this precious stink, which I am sure might be bestowed upon many far better uses. I read indeed of a knavish courtier, who for abusing the favour of the emperor Alexander Severus, his master, by taking bribes to intercede for sundry persons in his master's ear (for whom he never once opened his mouth), was justly choked with smoke, with this doom, *Fumo pereat, qui fumum vendidit* : but of so many smoke-buyers, as are at this present in this kingdom, I never read nor heard.

And for the vanities committed in this filthy custom, is it not both great vanity and uncleanness, that at the table, a place of respect, of cleanliness, of modesty, men should not be ashamed to sit tossing of tobacco pipes, and puffing of the smoke of tobacco one to another, making the filthy smoke and stink thereof to exhale athwart the dishes, and infect the air, when very often men that abhor it are at their repast ? Surely smoke becomes a kitchen far better than a dining chamber, and yet it makes a kitchen also oftentimes in the inward parts of men, soiling and infecting them, with an unctuous and oily kind of soot, as hath been found in some great tobacco takers, that after their death were opened. And not only meat time, but no other time nor action is exempted from the public use of this uncivil trick : so as if the wives of Dieppe list to contest with this nation for good manners, their worst manners would in all reason be found at least not so dishonest (as ours are) in this point. The public use whereof, at all times and in all places, hath now so far prevailed, as divers men very sound both in judgment and complexion, have been at last forced to take it also without desire, partly because they were ashamed to seem singular (like the two philosophers that were forced to duck themselves in that rain water, and so become fools as well as the rest of the people), and partly, to be as one that was content to eat garlic (which he did not love) that he might not be troubled with the smell of it in the breath of his fellows. And is it not a great vanity, that a man cannot heartily welcome his friend now, but straight they must be in hand with tobacco ?

TOBACCO

No, it is become in place of a cure a point of good fellowship, and he that will refuse to take a pipe of tobacco among his fellows (though by his own election he would rather feel the savour of a sink), is accounted peevish and no good company, even as they do with tippling in the cold eastern countries. Yea the mistress cannot in a more mannerly kind entertain her servant, than by giving him out of her fair hand a pipe of tobacco. But herein is not only a great vanity, but a great contempt of God's good gifts, that the sweetness of man's breath, being a good gift of God, should be wilfully corrupted by this stinking smoke, wherein I must confess, it hath too strong a virtue : and so that which is an ornament of nature, and can neither by any artifice be at the first acquired, nor once lost, be recovered again, shall be filthily corrupted with an incurable stink, which vile quality is as directly contrary to that wrong opinion which is holden of the wholesomeness thereof, as the venom of putrifaction is contrary to the virtue preservative.

Moreover, which is a great iniquity and against all humanity, the husband shall not be ashamed to reduce thereby his delicate, wholesome, and clean complexioned wife to that extremity, that either she must also corrupt her sweet breath therewith, or else resolve to live in a perpetual stinking torment.

Have you not reason then to be ashamed, and to forbear this filthy novelty, so basely grounded, so foolishly received and so grossly mistaken in the right use thereof ? In your abuse thereof sinning against God, harming yourselves both in persons and goods, and raking [? taking] also thereby the marks and notes of vanity upon you : by the custom thereof making yourselves to be wondered at by all foreign civil nations, and by all strangers that come among you, to be scorned and contemned. A custom loathsome to the eye, hateful to the nose, harmful to the brain, dangerous to the lungs, and in the black stinking fume thereof nearest resembling the horrible Stigian smoke of the pit that is bottomless.

KING JAMES I., *A counter-blast to Tobacco* 1672 (written 1604)

C. Dicing and Gaming

For gourd and fullam holds,
And high and low beguile the rich and poor.

The Merry Wives of Windsor, I. iii. 92

He won it of me with false dice.

Much Ado About Nothing, II. i. 291

Multitude of cheaters

Now, such is the misery of our time, or such is the
licentious outrage of idle misgoverned persons, that of only
dicers a man might have half an army, the greatest number so
gaily be-seen, and so full of money, that they 'bash not to
insinuate themselves into the company of the highest, and look
for a good hour to creep into a gentleman's room of the privy
chamber. And hereof you may right well assure yourself, that
if their cost were not exceeding great, it were not possible by
the only help thereof to lead so sumptuous a life as they do,
always shining like blazing stars in their apparel, by night
taverning with strumpets, by day spoiling gentlemen of their
inheritance. And to speak all at once, like as all good and
liberal sciences had a rude beginning, and by the industry of
good men, being augmented by little and by little, at last grow
to a just perfection ; so this detestable privy robbery, from a
few and deceitful rules, is in few years grown to the body of
an art, and hath his peculiar terms and thereof as great a
multitude applied to it, as hath grammar, or logic, or any other
of the approved sciences.

A Gaming-house (catching a " cousin ")

I told him I was yet but a raw courtier, as one that came
from school not many months afore, and was now become
servant to my lord Chancellor of England ; partly to see
experience of things the better to govern myself hereafter, and,
chiefly to have a staff to lean unto to defend mine own. And
he again commended me much therein, declaring how divers
notable persons, rashly by ignorance misguiding themselves,
were suddenly shaken asunder, and fallen on the rocks of
extreme penury : and how some other, even goodly wits,

circumspectly working in all their doings, have, by want of such a leaning-stock, been overthrown with tyrants' power. "For which cause," quoth he, "like as I cannot but praise your wary working in this your first courting, so for my lord your master's sake you shall not lack the best that I may do for you : for, albeit that I am much beholding to all the lords of the counsel (as whom they stick not at all times to take to their board, and use sometime for a companion at play), yet is he my singular good lord above all the rest ; and, if I shall confess the truth, a great part of my living hath risen by his friendly pre-ferment ; and, though I say it myself, I am too old a courtier, and have seen too much, to bear nothing away ; and, in case our acquaintance hold, and, by daily company, gather deep root, I shall now and then shew you a lesson worth the learning ; and to the end hereafter each of us may be the bolder of the other, I pray you, if ye be not otherwise bespoken, take a capon with me at dinner. Though your fare be but homely and scant, yet a cup of good wine I can promise you, and all other lacks shall be supplied with a friendly welcome."...

Soon after we came home to his house, the table was fair spread with diaper cloths, the cupboard garnished with much goodly plate, and last of all came forth the gentlewoman, his wife, clothed in silks and embroidered works : the attire of her head broidered with gold and pearl ; a carcanet about her neck, agreeable thereto, with a flower of diamonds pendant thereat, and many fair rings on her finger. "Bess," quoth he, "bid this gentleman welcome" : and with that she courteously kissed me ; and, after, moved communication of my name, my natural country, what time my father died, and whether I were married yet or not, always powdering our talk with such pretty devices, that I saw not a woman in all my life whose fashions and entertainment I liked better. The good man, in the mean season, had been in the kitchen ; and suddenly returning and breaking our talk, somewhat sharply blamed his wife that the dinner was no further forward ; and whiles she withdrew her from us, by like to put all things in a good readiness, "Come on," quoth he, "you shall go see my house the while ; it is not like your large country houses ; rooms, ye wot, in London be strait, but yet the furniture of them be costly enough ; and victuals be here at such high prices, that much money is soon consumed, specially with them that maintain an idle household; nevertheless, assure yourself that no man is welcomer than you to such cheer as ye find ": and, consequently, bringing me through divers well-trimmed chambers, the worst of them apparelled with verdures, some with rich cloth of arras, all with beds, chairs, and cushions of silk and gold, of sundry colours, suitably wrought. " Lo ! here," quoth he, " a poor man's lodging ; which if ye think it may do you any pleasure (for the inns of London be the worst of England), take your choice, and heartily welcome ; reserving but one for my lord, my wife's cousin, whom I dare not disappoint, lest happily he should lower, and make the house too hot for us." I gave him thanks, as meet it was I should, neither yet refusing his gentle offer (for, indeed, mine own lodging is somewhat loathsome, and pestered with company), nor yet embracing it, because hitherto I had not by any means deserved so great a pleasure. So down we came again into the parlour, and found three divers gentlemen, all strangers to me ; and what should I say more, but to dinner we went....

As touching our fare, though partridge and quail were no dainties, and wines of sundry grapes flowed abundantly, yet spare I to speak thereto....So soon as we had well victualled ourselves, I wot not how, but easily it came to pass that we talked of news: namely, of Boulogne ; how hardly it was won; what policy then was practised to get it ; and what case the soldiers had in the siege of it ; insomuch that the least progress the king maketh into the inland parts of the realm dislodgeth more of his train, and leaveth them to their own provision, with less relief of victuals than had the worst unwaged adventurer there. From this the good man led us to talk of home pleasures ; enlarging the beauties of peace and London pastimes, and made so jolly a discourse thereof, that, to my judgment, he seemed skilful in all things. " Methinks," quoth he, " such simple fare as this, taken in peace, without fear and danger of gun-shot, is better than a prince's purveyance in war, where each morsel he eateth shall bring with it a present fear of sudden mischance, or violent hostility : and though that in the open camp none [?one] might have more familiar access to the nobility than here at home, yet, for my part, I thank God, I have no cause to complain either, because of their gentleness; no usher keeps the door between me and them when I come to visit them, or that the greatest princes refuse not sometimes to hallow my poor table and house with their person; which (be it spoken without boast, or embraiding) doth sometime cost me twenty pounds a-day. I am sure that some of this company do remember what a brave company of lords supped with me the last term, and I think how ye have heard how some of them gat an hundred pounds or two by their coming." With this and that like talk, consumed was our dinner. And, after the table was removed, in came one of the waiters with a fair silver bowl, full of dice and cards. "Now, masters" quoth the goodman, "who is so disposed to fall to: here is my twenty pounds; win it, and wear it." Then each man chose his game: some kept the goodman company at the hazard, some matched themselves at a new game called primero....

They egged me to have made one at dice, and told me it was a shame for a gentleman not to keep gentlemen company for his twenty or forty crowns: nevertheless, because I alleged ignorance, the gentlewoman said I should not sit idle, all the rest being occupied, and so we two fell to saunt, five games a crown....I passed not for the loss of twenty or forty shillings for acquaintance, and so much I think it cost me, and then I left off. Marry the dice-players stuck well by it and made very fresh play, saving one or two, that were clean shriven, and had no more money to lose. In the end, when I should take my leave to depart, I could not by any means be suffered so to break company, unless I would deliver the gentlewoman a ring for a gage of my return to supper, and so I did; and, to tell you all in few words, I have haunted none other since I got that acquaintance: my meat, and drink and lodging is every way so delicate, that I make no haste to change it.

Cheating and False Dice (a cheater speaks)

Ye know that this outrageous swearing and quarrelling that some use in play, giveth occasion to many to forbear that else would adventure much money at it; for this we have a device amongst us, that rather we relent and give place to a wrong, than we would cause the play, by strife, to cause any company to break ; neither have we any oaths in use but lightly these : "of honesty," "of truth," "by salt," "Martin !" which, when we use them affirmatively, we mean always directly the contrary. As for example, if haply I say unto you when the dice cometh to your hands, " Of honesty cast at all," my meaning is that ye shall cast at the board or else at very little. If, when a thing is offered in gage, I swear, "By Saint Martin I think it fine gold," then mean I the contrary, that it is but copper. And like as it is a gentle and old proverb : let losers have their words ; so by the way take forth this lesson, ever to shew gentleness to the silly fools, and creep if ye can into their very bosoms. For harder it is to hold them when ye have them, than for the first time to take them up ; for these young wits be so light and so wavering, that it requireth great travail to make them always dance after one pipe. But to follow that we have in hand, be they young, be they old that falleth into our laps, and be ignorant of our art, we call them all by the name of a "cousin" ; as men that we make as much of as if they were of our kin. Indeed, the greatest wisdom of our faculty resteth in this point ; diligently to foresee to make the "cousin" sweat, that is to have a will to keep play and company, and always to beware that we cause him not smoke, lest that, having any feel or savour of guile intended against him, he slip the collar as it were a hound, and shake us off for ever. And whensoever ye take up a "cousin," be sure, as near as ye can, to know aforehand what store of bit he hath in his bag, that is, what money he hath in his purse, and whether it be in great coggs or in small, that is, gold or silver ; and at what game he will soonest stoop, that we may feed him with his own humour, and have cauls ready for him ; for thousands there be that will not play a groat at novem, and yet will lose a hundred pound at the hazard ; and he that will not stoop a dodkin at the dice, perchance at cards will spend God's cope ; therefore they must be provided for every way. Generally your fine cheats, though they be good made both in the King's Bench and in the Marshalsea, yet Bird in Holborn is the finest workman; acquaint yourself with him, and let him make you a bale or two of quarters [?caters] of sundry sizes, some less, some more, to throw into the first play, till ye perceive what your company is. Then have in a readiness, to be foisted in when time shall be, your fine cheats of all sorts; be sure to have in store of such as these be :—a bale of barred cinque-deuces and flat cinque-deuces, a bale of barred six-aces and flat six-aces, a bale of barred cater-treys and flat cater-treys*, the advantage whereof is all on the one side and consisteth in the forging. Provide also a bale or two of fullams, for they have great use at the hazard : and though they be square outward, yet, being within at the corner with lead or other ponderous matter stopped, minister as great an advantage as any of the rest ; ye must also be furnished with high men and low men for a mumchance and for passage. Yea, and a long die for even and odd is good to strike a small stroke withal, for a crown or two, or the price of a dinner. As for gourds and bristle dice, they be now too gross a practice to be put in use ; light graviers there be, demies, contraries, and of all sorts, forged clean against the apparent vantage, which have special and sundry uses. But it is enough at this time to put you in a remembrance what tools ye must prepare to make you a workman.

Card-sharping

Is there as much craft at cards as ye have rehearsed at the dice ?

Altogether, I would not give a point to choose ; they have such a sleight in sorting and shuffling of the cards, that play at what game ye will, all is lost aforehand. If two be confederated to beguile the third, the thing is compassed with the more ease than if one be but alone, yet are there many ways to deceive. Primero, now as it hath most use in court, so is there most deceit in it : some play upon the prick ; some pinch the cards privily with their nails ; some turn up the corners ; some mark them with fine spots of ink. One fine trick brought in a Spaniard : a finer than this invented an Italian, and won much money with it by our doctors, and yet, at the last, they were both overreached by new sleights devised here at home. At trump, saint, and such other like, cutting at the neck is a great vantage, so is cutting by a bum card (finely) under and over,

* See glossary under " False Dice."

stealing the stock of the decarded cards, if there be broad laws beforced aforehand. At decoy, they draw easily twenty hands together, and play all upon assurance when to win or lose. Other helps I have heard of besides ; as, to set the " cousin" upon the bench with a great looking-glass behind him on the wall, wherein the cheater might always see what cards were in his hand. Sometimes they work by signs made by some of the lookers-on. Wherefore methinks this, among the rest, proceeded of a fine invention. A gamester, after he had been oftentimes bitten among cheaters, and after much loss, grew very suspicious in his play, that he could not suffer any of the sitters by to be privy to his game ; for this the cheaters devised a new shift. A woman should sit sewing besides him ; and by the shift, or slow drawing her needle, give a token to the cheater what was the " cousin's " game. So that from a few examples instead of infinite that might be rehearsed, this one universal conclusion may be gathered, that give you to play, and yield yourself to loss.

GILBERT WALKER ? *A Manifest detection of Dice-play* 1532

D. Debt and Usury

Falstaff. Boy !
Page. Sir !
Falstaff. What money is in my purse ?
Page. Seven groats and twopence.
Falstaff. I can get no remedy against this consumption of the purse : borrowing only lingers and lingers it out, but the disease is incurable.

2 Henry IV., I. ii. 264—270

First, here's young Master Rash ; he's in for a commodity of brown paper, and old ginger, nine-score and seventeen pounds, of which he made five marks, ready money....Then is there here one Master Caper, at the suit of Master Three-pile the mercer, for some four suits of peach-coloured satin, which now peaches him a beggar.

Measure for Measure, IV. iii. 4—21

A Portrait of a Usurer

The first of them is Usury (a devil of good credit in the city) who having privily stolen a sufficient stock from the old miser his father, hath lately set up for himself, and hath four of his brothers his apprentices. The first of them is Hardness-of-

118

DEBT

Heart, who bringing into his bank contempt-of-the-poor, is set by him to beat beggars from his door, and arrest his debtors by latitats. The second is, Unmeasurable-Care-and-Trouble-of-Mind, who hath brought this portion to be employed: destruction-of-the-mind, neglect-of-God's-service, want-of-faith, jealousy-of-loss: he keeps the cash, and suffers not a mouse to enter, but he scores him. The third is Violence, and for him he hath bought a sergeant's office, who hath so many eyes like Argus to watch that no poor creditor can escape him: his stock is a bunch of writs, and a hanger, and ordinarily he wears his mace at his back instead of a dagger. The fourth is Rapine, and he jets about the streets to steal for him: he is a passing good hooker and picklock; and for a short knife and a horn thimble, turn him loose to all the fraternity: his stock is false keys, engines, and sword-and-buckler: him he employs to rob from them he hath lent money to, to the end they may be the fitter to commit a forfeiture.

This Usury is jump of the complexion of the baboon his father; he is haired like a great ape, and swart like a tawny Indian, his horns are sometimes hidden in a button cap (as Th. Nashe described him), but now he is fallen to his flat cap, because he is chief warden of his company: he is narrow-browed, and squirrel-eyed, and the chiefest ornament of his face is, that his nose sticks in the midst like an embossment in terrace work, here and there embellished and decked with *verucæ* for want of purging with agaric; some authors have compared it to a rutter's cod-piece, but I like not the allusion so well, by reason the tyings have no correspondence. His mouth is always mumbling, as if he were at his matins: and his beard is bristled here and there like a sow that had the lousy. Double-chinned he is, and over his throat hangs a bunch of skin like a money-bag. Band wears he none, but a welt of coarse holland, and if you see it stitched with blue thread, it is no workaday wearing. His truss is the piece of an old packcloth, the mark washed out; and if you spy a pair of Bridges' satin sleeves to it, you may be assured it is a holiday. His points are the edging of some cast packsaddle, cut out sparingly (I warrant you) to serve him and his household for trussing leather. His jacket forsooth is faced with moth-eaten budge, and it is no less than Lisle grogram of the worst. It is bound to his body with a cordelier's girdle, dyed black for comeliness sake: and in his bosom he bears his handkerchief made of the reversion of his old tablecloth. His spectacles hang beating over his codpiece like the flag in the top of a maypole. His breeches and stockings are of one piece I warrant you, which, having served him in pure kersey for the tester of a bed some twenty years, is by the frugality of a dyer and the courtesy of a tailor for this present made a sconce for his buttocks. His shoes of the old cut, broad at the toes and cross-buckled with brass, and have loop-holes like a sconce for his toes to shoot out at. His gown is suitable, and as seemly as the rest, full of threads I warrant you, wheresoever the wool is employed, welted on the back with the clipping of a bare cast velvet hood, and faced with foins that had kept a widow's tail warm twenty winters before his time.

Thus attired, he walks Paul's, coughing at every step as if he were broken-winded, grunting sometime for the pain of the stone and strangury: and continually thus old, and seeming ready to die, he notwithstanding lives to confound many families. If you come to borrow money, he will take no usury, no marry will he not: but if you require ten pound, you shall pay him forty shillings for an old cap, and the rest is yours in ready money; the man loves good dealing. If you desire commodities at his hand, why sir you shall have them, but how? not (as the caterpillars wont to sell) at high prices, but at the best and easiest pennyworth, as in conscience you can desire them: only this, at the insealing of the assurance, if you help him away with a chest of glass for ten pound of ten shillings price, you shall command his warehouse another time. Tut he is for you at casual marts, commodities of proclamations and hobby-horses, you shall have all that you please, so he receive what he desires. It is a common custom of his to buy up cracked angels at nine shillings the piece. Now sir if a gentleman (on good assurance of land) request him of money, "Good sir," saith he, with a counterfeit sigh "I would be glad to please your worship, but my good money is abroad, and that I have, I dare not put in your hands." The gentleman thinking this conscience, where it is subtlety, and being beside that in some necessity, ventures on the cracked angels, some of which cannot fly for soldering, and pays double interest to the miser, under the cloak of honesty. If he fails his day, God forbid he should take the forfeiture, he will not thrive by other men's curses, but because men must live, and we are infidels if we provide not for our families, he is content with this his own; only a leaf, a toy of this or that manor, worth both his principal and ten times the interest; this is easy for the gentleman to pay, and reasonable in him to receive. If a citizen come to borrow, "My friend" quoth he, "you must keep day, I am glad to help young men without harming myself": then paying him out the money and receiving his assurance, he casts Jolly Robins in his head how to cozen the simple fellow. If he have a shop well furnished, a stock to receive out of the Chamber, possibility after the death of his father, all this he hearkens after: and if he fail of his day, "Well," saith he, "for charity sake I will forbear you, mine interest paid": meanwhile (unknown to the wretch) he sues him upon the original to an outlawry, and if the second time he fail (as by some slight encouragement he causes him to do) he turns him out a doors like a careless young man, yet for Christianity sake, he lets him at liberty, and will in charity content him with his goods.

THOMAS LODGE, *Wits Miserie* 1596

The Debtors' Prison

Shylock.   Gaoler, look to him : tell me not of mercy.
The Merchant of Venice, III. iii. 1

Portia.   But mercy is above this sceptred sway
It is enthroned in the hearts of kings,
It is an attribute to God himself,
And earthly power doth then show likest God's
When mercy seasons justice.   *Ibid.* IV. i. 193—197

You have another cruelty in keeping men in prison so long, till sickness and death deal mildly with them, and (in despite of all tyranny) bail them out of all executions. When you see a poor wretch that to keep life in a loathed body hath not a house left to cover his head from the tempests, nor a bed (but the common bed which our mother the earth allows him) for his cares to sleep upon, when you have (by keeping or locking him up) robbed him of all means to get, what seek you to have him lose but his life? The miserable prisoner is ready to famish, yet that cannot move you; the more miserable wife is ready to run mad with despair, yet that cannot melt you; the most of all miserable, his children lie crying at your doors, yet nothing can awaken in you compassion. If his debts be heavy, the greater and more glorious is your pity to work his freedom; if they be light, the sharper is the vengeance that will be heaped upon your heads for your hardness of heart. We are most like to God that made us, when we shew love one to another, and do most look like the devil that would destroy us, when we are one another's tormentors. If any have so much flint growing about his bosom, that he will needs make dice of men's bones, I would there were a law to compel him to make drinking bowls of their skulls too: and that every miserable debtor that so dies, might be buried at his creditor's door, that when he strides over him he might think he still rises up (like the Ghost in *Ieronimo*) crying ' Revenge.'

THOMAS DEKKER, *The Seuen Deadly Sinnes of London* 1606

§ 5. Dress and Fashion

> One touch of nature makes the whole world kin,
> That all with one consent praise new-born gawds.
> *Troilus and Cressida*, III. iii. 174—175

Nerissa. What say you, then, to Falconbridge, the young baron of England ?

Portia. ...How oddly he is suited! I think he bought his doublet in Italy, his round hose in France, his bonnet in Germany, and his behaviour every where. *The Merchant of Venice*, I. ii. 70—81

Petruchio. We will return unto thy father's house,
And revel it as bravely as the best,
With silken coats and caps and golden rings,
With ruffs and cuffs and farthingales and things;
With scarfs and fans and double change of bravery,
With amber bracelets, beads and all this knavery.

> *   *   *   *   *   *

Haberdasher. Here is the cap your worship did bespeak.
Petruchio. Why, this was moulded on a porringer;
A velvet dish: fie, fie! 'tis lewd and filthy:
Why, 'tis a cockle or a walnut-shell,
A knack, a toy, a trick, a baby's cap:
Away with it! come, let me have a bigger.

> *   *   *   *   *

DRESS AND FASHION

Petruchio.	Thy gown? why, ay: come, tailor, let us see't.
	Oh mercy, God! what masquing stuff is here?
	What's this? a sleeve? 'tis like a demi-cannon:
	What! up and down, carv'd like an apple-tart?
	Here's snip and nip and cut and slish and slash,
	Like to a censer in a barber's shop.
	* * * * * *
Tailor.	You bid me make it orderly and well,
	According to the fashion of the time.

The Taming of the Shrew, IV. iii. 53—95

Fashion in general

The fantastical folly of our nation (even from the courtier to the carter), is such that no form of apparel liketh us longer than the first garment is in the wearing, if it continue so long, and be not laid aside to receive some other trinket newly devised by the fickle-headed tailors, who covet to have several tricks in cutting, thereby to draw fond customers to more expense of money. For my part, I can tell better how to inveigh against this enormity than describe any certainty of our attire ; sithence such is our mutability, that to-day there is none to the Spanish guise, to-morrow the French toys are most fine and delectable, ere long no such apparel as that which is after the high Almain fashion, by-and-bye the Turkish manner is generally best liked of, otherwise the Morisco gowns, the Barbarian fleeces, the mandilion worn to Colleyweston ward, and the short French breeches make a comely vesture that, except it were a dog in a doublet, you shall not see any so disguised as are my countrymen of England. And as these fashions are diverse, so likewise it is a world to see the costliness and the curiosity, the excess and the vanity, the pomp and the bravery, the change and the variety, and finally the fickleness and the folly, that is in all degrees, insomuch that nothing is more constant in England than inconstancy of attire. Oh, how much cost is bestowed nowadays upon our bodies, and how little upon our souls! How many suits of apparel hath the one, and how little furniture hath the other! How long time is asked in decking up of the first, and how little space left wherein to feed the latter! How curious, how nice also, are a number of men and women, and how hardly can the tailor please them in making it fit for their bodies! How many times must it be sent back again to him that made it! What chafing, what fretting, what reproachful language, doth the poor workman bear away! And many times when he doth nothing to it at all, yet when it is brought home again it is very fit and handsome. Then must we put it on, then must the long seams of our hose be set by a plumb-line, then we puff, then we blow, and finally sweat till we drop, that our clothes may stand well upon us. I will say nothing of our heads, which sometimes are polled, sometimes curled, or suffered to grow at length like woman's locks, many times cut off, above or under the ears, round as by a wooden dish. Neither will I meddle with our variety of beards, of which some are shaven from the chin like those of Turks, not a few cut short like to the beard of Marquess Otto, some made round like a rubbing-brush, others with a *pique de vant* (O! fine fashion), or now and then suffered to grow long, the barbers being grown to be so cunning in this behalf as the tailors. And therefore if a man have a lean and straight face, a Marquess Otto's cut will make it broad and large; if it be platter-like, a long, slender beard will make it seem the narrower; if he be weasel-beaked, then much hair left on the cheeks will make the owner look big like a bowdled hen, and so grim as a goose, if Cornelis of Chelmsford say true. Many old men do wear no beards at all. Some lusty courtiers also and gentlemen of courage do wear either rings of gold, stones, or pearl in their ears, whereby they imagine the workmanship of God not to be a little amended. But herein they rather disgrace than adorn their persons, as by their niceness in apparel, for which I say most nations do not unjustly deride us, as also for that we do seem to imitate all nations round about us, wherein we be like to the polypus or chameleon; and thereunto bestow most cost upon our arses, and much more than upon all the rest of our bodies, as women do likewise upon their heads and shoulders. In women also, it is most to be lamented, that they do now far exceed the lightness of our men (who nevertheless are transformed from the cap even to the very shoe), and such staring attire, as in time past was supposed meet for none but light housewives only, is now become a habit for chaste and sober matrons. What should I say of their doublets with pendant codpieces on the breast, full of jags and cuts, and sleeves of sundry colours? Their galligaskins to bear out their bums and make their attire to fit plum round (as they term it) about them. Their farthingales, and diversely coloured nether stocks of silk, jersey, and such like, whereby their bodies are rather deformed than commended? I have met with some of these trulls in London so disguised that it hath passed my skill to discern whether they were men or women.

Thus it is now come to pass, that women are become men, and men transformed into monsters.

WILLIAM HARRISON, *Description of England* 1587 (2nd ed.)

The sin of gorgeous attire

England, the players' stage of gorgeous attire, the ape of all nations' superfluities, the continual masquer in outlandish habiliments, great plenty-scanting calamities art thou to await, for wanton disguising thyself against kind, and digressing from the plainness of thy ancestors. Scandalous and shameful is it, that not any in thee (fishermen and husbandmen set aside) but live above their ability and birth; that the outward habit (which in other countries is the only distinction of honour) should yield in thee no difference of persons: that all thy ancient nobility (almost), with this gorgeous prodigality, should be devoured and eaten up, and upstarts inhabit their stately palaces, who from far have fetched in this variety of pride to entrap and to spoil them. Those of thy people that in all other things are miserable, in their apparel will be prodigal. No land can so unfallibly experience this proverb, *The hood makes not the monk*, as thou; for tailors, serving-men, make-shifts, and gentlemen in thee are confounded. For the compassment of bravery, we have them will rob, steal, cozen, cheat, betray their own fathers, swear and forswear, or do any thing. Take away bravery, you kill the heart of lust and incontinency. Wherefore do men make themselves brave, but to riot and to revel? Look after what state their apparel is, that state they take to them and carry, and after a little accustoming to that carriage, persuade themselves they are such indeed....

We here in London, what for dressing ourselves, following our worldly affairs, dining, supping, and keeping company, have no leisure, not only not to watch against sin, but not so much as once to think of sin. In bed, wives must question their

125

husbands about housekeeping, and providing for their children and family. No service must God expect of us, but a little in Lent, and in sickness and adversity. Our gorgeous attire we make not to serve Him, but to serve the flesh. If He were pleased with it, why did they ever in the old law, (when they presented themselves before Him, in fasting and prayer), rend it off their backs, and put on coarse sackcloth and ashes? No lifting up a man's self that God likes, but the lifting up of the spirit in prayer.

One thing it is for a man to lift up himself to God, another thing to lift up himself against God. In pranking up our carcasses too proudly, we lift up our flesh against God. In lifting up our flesh, we depress our spirits. London, lay off thy gorgeous attire, and cast down thyself before God in contrition and prayer, lest He cast thee down in His indignation into hell fire.

THOMAS NASHE, *Christs Teares over Ierusalem* 1593

The portrait of a dandy

At last, to close up the lamentable tragedy of us ploughmen, enters our young landlord, so metamorphosed into the shape of a French puppet, that at the first we started, and thought one of the baboons had marched in in man's apparel. His head was dressed up in white feathers like a shuttlecock, which agreed so well with his brain, being nothing but cork, that two of the biggest of the guard might very easily have tossed him with battledores, and made good sport with him in his majesty's great hall. His doublet was of a strange cut; and shew the fury of his humour, the collar of it rose up so high and sharp as if it would have cut his throat by daylight. His wings, according to the fashion now, were as little and diminutive as a puritan's ruff, which shewed he ne'er meant to fly out of England, nor do any exploit beyond sea, but live and die about London, though he begged in Finsbury. His breeches, a wonder to see, were full as deep as the middle of winter, or the roadway between London and Winchester, and so large and wide withal, that I think within a twelvemonth he might very well put all his lands in them; and then you may imagine they were big enough, when they would outreach a thousand acres. Moreover, they differed so far from our fashioned hose in

126

the country, and from his father's old gascoins, that his back-part seemed to us like a monster; the roll of the breeches standing so low, that we conjectured his house of office, sir-reverence, stood in his hams. All this while his French monkey bore his cloak of three pounds a yard, lined clean through with purple velvet, which did so dazzle our coarse eyes, that we thought we should have been purblind ever after, what with the prodigal aspect of that and his glorious rapier and hangers all bossed with pillars of gold, fairer in show than the pillars in Paul's or the tombs at Westminster. Beside, it drunk up the price of all my plough-land in very pearl, which stuck as thick upon those hangers as the white measles upon hogs' flesh. When I had well viewed that gay gaudy cloak and those unthrifty wasteful hangers, I muttered thus to myself: "That is no cloak for the rain, sure; nor those no hangers for Derrick": when of a sudden, casting mine eyes lower, I beheld a curious pair of boots of king Philip's leather, in such artificial wrinkles, sets and plaits, as if they had been starched lately and came new from the laundress's, such was my ignorance and simple acquaintance with the fashion, and I dare swear my fellows and neighbours here are all as ignorant as myself. But that which struck us most into admiration, upon those fantastical boots stood such huge and wide tops, which so swallowed up his thighs, that had he sworn as other gallants did, this common oath, "Would I might sink as I stand!" all his body might very well have sunk down and been damned in his boots. Lastly he walked the chamber with such a pestilent gingle that his spurs oversqueaked the lawyer, and made him reach his voice three notes above his fee; but after we had spied the rowels of his spurs, how we blest ourselves! they did so much and so far exceed the compass of our fashion, that they looked more like the forerunners of wheelbarrows. Thus was our young landlord accoutred in such a strange and prodigal shape that it amounted to above two years' rent in apparel.

THOMAS MIDDLETON ? *Father Hubburds Tales* 1604

LONDON

Fashion descends

All manners of attire came first into the city and country from the court, which, being once received by the common people, and by very stage-players themselves, the courtiers justly cast off, and take new fashions, (though somewhat too curiously); and whosoever wears the old, men look upon him as a picture in arras hangings. For it is proverbially said, that we may eat according to our own appetite, but in our apparel must follow the fashion of the multitude, with whom we live. But in the meantime it is no reproach to any, who of old did wear those garments, when they were in fashion. In like sort, many dances and measures are used in Court, but when they come to be vulgar and to be used upon very stages, courtiers and gentlemen think them uncomely to be used, yet is it no reproach to any man who formerly had skill therein.

FYNES MORYSON, *Itinerary* 1617

Barbers

Claudio. If he be not in love with some woman, there is no believing old signs: a' brushes his hat a mornings; what should that bode?
Don Pedro. Hath any man seen him at the barber's?
Claudio. No, but the barber's man hath been seen with him; and the old ornament of his cheek hath already stuffed tennis balls.
Leonato. Indeed he looks younger than he did, by the loss of a beard.

Much Ado About Nothing, III. ii. 40—49

How many cowards, whose hearts are all as false
As stairs of sand, wear yet upon their chins
The beards of Hercules and frowning Mars,
Who, inward search'd, have livers white as milk;
And these assume but valour's excrement
To render them redoubted!

The Merchant of Venice, III. ii. 83—88

Theodorus. What say you of the barbers and trimmers of men? are they so neat, and so fine fellows as they are said to be?
Amphilogus. There are no finer fellows under the sun, nor experter in their noble science of barbing than they be. And therefore in the fulness of their overflowing knowledge (oh ingenious heads, and worthy to be dignified with the diadem of

128

folly and vain curiosity!) they have invented such strange
fashions and monstrous manners of cuttings, trimmings, shavings
and washings, that you would wonder to see. They have one
manner of cut called the French cut, another the Spanish cut;
one the Dutch cut, another the Italian; one the new cut, another
the old; one of the bravado fashion, another of the mean fashion;
one a gentleman's cut, another the common cut; one cut of
the court, another of the country, with infinite the like varieties,
which I overpass. They have also other kinds of cuts innumer-
able; and therefore when you come to be trimmed, they will
ask you whether you will be cut to look terrible to your enemy,
or amiable to your friend, grim and stern in countenance, or
pleasant and demure (for they have divers kinds of cuts for all
these purposes, or else they lie). Then, when they have done
all their feats, it is a world to consider, how their mustachios
must be preserved and laid out, from one cheek to another, yea,
almost from one ear to another, and turned up like two horns
towards the forehead. Besides that, when they come to the
cutting of the hair, what snipping and snapping of the scissors
is there, what tricking and trimming, what rubbing, what
scratching, what combing and clawing, what trickling and
toying, and all to tawe out money, you may be sure. And
when they come to washing, oh how gingerly they behave
themselves therein. For then shall your mouth be bossed
with the lather or foam that riseth of the balls (for they
have their sweet balls wherewithal they use to wash); your
eyes closed must be anointed therewith also. Then snap
go the fingers, full bravely, God wot. Thus this tragedy
ended, comes me warm cloths to wipe and dry him withal;
next, the ears must be picked, and closed together again
artificially forsooth; the hair of the nostrils cut away, and
every thing done in order comely to behold. The last
action in this tragedy is the payment of money. And lest
these cunning barbers might seem unconscionable in asking
much for their pains, they are of such a shamefast modesty, as
they will ask nothing at all, but standing to the courtesy and
liberality of the giver, they will receive all that comes, how
much soever it be, not giving any again, I warrant you: for
take a barber with that fault, and strike off his head. No, no,
such fellows are *rarae aves in terris, nigrisque simillimi cygnis:*

rare birds upon the earth, and as geason as black swans. You shall have also your orient perfumes for your nose, your fragrant waters for your face, wherewith you shall be all to besprinkled: your music again, and pleasant harmony, shall sound in your ears, and all to tickle the same with vain delight. And in the end your cloak shall be brushed, and 'God be with you, gentleman!'

Philip Stubbes, Anatomie of Abuses (Part ii) 1583

A Denunciation of Fashionable Ladies

Hamlet (to Yorick's skull). Now get you to my lady's chamber, and tell her, let her paint an inch thick, to this favour she must come; make her laugh at that.

Hamlet, v. i. 211—214

> Look on beauty,
> And you shall see 'tis purchas'd by the weight;
> Which therein works a miracle in nature,
> Making them lightest that wear most of it:
> So are those crisped snaky golden locks
> Which make such wanton gambols with the wind,
> Upon supposed fairness, often known
> To be the dowry of a second head,
> The skull that bred them, in the sepulchre.

Merchant of Venice, iii. ii. 88—96

Ever since Evah was tempted, and the serpent prevailed with her, women have took upon them both the person of the tempted and the tempter. They tempt to be tempted, and not one of them, except she be tempted, but thinks herself contemptible. Unto the greatness of their great-grand-mother Evah they seek to aspire, in being tempted and tempting. If not to tempt and be thought worthy to be tempted, why dye they and diet their faces with so many drugs as they do, as it were to correct God's workmanship, and reprove Him as a bungler, and one that is not his craftsmaster? Why ensparkle they their eyes with spiritualized distillations? Why tip they their tongues with *aurum potabile*? Why fill they age's frets with fresh colours? Even as roses and flowers in winter are preserved in close houses under earth, so preserve they their beauties by continual lying in bed.

Just to dinner they will arise, and after dinner go to bed again, and lie until supper. Yea, sometimes (by no sickness occasioned) they will lie in bed three days together : provided every morning before four o'clock, they have their broths and their cullises, with pearl and gold sodden in them. If haply they break their hours and rise more early to go a banquetting, they stand practising half a day with their looking-glasses, how to pierce and to glance and look alluringly amiable. Their feet are not so well framed to the measures, as are their eyes to move and bewitch. Even as angels are painted in Church-windows with glorious golden fronts beset with sunbeams, so beset they their foreheads on either side with glorious borrowed gleamy bushes; which, rightly interpreted, should signify beauty to sell, since a bush is not else hanged forth but to invite men to buy. And in Italy, when they set any beast to sale, they crown his head with garlands, and bedeck it with gaudy blossoms, as full as ever it may stick.

Their heads, with their top and top-gallant lawn baby-caps, and snow-resembled silver curlings, they make a plain puppet stage of. Their breasts they embusk up on high, and their round roseate buds immodestly lay forth, to shew at their hands there is fruit to be hoped. In their curious antic-woven garments, they imitate and mock the worms and adders that must eat them. They shew the swellings of their mind, in the swellings and plumpings out of their apparel. Gorgeous ladies of the court, never was I admitted so near any of you, as to see how you torture poor old Time with sponging, pinning, and pouncing ; but they say his sickle you have burst in twain, to make your periwigs more elevated arches of.

I dare not meddle with ye, since the philosopher that too intentively gazed on the stars, stumbled and fell into a ditch ; and many gazing too immoderately on our earthly stars, fall in the end into the ditch of all uncleanness. Only this humble caveat let me give you by the way, that you look the devil come not to you in the likeness of a tailor or a painter ; that however you disguise your bodies, you lay not on your colours so thick that they sink into your souls; that your skins being too white without, your souls be not all black within.

It is not your pinches, your purls, your flowery jaggings, superfluous interlacings, and puffings up, that can any way offend God, but the puffing up of your souls, which therein you express. For as the biting of a bullet is not that which poisons the bullet, but the lying of the gunpowder in the dint of the biting: so it is not the wearing of costly burnished apparel that shall be objected unto you for sin, but the pride of your hearts, which (like the moth) lies closely shrouded amongst the threads of that apparel. Nothing else is garish apparel but pride's ulcer broken forth. How will you attire yourselves, what gown, what head-tire will you put on, when you shall live in hell amongst hags and devils?

As many jags, blisters and scars shall toads, cankers and serpents make on your pure skins in the grave, as now you have cuts, jags or raisings, upon your garments. In the marrow of your bones snakes shall breed. Your morn-like crystal countenances shall be netted over and (masquer-like) caul-visarded with crawling venomous worms. Your orient teeth toads shall steal into their heads for pearl; of the jelly of your decayed eyes shall they engender them young. In their hollow caves (their transplendent juice so pollutionately employed), shelly snails shall keep house.

Oh, what is beauty more than a wind-blown bladder, that it should forget whereto it is born? It is the food of cloying concupiscence, living; and the substance of the most noisome infection, being dead. The mothers of the justest men are not freed from corruption, the mothers of kings and emperors are not freed from corruption. No gorgeous attire (man or woman) hast thou in this world, but the wedding garment of faith. Thy winding-sheet shall see thee in none of thy silks or shining robes; to show they are not of God, when thou goest to God, thou shalt lay them all off. Then shalt thou restore to every creature what thou hast robbed him of. All the leases which dust let out to life, at the day of death shall be returned again into his hands. In skins of beasts Adam and Eve were clothed; in nought but thine own skin at the day of Judgment shalt thou be clothed. If thou beest more deformed than the age wherein thou diedst should make thee, the devil shall stand up and certify, that with painting and physicing thy visage thou so deformedst it; whereto God shall reply, "What have I to do with thee, thou painted sepulchre? Thou hast so differenced and divorced thyself from thy creation, that I know thee not for my creature. The print of my finger thou hast defaced, and with arts-vanishing varnishment made thyself a changeling from the form I first cast thee in ; Satan, take her to thee, with black boiling pitch rough-cast over her counterfeit red and white ; and whereas she was wont in ass's milk to bathe her to engrain her skin more gentle, pliant, delicate and supple, in bubbling scalding lead, and fatty flame-feeding brimstone see thou unceasingly bathe her. With glowing hot irons, singe and suck up that adulterized sinful beauty, wherewith she hath branded herself to infelicity."

Oh female pride, this is but the dalliance of thy doom, but the intermissive recreation of thy torments. The greatness of thy pains I want portentous words to portray. Whereinsoever thou hast took extreme delight and glory, therein shalt thou be plagued with extreme and despiteous malady. For thy flaring frounced periwigs low dangled down with love-locks, shalt thou have thy head side dangled down with more snakes than ever it had hairs. In the mould of thy brain shall they clasp their mouths, and gnawing through every part of thy skull, ensnarl their teeth amongst thy brains, as an angler ensnarleth his hook amongst weeds.

For thy rich borders, shalt thou have a number of dis-coloured scorpions rolled up together, and cockatrices that kill with their very sight shall continually stand spurting fiery poison in thine eyes. In the hollow cave of thy mouth, basilisks shall keep house, and supply thy talk with hissing when thou strivest to speak. At thy breasts (as at Cleopatra's), aspices shall be put out to nurse. For thy carcanets of pearl, shalt thou have carcanets of spiders, or the green venomous flies cantharides. Hell's torments were no torments, if invention might conceit them. As no eye hath seen, no ear hath heard, no tongue can express, no thought comprehend the joys pre-pared for the elect, so no eye hath seen, no ear hath heard, no thought can comprehend the pains prepared for the rejected.

THOMAS NASHE, *Christs Teares over Ierusalem* 1593

The Pride of Merchants' Wives

Mistress Minx, a merchant's wife, that will eat no cherries, forsooth, but when they are at twenty shillings a pound, that looks as simperingly as if she were besmeared, and jets it as gingerly as if she were dancing the canaries : she is so finical in her speech, as though she spake nothing but what she had first sewed over before in her samplers, and the puling accent of her voice is like a feigned treble, or one's voice that interprets to the puppets. What should I tell how squeamish she is in her diet, what toil she puts her poor servants unto, to make her looking-glasses in the pavement? how she will not go into the fields, to cower on the green grass, but she must have a coach for her convoy; and spends half a day in pranking herself if she be invited to any strange place? Is not this the excess of pride, signior Satan? Go to, you are unwise, if you make her not a chief saint in your calendar.

THOMAS NASHE, *Pierce Penilesse* 1592

Lap-dogs

The third sort of dogs of the gentle kind is the spaniel gentle, or comforter, or (as the common term is) the fisting-hound, and those are called Meltei, of the Island Malta, from whence they were brought hither. These are little and pretty, proper and fine, and sought out far and near to satisfy the nice delicacy of dainty dames, and wanton women's wills; instruments of folly to play and dally withal, in trifling away the treasure of time, to withdraw their minds from more commendable exercises, and to content their corrupt concupiscences with vain disport, a silly poor shift to shun their irksome idleness. These sybaritical puppies, the smaller they be (and thereto if they have an hole in the foreparts of their heads) the better they are accepted, the more pleasure also they provoke, as meet playfellows for mincing mistresses to bear in their bosoms, to keep company withal in their chambers, to succour with sleep in bed, and nourish with meat at board, to lie in their laps, and lick their lips, as they lie (like young Dianas) in their waggons and coaches. And good reason it should be so, for coarseness with fineness hath no fellowship, but featness with neatness hath neighbourhead enough. That plausible proverb, therefore, verified sometime upon a tyrant, namely that he loved his sow better than his son, may well be applied to some of this kind of people, who delight more in their dogs, that are deprived of all possibility of reason, than they do in children that are capable of wisdom and judgment. Yea, they oft feed them of the best, where the poor man's child at their doors can hardly come by the worst. But the former abuse peradventure reigneth where there hath been long want of issue, else where barrenness is the best blossom of beauty, or, finally, where poor men's children for want of their own issue are not ready to be had.   It is thought of some that it is very wholesome for a weak stomach to bear such a dog in the bosom, as it is for him that hath the palsy to feel the daily smell and savour of a fox.   But how truly this is affirmed, let the learned judge: only it shall suffice for Dr Caius to have said thus much of spaniels and dogs of the gentle kind.

WILLIAM HARRISON, *Description of England* 1587 (2nd ed.)

§ 6. The Plague

[In Shakespeare's day the plague was an annual visitor to London. When there were over 30 deaths a week the theatres were closed.   There were very few summers in which this did not happen.]

It's an ill wind (a beggar speaks)

If such plague do ensue it is no great loss.   For, first, it shall not only deliver the miserable poor man, woman and bairns from hurt and carefulness into a better world, but also cut off many covetous usurers, which be like fat unclean swine, which do never good until they come to the dish, but root out every plant that they can come by; and like unto great stinking mickle midden-hills, which never do pleasure unto the land or ground until their heaps are cast abroad to the profits of many, which are kept neither to their own comforts nor others, but only in beheading them; like unto cruel dogs lying in a manger, neither eating the hay themselves nor suffering the horse to feed thereof himself.   And in such plagues we poor people have mickle good.   Their loss is our luck; when they do become naked, we then are clothed against their wills; with their doles and alms we are relieved; their sickness is our health, their death our life.   Besides us pakers, many more men have good luck, as the vicar, parish clerk and the bell-man; oftentimes the executors be no losers by this game.   And in fine, in my fantasy it is happy to the huntsman when he have nothing of the cat but the silly skin.   We beggars reck nought of the carcase of the dead body, but do defy it; we look for old cast coats, jackets, hose, caps, belts and shoes, by their deaths which in their lives they would not depart from, and this is our hap. God send me of them.

WILLIAM BULLEIN, *A Dialogue against the Pestilence* 1573 (1st ed. 1564)

Treatment for the plague

To preserve your body from the infection of the plague, you shall take a quart of old ale, and after it hath risen upon the fire and hath been scummed, you shall put thereinto of aristolochia longa, of angelica and of celandine of each half an handful, and boil them well therein ; then strain the drink through a clean cloth, and dissolve therein a drachm of the best mithridate, as much ivory finely powdered and searced, and six spoonful of dragon-water, then put it up in a close glass ; and every morning fasting take five spoonful thereof, and after bite and chew in your mouth the dried root of angelica, or smell, as on a nosegay, to the tasselled end of a ship rope, and they will surely preserve you from infection.

But if you be infected with the plague, and feel the assured signs thereof, as pain in the head, drought, burning, weakness of stomach and such like : then you shall take a drachm of the best mithridate, and dissolve it in three or four spoonful of dragon-water, and immediately drink it off, and then with hot cloths or bricks, made extreme hot and laid to the soles of your feet, after you have been wrapt in woollen cloths, compel the sick party to sweat, which if he do, keep him moderately therein till the sore begin to rise ; then to the same apply a live pigeon cut in two parts, or else a plaster made of the yolk of an egg, honey, herb of grace chopped exceeding small, and wheat flour, which in very short space will not only ripen, but also break the same without any other incision ; then after it hath run a day or two, you shall apply a plaster of melilot unto it until it be whole.

GERVASE MARKHAM, *The English Hus-wife* 1615

The flight from London

Civis. Good wife, the daily jangling and ringing of the bells, the coming in of the minister to every house in ministring the communion, in reading the homily of death, the digging up of graves, the sparring in of windows, and the blazing forth of the blue cross, do make my heart tremble and quake. Alas, what shall I do to save my life ?

Uxor. Sir, we are but young, and have but a time in this world, what doth it profit us to gather riches together, and can not enjoy them? Why tarry we here so long? I do think every hour a year until we be gone; my heart is as cold as a stone, and as heavy as lead, God help me. Seeing that we have sent our children forth three weeks past into a good air and a sweet country, let us follow them. We shall be welcome to your brother's house, I dare say; my sister will rejoice in our coming, and so will all our friends there. Let us take leave of our neighbours, and return merely home again when the plague is past, and the dog days ended; and there you may occupy your stock, and have gain thereof.

Civis. Oh, wife, we know not our return, for the Apostle saith to you that will say, "To-day or to-morrow we will go to such a city, and buy and sell, and have gain, and know not what shall happen to-morrow," "What is our life? It is as a vapour that appeareth for a little time, and afterward vanisheth away." For that ye ought to say, "If the Lord will and we live, we will to this or that place; and if it please God we will both depart and return again at His good will and pleasure"; for we are in His hands whither so ever we do go; and I trust it is not against God's commandment or pleasure that we depart from this infected air.

Uxor. I know not what God will in our departing, but my flesh trembles when I do hear the death-bell ring.

Civis. Yes surely, we have the Apostle saying (for our defence in flying), "No man ever yet hath hated his own flesh, but nourisheth and cherisheth it": therefore, who can nourish his flesh in a corrupted air, but rather do kill it? Further, I hear a doctor of physic say that one called Galen, in a book of treacle, [wrote] to one Pison, his friend, that the pestilence was like a monstrous hungry beast, devouring and eating not a few but sometimes whole cities, that by respiration or drawing in their breath do take the poisoned air. He lauded Hippocrates, which saith that to remove from the infected air into a cleaner, thereby, saith he, they did not draw in more foul air, and this was his only remedy for the plague. To them that did remain he commanded not only simple wood to be burned within the city of Athens, but also most sweet flowers and spices, perfumes, as gums and ointments, to purge the air. And, wife, fear of death enforced many holy men to fly: as

Jacob from his cruel brother Esau, David from Saul, Elias from Jezebel. The Christian men from fear of death did fly the tyranny of the papists, and although these men did not fly the pestilence, yet they fled all for fear of death; and so will we by God's grace observe such wholesome means, and obey His Divine providence. Also I will leave my house with my faithful friends, and take the keys of my chests with me. Where are our horses?

Uxor. Our things are ready; have you taken your leave of our neighbours, man?

Civis. I have done; so now let us depart, a God's blessing, good wife.

Uxor. Give me my horse, Roger.

Roger. Mistress, he is here ready at your hand, a good gelding. God bless him and sweet Saint Loye.

Civis. Bring forth mine also, and let the servants forget nothing behind them, specially the steel casket. Let us ride fair and softly until we be out of the town.

Uxor. How pleasant are these sweet fields, garnished with fair plants and flowers! the birds do sing sweetly and pitifully in the bushes; here are pleasant woods. Jesus, man, who would be in the city again? Not I, for an hundred pound. Oh, help me! my horse starteth, and had like to have been unsaddled; let me sit faster for falling.

Civis. He is a bird-eyed jade, I warrant you, and you are no good horsewoman, for I did never see you ride before in all my life; but exercise will make you perfect. Your mother was a good horsewoman, and loved riding well as any gentlewoman that ever I knew in my life. Well, she is gone, and we must follow · this is the world.

Uxor. I never was so far from London in all my life. How far have we ridden already, sir, I pray you?

Civis. Wife, we have ridden ten miles this morning.

Uxor. What town is this, I pray you, sir?

Civis. This is Barnet, whereas Samuel your son was nursed; and yonder is Richard Higmer's house; we will see him as we do return home again; we will not tarry now, because every inn is pestered with Londoners and carriers, and it is early days. How like you this town, dame?

138

THE PLAGUE

Uxor. A pretty street; but methink the people go very
plain; it is no city as I do suppose by their manners. What
house is this at the town's end, compassed with a moat?

Civis. Here dwelleth a friend of ours; this is called the
Fold. And here before is Dancers' Hill, and Rig Hill.

Uxor. What great smoke is in yonder wood? God grant
it be well.

Civis. It is nothing but making of charcoal in that place.

Uxor. Why, is charcoal made? I had thought all things
had been made at London, yet I did never see no charcoals
made there: by my troth, I had thought that they had grown
upon trees, and had not been made.

WILLIAM BULLEIN, *A Dialogue against the Pestilence* 1573 (1st ed. 1564)

CHAPTER VI

BOOKS AND AUTHORS

Polonius. What do you read, my lord?
Hamlet. Words, words, words. *Hamlet,* II. ii. 189—190

Slender. I had rather than forty shillings I had my Book of Songs and Sonnets here. How now, Simple! where have you been? I must wait on myself, must I? You have not the Book of Riddles about you, have you?
Simple. Book of Riddles! why, did you not lend it to Alice Shortcake upon All-Hallowmas last, a fortnight afore Michaelmas?
The Merry Wives of Windsor, I. i. 205—212

Patronage

To the right honourable Henry Wriothesly,
Earl of Southampton and Baron of Tichfield.

The love I dedicate to your lordship is without end; whereof this pamphlet, without beginning, is but a superfluous moiety. The warrant I have of your honourable disposition, not the worth of my untutored lines, makes it assured of acceptance. What I have done is yours; what I have to do is yours; being part in all I have, devoted yours. Were my worth greater, my duty would show greater; meantime, as it is, it is bound to your lordship, to whom I wish long life, still lengthened with happiness.

Your lordship's in all duty,

William Shakespeare

Dedication of The Rape of Lucrece 1594

A sixteenth century printer's office

Most gracious and dread Sovereign,

    ...Thirteen years your Highness's servant, but yet nothing. Twenty friends that though they say they will be sure, I find them sure too slow. A thousand hopes, but all nothing. A hundred promises, but yet nothing. Thus casting up an inventory of my friends, hopes, promises and times, the sum total amounteth to just nothing. My last will is shorter than mine invention. But three legacies I bequeath, Patience to my creditors, Melancholy without measure to my friends, and Beggary without shame to my family...

    The last and the least, that if I be born to have nothing, I may have protection to pay nothing, which suit is like his, who having followed the court ten years, for recompense of his service committed a robbery, and took it out in a pardon.

John Lyly to Queen Elizabeth 1598

Portrait of a poet

    I espied afar off a certain kind of an overworn gentleman attired in velvet and satin, but it was somewhat dropped and greasy, and boots on his legs, whose soles waxed thin and seemed to complain of their master, which treading thrift under his feet had brought them unto that consumption. He walked not as other men in the common beaten way, but came compassing *circumeirca*, as if we had been devils, and he would draw a circle about us, and at every third step he looked back as if he were afraid of a bailey or a sergeant....

    A poet is a waste-good and an unthrift, that he is born to make the taverns rich and himself a beggar. If he have forty pound in his purse together, he puts it not to usury, neither buys land nor merchandise with it, but a month's commodity of wenches and capons. Ten pound a supper, why 'tis nothing, if his plough goes and his ink-horn be clear. Take one of them with twenty thousand pounds and hang him. He is a king of his pleasure, and counts all other boors and peasants that, though they have money at command, yet know not like him how to domineer with it to any purpose as they should. But to speak plainly, I think him an honest man, if he would but live within his compass, and generally no man's foe but his own.

ROBERT GREENE, A Quip for an Upstart Courtier 1592

BOOKS AND AUTHORS

An author's complaint

I tossed my imagination a thousand ways, to see if I could find any means to relieve my estate : but all my thoughts consorted to this conclusion, that the world was uncharitable, and I ordained to be miserable. Thereby I grew to consider how many base men that wanted those parts which I had, enjoyed content at will, and had wealth at command : I called to mind a cobbler, that was worth five hundred pound, an hostler that had built a goodly inn, and might dispend forty pound yearly by his land, a carman in a leather pilch, that had whipped out a thousand pound out of his horse tail : and have I more wit than all these (thought I to myself) ? am I better born ? am I better brought up ? yea, and better favoured ? and yet am I a beggar ? What is the cause ? how am I crossed ? or whence is this curse ?

Even from hence, that men that should employ such as I am, are enamoured of their own wits, and think whatever they do is excellent, though it be never so scurvy : that learning (of the ignorant) is rated after the value of the ink and paper: and a scrivener better paid for an obligation, than a scholar for the best poem he can make ; that every gross-brained idiot is suffered to come into print, who if he set forth a pamphlet of the praise of pudding-pricks, or write a treatise of *Tom Thumme,* or the exploits of *Untrusse,* it is bought up thick and threefold, when better things lie dead. How then can we choose but be needy, when there are so many drones amongst us ? or ever prove rich, that toil a whole year for fair looks ?

Gentle Sir Philip Sidney, thou knewest what belonged to a scholar, thou knewest what pains, what toil, what travail, conduct to perfection : well couldst thou give every virtue his encouragement, every art his due, every writer his desert : 'cause none more virtuous, witty, or learned than thyself. But thou art dead in thy grave, and hast left too few successors of thy glory, too few to cherish the sons of the Muses, or water those budding hopes with their plenty, which thy bounty erst planted.

Believe me, gentlemen, for some cross mishaps have taught me experience, there is not that strict observation of honour, which hath been heretofore. Men of great calling take it of merit, to have their names eternized by poets ; and whatsoever pamphlet or dedication encounters them, they put it up their sleeves, and scarce give him thanks that presents it. Much better is it for those golden pens to raise such ungrateful peasants from the dunghill of obscurity, and make them equal in fame to the worthies of old, when their doting self-love shall challenge it of duty, and not only give them nothing themselves, but impoverish liberality in others.

This is the lamentable condition of our times, that men of art must seek alms of cormorants, and those that deserve best, be kept under by dunces, who count it a policy to keep them bare, because they should follow their books the better: thinking belike, that, as preferment hath made themselves idle that were erst painful in meaner places, so it would likewise slacken the endeavours of those students that as yet strive to excel in hope of advancement. A good policy to suppress superfluous liberality. But, had it been practised when they were promoted, the yeomanry of the realm had been better to pass than it is, and one drone should not have driven so many bees from their honeycombs.

THOMAS NASHE, Pierce Penilesse 1592

A Pot-poet

Is the dregs of wit; yet mingled with good drink may have some relish. His inspirations are more real than others; for they do but feign a god, but he has his by him. His verses run like the tap, and his invention, as the barrel, ebbs and flows at the mercy of the spiggot. In thin drink he aspires not above a ballad, but a cup of sack inflames him, and sets his muse and nose afire together. The press is his mint, and stamps him now and then a sixpence or two in reward of the baser coin, his pamphlet. His works would scarce sell for three halfpence, though they are given oft for three shillings, but for the pretty title that allures the country gentleman: for which the printer maintains him in ale a fortnight. His verses are like his clothes, miserable centos and patches, yet their pace is not altogether so hobbling as an almanac's. The death of a great man or the burning of a house furnish him with an argument, and the nine Muses are out straight in mourning gown, and Melpomene cries "Fire, Fire." His other poems are but briefs in rhyme, and like the poor Greeks' collections to redeem from captivity. He is a man now much employed in commendations of our navy, and a bitter inveigher against the Spaniard. His frequentest works go out in single sheets, and are chanted from market to market, to a vile tune and a worse throat, whilst the poor country wench melts like her butter to hear them. And these are the stories of some men of Tyburn or a strange monster out of Germany, or, sitting in a bawdy-house, he writes God's judgment. He ends at last in some obscure painted cloth, to which himself made the verses, and his life, like a can too full, spills upon the bench. He leaves twenty shillings on the score, which my hostess loses.

JOHN EARLE, *Micro-cosmographie* 1628

A worthy poet

[Had the writer Shakespeare in mind while penning the following ?]

A worthy poet is the purest essence of a worthy man: he is confident of nature in nothing but the form and an ingenious fitness to conceive the matter. So he approves nature as the motive, not the foundation or structure of his worthiness. His works do every way pronounce both nourishment, delight and admiration to the reader's soul: which makes him neither rough, effeminate, nor windy: for by a sweet contemperature of tune and ditty he entices others to goodness, and shows himself perfect in the lesson. He never writes upon a full stomach and an empty head, or a full head and an empty stomach. For he cannot make so divine a receptable stoop to the sordid folly of gall or envy without strength: or strength of brain stoop, and debase itself with hunting out the body's succour. He is not so impartial as to condemn every new fashion, or tax idle circumstance; nor so easy as to allow vices, and account them generous humours. So he neither seeks to enlarge his credit of bitterness by a snarling severity; nor to augment his substance by insinuating courtship. He hath more debtors in knowledge among the present writers than creditors among the ancient poets. He is possessed with an innocent liberty, which excludes him from the slavish labour and means of setting a gloss upon frail commodities. Whatsoever therefore proceeds from him, proceeds without a meaning to supply the worth, when the work is ended, by the addition of preparative verses at the beginning, or the dispersed hire of acquaintance to extol things indifferent. Neither does he passionately affect high

144

patronage, or any, further than he may give freely, and so receive back honest thanks. The dangerous name and the contempt of poets, sprung from their multitude of corruptions, prove no disadvantage or terror to him: for such be his antidotes that he can walk untouched, even through the worst infection. And indeed that mountebank's preparing oil which kept his hands unscalded, was a toy of nothing to this poet's rarity of discretion, which so prepares his mind, that he can bathe it in the strains of burning lust, fury, malice, or despite, and yet be never scalded, or endangered by them. He only among men is nearest infinite: for in the scenical composures, of a tragedy or comedy, he shows the best resemblance of his high Creator: turning his quick passions, and witty humours to replenish and overcome into matter and form as infinite as God's pleasure to diversify mankind. He is no miserable self-lover, nor no unbounded prodigal: for he can communicate himself wisely to avoid dull reservedness, but not make every thought common to maintain his market. It must be imputed to his perfect eyesight, that he can see error and avoid it without the hazard of a new one: as in poems, so in projects, by an easy conjecture. He cannot flatter, nor be flattered: if he gives desert, he gives no more, and leaves hyperbole in such a matter of importance. As for himself, he is so well known unto himself, that neither public fame, nor yet his own conceit, can make him over-valued in himself. He is an enemy to atheists; for he is no fatist nor naturalist: he therefore excludes luck and rhyme from the acceptance of his poems; scorning to acknowledge the one as an efficient, the other as an essence, of his muse's favour. He pays back all his imitation with interest; whilst his authors (if revived) would confess their chief credit was to be such a pattern: otherwise (for the most part) he proves himself the pattern, and the project in hand. Silver only and sound metal comprehend his nature: rubbing, motion, and customary usage, make the brightness of both more eminent. No marvel though he be immortal, seeing he converts poison into nourishment, even the worst objects and societies to a worthy use. When he is lastly silent (for he cannot die) he finds a monument prepared at others' cost and remembrance, whilst his former actions be a living epitaph.

JOHN STEPHENS, *Essayes and Characters* 1615

BOOKS AND AUTHORS

Ballads and Monsters

I will get Peter Quince to write a ballad of this dream : it shall be
called Bottom's Dream, because it hath no bottom.

A Midsummer Night's Dream, IV. i. 221

Falstaff. An I have not ballads made on you all, and sung to filthy
tunes, let a cup of sack be my poison.

1 Henry IV., II. ii. 50

Clown. What hast here ? ballads ?

Mopsa. Pray now, buy some : I love a ballad in print, o' life, for then
we are sure they are true.

Autolycus. Here 's one to a very doleful tune, how a usurer's wife was
brought to bed of twenty money-bags at a burden ; and how she longed
to eat adders' heads and toads carbonadoed.

Mopsa. Is it true, think you ?

Autolycus. Very true, and but a month old.

Dorcas. Bless me from marrying a usurer !

*　　*　　*　　*　　*　　*　　*

Autolycus. Here's another ballad of a fish that appeared upon the coast
on Wednesday the fourscore of April, forty thousand fathom above water,
and sung this ballad against the hard hearts of maids : it was thought she
was a woman and was turned into a cold fish for she would not exchange
flesh with one that loved her. The ballad is very pitiful and as true.

Dorcas. Is is true, think you ?

Autolycus. Five justices' hands at it, and witnesses more than my pack
will hold.

The Winter's Tale, IV. iii. 261—287

Another sort of men there are, who, though not addicted to
such counterfeit curiosity, yet are they infected with a farther
improbability; challenging knowledge unto themselves of
deeper mysteries, whenas with Thales Milesius they see not
what is under their feet; searching more curiously into the
secrets of nature, whenas in respect of deeper knowledge,
they seem mere naturals; coveting with the phœnix to
approach so nigh to the sun, that they are scorched with his
beams and confounded with his brightness. Who made them
so privy to the secrets of the Almighty, that they should foretell the tokens of his wrath, or terminate the time of his
vengeance? But lightly some news attends the end of every
term, some monsters are booked, though not bred, against
vacation times, which are straightway diversely dispersed into
every quarter, so that at length they become the alehouse talk
of every carter: yea, the country ploughman feareth a Calabrian
flood in the midst of a furrow, and the silly shepherd com-
mitting his wandering sheep to the custody of his wap, in his

146

field-naps dreameth of flying dragons, which for fear lest he should see to the loss of his sight, he falleth asleep; no star he seeth in the night but seemeth a comet; he lighteth no sooner on a quagmire, but he thinketh this is the foretold earthquake, whereof his boy hath the ballad.

Thus are the ignorant deluded, the simple misused, and the sacred science of astronomy discredited; and in truth what leasings will not make-shifts invent for money? What will they not feign for gain? Hence come our babbling ballads, and our new found songs and sonnets, which every rednose fiddler hath at his fingers' ends, and every ignorant ale-knight will breathe forth over the pot, as soon as his brain waxeth hot. Be it a truth which they would tune, they interlace it with a lie or two to make metre, not regarding verity, so they may make up the verse; not unlike to Homer, who cared not what he feigned, so he might make his countrymen famous. But as the straightest things being put into water seem crooked, so the crediblest truths if once they come within compass of these men's wits, seem tales. Were it that the infamy of their ignorance did redound only upon themselves, I could be content to apply my speech otherwise than to their Apuleian ears, but sith they obtain the name of our English poets, and thereby make men think more basely of the wits of our country, I cannot but turn them out of their counterfeit livery, and brand them in the forehead, that all men may know their falsehood. Well may that saying of Campanus be applied to our English poets, which he spake of them in his time: " They make (saith he) poetry an occupation, lying is their living, and fables are their movables; if thou takest away trifles, silly souls, they will famish for hunger." It were to be wished that the acts of the venturous, and the praise of the virtuous were, by public edict, prohibited by such men's merry mouths to be so odiously extolled, as rather breeds detestation than admiration, loathing than liking. What politic councillor or valiant soldier will joy or glory of this, in that some stitcher, weaver, spendthrift or fiddler hath shuffled or slubbered up a few ragged rimes, in the memorial of the one's prudence, or the other's prowess? It makes the learned sort to be silent when they see unlearned sots so insolent.

THOMAS NASHE, *The Anatomie of Absurditie* 1589

BOOKS AND AUTHORS

The Troubles of Authorship

Theft of Manuscripts

As touching this short gloss or annotation on the foolish *Terrors of the Night*, you partly are acquainted from whose motive imposition it first proceeded, as also what strange sudden cause necessarily produced that motion. A long time since hath it lain suppressed by me, until the urgent importunity of a kind friend of mine (to whom I was sundry ways beholding) wrested a copy from me. That copy progressed from one scrivener's shop to another, and at length grew so common that it was ready to be hung out for one of their signs, like a pair of indentures. Whereupon I thought it as good for me to reap the fruit of my own labours, as to let some unskilful pen-man or noverint-maker starch his ruff and newspade his beard with the benefit he made of them.

Thomas Nashe, The Terrors of the Night 1594

Decipherers and Informers

If but carelessly betwixt sleeping and waking I write I know not what against plebeian publicans and sinners (no better than the sworn brothers of candlestick-turners and tinkers) and leave some terms in suspense that my post-haste want of argent will not give me elbow-room enough to explain or examine as I would, out steps me an infant squib of the Inns of Court, that hath not half greased his dining-cap or scarce warmed his lawyer's cushion, and he, to approve himself an extravagant statesman, catcheth hold of a rush, and absolutely concludeth it is meant of the Emperor of Russia, and that it will utterly mar the traffic into that country if all the pamphlets be not called in and suppressed, wherein that libelling word is mentioned....

O, for a legion of mice-eyed decipherers and calculators upon characters, now to augurate what I mean by this,...men that have no means to purchase credit with their prince, but by putting him still in fear and beating into his opinion that they are the only preservers of his life, in sitting up night and day in sifting out treasons, when they are the most traitors themselves to his life, health and quiet, in continual commacerating him with dread and terror, when, but to get a pension or bring him in their debt, next to God, for upholding his vital breath, it is neither so, nor so, but some fool, some drunken man, some madman in an intoxicate humour hath uttered he knew not what, and they, being starved for intelligence or want of employment, take hold of it with tooth and nail, and in spite of the waiters, will violently break into the king's chamber, and awake him at midnight to reveal it....

I am not against it, (for God forbid I should), that it behoves all loyal true subjects to be vigilant and jealous for their prince's safety, and, certain, too jealous and vigilant of it they cannot be, if they be good princes that reign over them, nor use too many means of disquisition by tortures or otherwise to discover treasons pretended against them. But upon the least wagging of a straw to put them in fear where no fear is, and to make a hurly-burly in the realm upon had-I-wist, not so much for any zeal or love to their princes or tender care of their preservation, as to pick thanks and curry a little favour, that thereby they may lay the foundation to build a suit on, or cross some great enemy they have, I maintain it is most lewd and detestable. I accuse none, but such there have been belonging to princes in former ages, if there be not at this hour.

THOMAS NASHE, *Lenten Stuffe* 1599

Prison

About the time of the last convocation, I composed a little poem, well known throughout this kingdom; wherein, having to conscionable purposes expressed such resolutions as every reasonable man should endeavour to entertain, and having, as opportunity was offered, glanced also in general terms at the reproof of a few things of such nature as I feared might disparage or prejudice the commonwealth, some particulars, not then in season to be meddled withal, were at unawares so nearly touched upon, that I unhappily fell into the displeasure of the State: and all my apparent good intentions were so mistaken by the aggravations of some ill-affected towards my endeavours, that I was shut up from the society of mankind, and, as one unworthy the compassion vouchsafed to thieves and murderers, was neither permitted the use of my pen, the access or sight of acquaintance, the allowance usually afforded other close prisoners, nor means to send for necessaries befitting my present condition. By which means I was for many days compelled to feed on nothing but the coarsest bread, and sometimes locked up four and twenty hours together, without so much as a drop of water to cool my tongue. And being at the same time in one of the greatest extremities of sickness that was ever inflicted upon my body, the help both of physician and apothecary was uncivilly denied me. So that if God had not by resolutions of the mind, which he infused into me, extraordinarily enabled me to wrestle with those and such other afflictions as I was then exercised withal, I had been dangerously and everlastingly overcome.

GEORGE WITHER, *The Schollers Purgatory*, c. 1625

Fashions in books

I was driven into a quandary, gentlemen, whether I might send this my pamphlet to the printer or to the pedlar. I thought it too bad for the press, and too good for the pack. But seeing my folly in writing to be as great as others', I was willing my fortune should be as ill as any man's. We commonly see the book that at Christmas lieth bound on the stationer's stall, at Easter to be broken in the haberdasher's shop, which sith it is the order of proceeding, I am content this winter to have my doings read for a toy, that in summer they may be ready for trash. It is not strange whenas the greatest wonder lasteth but nine days, that a new work should not endure but three months. Gentlemen use books as gentlewomen handle their flowers, who in the morning stick them in their heads, and at night straw them at their heels. Cherries be fulsome when they be through ripe, because they be plenty, and books be stale when they be printed, in that they be common. In my mind printers and tailors are bound chiefly to pray for gentlemen : the one hath so many fantasies to print, the other such divers fashions to make, that the pressing iron of the one is never out of the fire, nor the printing press of the other at any time lieth still. But a fashion is but a day's wearing and a book but an hour's reading: which seeing it is so, I am of a shoemaker's mind who careth not so the shoe hold the plucking on, nor I, so my labours last the running over. He that cometh in print because he would be known, is like

the fool that cometh into the market because he would be seen.
I am not he that seeketh praise for his labour, but pardon for
his offence, neither do I set this forth for any devotion in
print, but for duty which I owe to my patron. If one write
never so well, he cannot please all, and write he never so ill,
he shall please some. Fine heads will pick a quarrel with me
if all be not curious, and flatterers a thank if any thing be
current. But this is my mind: let him that findeth fault amend
it, and him that liketh it use it. Envy braggeth, but draweth
no blood: the malicious have more mind to quip, than might
to cut. I submit myself to the judgment of the wise, and
I little esteem the censure of fools. The one will be satisfied
with reason: the other are to be answered with silence. I
know gentlemen will find no fault without cause, and bear with
those that deserve blame, as for others I care not for their jests,
for I never meant to make them my judges.

JOHN LYLY, *Euphues, The Anatomy of Wyt* 1578 (preface)

Stationers, good and bad

An honest stationer is he, that exerciseth his mystery
(whether it be in printing, binding or selling of books) with
more respect to the glory of God and the public advantage,
than to his own commodity; and is both an ornament and
a profitable member in a civil commonwealth. He is the
caterer that gathers together provision to satisfy the curious
appetite of the soul and is careful, to his power, that whatsoever
he provides shall be such as may not poison or distemper the
understanding. And seeing the state entrusteth him with the
disposing of those books, which may both profit and hurt as
they are applied, like a discreet apothecary in selling poisonous
drugs, he observes by whom, and to what purpose, such books
are likely to be bought up, before he will deliver them out of his
hands. If he be a printer, he makes conscience to exemplify
his copy fairly and truly. If he be a book-binder, he is careful
his work may be strong and serviceable. If he be a seller of
books, he is no mere bookseller, that is one who selleth merely
ink and paper bundled up together for his own advantage only,
but he is the chapman of arts, of wisdom and of much experience
for a little money. He would not publish a book tending to
schism or profaneness, for the greatest gain; and if you see

in his shop any books vain or impertinent, it is not so much to be imputed his fault, as to the vanity of the times. For when books come forth allowed by authority, he holds it his duty rather to sell them than to censure them. Yet he meddles, as little as he can, with such as he is truly persuaded are pernicious or altogether unprofitable. The reputation of scholars is as dear unto him as his own, for he acknowledgeth that from them his mystery hath both beginning and means of continuance. He heartily loves and seeks the prosperity of his own corporation, yet he would not injure the universities to advantage it, nor be so saucy as to make comparisons between them. He loves a good author as his brother, and will be ready to yield him the due portion of his labours without wrangling. When he comes to be master or warden of his company, he labours truly to rectify what is amiss, but finds so many perversions, and so few of his good mind, that his year is out before he can bring any remedy to pass....

A mere stationer is he that imagines he was born altogether for himself, and exerciseth his mystery without any respect either to the glory of God or the public advantage. For which cause he is one of the most pernicious superfluities in a Christian government, and may well be termed the Devil's seedsman, seeing he is the aptest instrument to sow schisms, heresies, scandals and seditions through the world. What book soever he may have hope to gain by, he will divulge, though it contain matter against his prince, against the state, or blasphemy against God. And all his excuse will be that he knew not it comprehended any such matter. For (give him his right) he scarcely reads over one page of a book in seven year, except it be some such history as the *Wise men of Gotham*, and that he doth furnish himself with some foolish conceits to be thought facetious....He will fawn upon authors at his first acquaintance, and ring them to his hive by the promising sounds of some good advertisement; but as soon as they have prepared the honey to his hand, he drives the bees to seek another stall. If he be a printer, so his work have such appearance of being well done that he may receive his hire, he cares not how unworkmanlike it be performed, nor how many faults he let go to the author's discredit and the reader's trouble. If his employment be in binding books, so they will hold together but till his work-master hath sold them, he desireth not they should last a week longer; for by that means a book of a crown is marred in one month which would last a hundred years if it had twopence more workmanship, and so their gain and employment is increased to the subject's loss. If he be a seller of books, he makes no conscience what trash he puts off, nor how much he takes for that which is worth nothing....He makes no scruple to put out the right author's name and insert another in the second edition of a book. And when the impression of some pamphlet lies upon his hands, to imprint new titles for it (and so take men's moneys twice or thrice for the same matter under diverse names) is no injury in his opinion. If he get any written copy into his power likely to be vendible, whether the author be willing or no, he will publish it. And it shall be contrived and named also according to his own pleasure, which is the reason so many good books come forth imperfect and with foolish titles.

GEORGE WITHER, The Schollers Purgatory, c. 1625

A bookseller at his stall in Paul's Churchyard

If I were to paint Sloth...by Saint John the Evangelist I swear, I would draw it like a stationer that I know, with his thumb under his girdle, who if a man come to his stall and ask him for a book, never stirs his head, or looks upon him, but stands stone still, and speaks not a word: only with his little finger points backwards to his boy, who must be his interpreter, and so all the day, gaping like a dumb image, he sits without motion, except at such times as he goes to dinner or supper: for then he is as quick as other three, eating six times every day.

THOMAS NASHE, Pierce Penilesse 1592

CHAPTER VII

THE THEATRE

Duke.   This wide and universal theatre
            Presents more woful pageants than the scene
            Wherein we play in.
Jaques.   All the world's a stage,
            And all the men and women merely players:
            They have their exits and their entrances;
            And one man in his time plays many parts,
            His acts being seven ages.
                          As You Like It, II. vii. 137—143

            Life's but a walking shadow, a poor player
            That struts and frets his hour upon the stage,
            And then is heard no more. *Macbeth*, v. v. 24—26

            Alas! 'tis true I have gone here and there,
            And made myself a motley to the view,
            Gor'd mine own thoughts, sold cheap what is most dear,
            Made old offences of affections new.   *Sonnet* CX

            O! for my sake do you with Fortune chide,
            The guilty goddess of my harmful deeds,
            That did not better for my life provide
            Than public means which public manners breeds.
            Thence comes it that my name receives a brand,
            And almost thence my nature is subdu'd
            To what it works in, like the dyer's hand.
                                              Sonnet CXI

An Elizabethan Stage

as imagined by a modern scholar

THEATRICAL AND DRAMATIC CONDITIONS

§ 1. Theatrical and dramatic conditions in 1580

[About 1580 Elizabethan drama began its course. Shakespeare probably came to London in 1586.]

> And so our scene must to the battle fly;
> Where,—O for pity,—we shall much disgrace,
> With four or five most vile and ragged foils,
> Right ill dispos'd in brawl ridiculous,
> The name of Agincourt. Yet, sit and see;
> Minding true things by what their mockeries be.
>
> *Henry V.*, IV. chorus 48—53

Polonius. The best actors in the world, either for tragedy, comedy, history, pastoral, pastoral-comical, historical-pastoral, tragical-historical, tragical-comical-historical-pastoral, scene individable, or poem unlimited: Seneca cannot be too heavy, nor Plautus too light.

> *Hamlet*, II. ii. 424—429

Æsthetic condemnation

[Sir Philip Sidney criticizes the theatre of his day by classical standards, but his remarks throw considerable light upon the state of the drama.]

Our tragedies and comedies (not without cause cried out against), observing rules neither of honest civility nor of skilful poetry, excepting *Gorboduc* (again, I say, of those that I have seen), which, notwithstanding as it is full of stately speeches and well-sounding phrases, climbing to the height of Seneca his style, and as full of notable morality, which it doth most delightfully teach, and so obtain the very end of poesy, yet in troth it is very defectious in the circumstances; which grieveth me, because it might not remain as an exact model of all tragedies. For it is faulty both in place and time, the two necessary companions of all corporal actions. For where the stage should always represent but one place, and the uttermost time presupposed in it should be, both by Aristotle's precept and common reason, but one day, there is both many days and many places, inartificially imagined. But if it be so in *Gorboduc,* how much more in all the rest? where you shall have Asia of the one side, and Afric of the other, and so many other under-kingdoms, that the player, when he cometh in, must ever begin with telling where he is: or else, the tale will not be conceived. Now ye shall have three ladies walk to gather flowers, and then we must believe the stage to be a garden. By and by, we hear news of shipwreck in the same place, and then we are to blame, if we accept it not for a rock.

Upon the back of that, comes out a hideous monster with fire and smoke, and then the miserable beholders are bound to take it for a cave. While in the mean-time two armies fly in, represented with four swords and bucklers, and then what hard heart will not receive it for a pitched field? Now of time they are much more liberal, for ordinary it is that two young princes fall in love. After many traverses, she is got with child, delivered of a fair boy, he is lost, groweth a man, falls in love, and is ready to get another child; and all this in two hours' space: which how absurd it is in sense, even sense may imagine, and art hath taught, and all ancient examples justified, and at this day the ordinary players in Italy will not err in. Yet will some bring in an example of *Eunuchus* in Terence, that containeth matter of two days, yet far short of twenty years. True it is, and so was it to be played in two days, and so fitted to the time it set forth. And though Plautus hath in one place done amiss, let us hit with him, and not miss with him. But they will say, how then shall we set forth a story, which containeth both many places and many times? And do they not know, that a tragedy is tied to the laws of poesy, and not of history? not bound to follow the story, but having liberty either to feign a quite new matter, or to frame the history to the most tragical conveniency. Again many things may be told which cannot be shewed, if they know the difference betwixt reporting and representing. As for example, I may speak (though I am here) of Peru, and in speech digress from that to the description of Calicut: but in action, I cannot represent it without Pacolet's horse: and so was the manner the ancients took, by some Nuncius to recount things done in former time, or other place. Lastly, if they will represent an history, they must not (as Horace saith) begin *ab ovo*, but they must come to the principal of that one action which they will represent. By example this will be best expressed. I have a story of young Polidorus, delivered for safety's sake, with great riches, by his father Priamus to Polimnestor king of Thrace, in the Trojan war time: he after some years, hearing the overthrow of Priamus, for to make the treasure his own murdered the child: the body of the child is taken up by Hecuba: she the same day findeth a slight to be revenged most cruelly of the tyrant. Where now would one of our tragedy writers begin, but with the delivery of the child? Then should he sail over into

Thrace, and so spend I know not how many years, and travel
numbers of places. But where doth Euripides? Even with
the finding of the body, leaving the rest to be told by the spirit
of Polidorus. This need no further to be enlarged; the dullest
wit may conceive it. But besides these gross absurdities, how all their plays be
neither right tragedies nor right comedies : mingling kings and
clowns, not because the matter so carrieth it, but thrust in
clowns by head and shoulders, to play a part in majestical
matters, with neither decency nor discretion. So as neither the
admiration and commiseration nor the right sportfulness is by
their mongrel tragi-comedy obtained. I know Apuleius did
somewhat so, but that is a thing recounted with space of time,
not represented in one moment : and I know the ancients
have one or two examples of tragi-comedies, as Plautus hath
Amphitrio, but if we mark them well, we shall find, that they
never or very daintily match horn-pipes and funerals. So
falleth it out, that having indeed no right comedy, in that
comical part of our tragedy we have nothing but scurrility,
unworthy of any chaste ears, or some extreme shew of doltish-
ness, indeed fit to lift up a loud laughter and nothing else :
where the whole tract of a comedy should be full of delight, as
the tragedy should be still maintained in a well-raised admiration. But our comedians think there is no delight without
laughter; which is very wrong, for though laughter may come
with delight, yet cometh it not of delight, as though delight
should be the cause of laughter: but well may one thing breed
both together ; nay, rather in themselves they have as it were
a kind of contrariety. For delight we scarcely do but in things
that have a conveniency to ourselves or to the general nature.
Laughter almost ever cometh of things most disproportioned to
ourselves and nature. Delight hath a joy in it, either per-
manent or present. Laughter hath only a scornful tickling....
   But I have lavished out too many words of this play matter.
I do it because as they are excelling parts of poesy, so is there
none so much used in England and none can be more pitifully
abused : which like an unmannerly daughter, shewing a bad
education, causeth her mother Poesy's honesty to be called in
question.

Sir Philip Sidney, *An Apologie for Poetrie* 1595 (written in 1581)

157

THE THEATRE

Moral condemnation

The writers of our time are so led away with vainglory, that their only endeavour is to pleasure the humour of men; and rather with vanity to content their minds, than to profit them with good ensample. The notablest liar is become the best poet; he that can make the most notorious lie, and disguise falsehood in such sort that he may pass unperceived, is held the best writer. For the strangest comedy brings greatest delectation and pleasure. Our nature is led away with vanity, which the author perceiving frames himself with novelties and strange trifles to content the vain humours of his rude auditors, feigning countries never heard of; monsters and prodigious creatures that are not, as of the Arimaspi, of the Grips, the Pigmies, the Cranes, and other such notorious lies. And if they write of histories that are known, as the life of Pompey, the martial affairs of Caesar and other worthies, they give them a new face, and turn them out like counterfeits to show themselves on the stage. It was therefore aptly applied of him who likened the writers of our days unto tailors, who having their shears in their hand, can alter the fashion of anything into another form; and with a new face make that seem new which is old. The shreds of whose curiosity our historians have now stolen from them, being by practice become as cunning as the tailor to set a new upper body to an old coat, and a patch of their own to a piece of another.

A second and third blast of retrait from plaies and Theatres 1580

The argument of tragedies is wrath, cruelty, incest, injury, murder, either violent by sword or voluntary by poison; the persons, gods, goddesses, furies, fiends, kings, queens and mighty men. The ground-work of comedies, is love, cozenage, flattery, bawdry, sly conveyance of whoredom; the persons, cooks, queans, knaves, bawds, parasites, courtezans, lecherous old men, amorous young men. Therefore Plautus in his prologue before the comedy of *The Captives*, desiring to curry favour with his auditors, exhorteth them earnestly to mark that play, because it shall cast no such stench of impurity into their noses as others do. There is in it (saith he) neither forsworn bawd, nor harlot, nor bragging soldier. Why could he not give this commendation to all the rest? Because it was the practice of the devil, to weave in a thread of his own spinning. Why is this rather purged of filthiness than the rest? Because it is the juggling of the devil, to turn himself sometimes to an angel of light, to deceive us the sooner. The best play you can pick out, is but a mixture of good and evil, how can it be then the schoolmistress of life? The beholding of troubles and miserable slaughters that are in tragedies drive us to immoderate sorrow, heaviness, womanish weeping and mourning, whereby we become lovers of dumps and lamentation, both enemies to fortitude. Comedies so tickle our senses with a pleasanter vein, that they make us lovers of laughter and pleasure, without any mean, both foes to temperance. What schooling is this? Sometime you shall see nothing but the adventures of an amorous knight, passing from country to country for the love of his lady, encountering many a terrible monster made of brown paper, and at his return is so wonderfully changed, that he cannot be known but by some posy in his tablet, or by a broken ring, or a handkercher, or a piece of a cockle shell. What learn you by that? When the soul of your plays is either mere trifles, or Italian bawdry, or wooing of gentlewomen, what are ye taught? Peradventure you will say, that by these kind of plays the authors instruct us how to love with constancy, to sue with modesty, and to loath whatsoever is contrary unto us. In my opinion, the discipline we get by plays is like to the justice that a certain schoolmaster taught in Persia, which taught his scholars to lie and not to lie, to deceive and not to deceive, with a distinction how they might do it to their friends, and how to their enemies; to their friends, for exercise; to their foes, in earnest. Wherein many of his scholars became so skilful by practise, by custom so bold, that their dearest friends paid more for their learning than their enemies. I would wish the players to beware of this kind of schooling, lest that whilst they teach youthful gentlemen how to love and not to love, how to woo and not to woo, their scholars grow as cunning as the Persians.

STEPHEN GOSSON, *Playes Confuted in five Actions* 1582

THE THEATRE

§ 2. Playhouses and Bear-gardens

> But pardon, gentles all,
> The flat unraised spirits that have dar'd
> On this unworthy scaffold to bring forth
> So great an object: can this cockpit hold
> The vasty fields of France? or may we cram
> Within this wooden O the very casques
> That did affright the air at Agincourt?
>
> *Henry V.*, I. chorus, 8—14

The earliest London public theatres, erected 1575—1576

[Before this plays had mostly been performed in the inn-yards of the city.]

This priory [of Holywell] was valued at the suppression to have lands two hundred and ninety-three pounds by the year, and was surrendered 1539, the 31st of Henry VIII. The church thereof being pulled down, many houses have been built for the lodgings of noblemen, of strangers born and others. And near thereunto, are builded two public houses for the acting and shew of comedies, tragedies and histories, for recreation. Whereof the one is called the Curtain, the other the Theater: both standing on the south-west side towards the field.

JOHN STOW, *A Survey of London* 1598

A German describes English theatres and bear-gardens

Without the city are some theatres, where English actors represent almost every day comedies and tragedies to very numerous audiences; these are concluded with variety of dances, accompanied by excellent music and the excessive applause of those that are present. Not far from one of these theatres, which are all built of wood, lies the royal barge, close to the river Thames. It has two splendid cabins, beautifully ornamented with glass windows, painting and gilding; it is kept upon dry ground, and sheltered from the weather.

There is still another place, built in the form of a theatre, which serves for the baiting of bears and bulls. They are fastened behind, and then worried by those great English dogs and mastiffs, but not without great risk to the dogs from the teeth of the one and the horns of the other; and it sometimes

160

happens they are killed upon the spot. Fresh ones are immediately supplied in the places of those that are wounded or tired. To this entertainment there often follows that of whipping a blinded bear, which is performed by five or six men, standing in a circle with whips, which they exercise upon him without any mercy. Although he cannot escape from them because of his chain, he nevertheless defends himself, vigorously throwing down all who come within his reach and are not active enough to get out of it, and tearing the whips out of their hands and breaking them. At these spectacles and everywhere else, the English are constantly smoking the Nicotian weed which in America is called *Tobaca*—others call it *Paetum*—and generally in this manner : they have pipes on purpose made of clay, into the farther end of which they put the herb, so dry that it may be rubbed into powder, and lighting it, they draw the smoke into their mouths, which they puff out again through their nostrils, like funnels, along with it plenty of phlegm and defluxion from the head. In these theatres, fruits, such as apples, pears and nuts, according to the season, are carried about to be sold, as well as wine and ale.

PAUL HENTZNER, *Travels in England* 1598 [Rye]

Structure of an Elizabethan playhouse

[The Globe theatre, which is here taken as a model, was the playhouse in which Shakespeare acted.]

...The frame of the said house to be set square and to contain four score foot of lawful assize every way square without, and fifty-five foot of like assize square every way within, with a good, sure and strong foundation of piles, brick, lime and sand both without and within to be wrought one foot of assize at the least above the ground. And the said frame to contain three storeys in height, the first or lower storey to contain twelve foot of lawful assize in height, the second storey eleven foot of lawful assize in height, and the third or upper storey to contain nine foot of lawful assize in height. All which storeys shall contain twelve foot and a half of lawful assize in breadth throughout, besides a jutty forwards in either of the said two upper storeys of ten inches of lawful assize, with four convenient divisions for gentlemen's rooms and other sufficient and convenient divisions for two-penny rooms, with necessary seats to be placed and set as well in those rooms as throughout all the rest of the galleries of the said house and with such-like stairs, conveyances and divisions without and within as are made and contrived in and to the late erected playhouse on the Bank, in the said parish of St Saviour's, called the Globe; with a stage and tiring-house to be made, erected and set up within the said frame with a shadow or cover on the said stage...

And which stage shall contain in length forty and three foot of lawful assize and in breadth to extend to the middle of the yard of the said house. The same stage to be paled in below with good, strong and sufficient new oaken boards, and likewise the lower storey of the said frame withinside; and the same lower storey to be also laid over and fenced with strong iron pikes. And the said stage to be in all other proportions contrived and fashioned like unto the stage of the said play-house called the Globe, with convenient windows and lights glazed to the said tiring-house, and the said frame, stage and staircases to be covered with tile and to have a sufficient gutter of lead to carry and convey the water from the covering of the said stage to fall backwards. And also all the said frame and the staircases thereof to be sufficiently enclosed without with lath, lime and hair, and the gentlemen's rooms and two-penny rooms to be sealed with lath, lime and hair, and all the floors of the said galleries, storeys and stage to be boarded with good and sufficient new deal boards of whole thickness where need shall be. And the said house, and other things beforementioned, to be made and done, to be in all other contrivitions, conveyances, fashions, thing and things effected, finished and done, according to the manner and fashion of the said house called the Globe, saving only that all the principal and main posts of the said frame and stage forward shall be square and wrought pilaster-wise with carved proportions called satyrs to be placed and set on the top of every of the same posts....

Contract for building the Fortune Theatre at the cost of £440
(dated Jan. 8, 1600)

PLAYHOUSES AND BEAR-GARDENS

Playhouses

Time, place, subject, actors and clothes either make or mar a play. The prologue and epilogue are like to an host and hostess, one bidding their guests welcome, the other bidding them farewell. The actors are like servingmen, that bring in the scenes and acts as their meat, which are liked or disliked, according to every man's judgment; the neatest drest and fairest delivered doth please most. They are as crafty with an old play, as bawds with old faces; the one puts on a new fresh colour, the other a new face and name. They practise a strange order, for most commonly the wisest man is the fool. They are much beholden to scholars that are out of means, for they sell them ware the cheapest. They have no great reason to love Puritans, for they hold their calling unlawful. New plays and new clothes many times help bad actions. They pray the company that's in to hear them patiently, yet they would not suffer them to come in without payment. They say as scholars now use to say, there are so many, that one fox could find in his heart to eat his fellow. A player often changes: now he acts a monarch, to-morrow a beggar; now a soldier, next a tailor. Their speech is loud, but never extempore; he seldom speaks his own mind, or in his own name. When men are here, and when at church, they are of contrary minds; there they think the time too long, but here too short. Most commonly when the play is done, you shall have a jig or dance of all treads; they mean to put their legs to it, as well as their tongues. They make men wonder when they have done, for they all clap their hands. Sometimes they fly into the country; but 'tis a suspicion that they are either poor, or want clothes, or else company, or a new play : or do, as some wandering sermonists, make one sermon travail [? travel] and serve twenty churches. All their care is to be like apes, to imitate and express other men's actions in their own persons. They love not the company of geese or serpents, because of their hissing. They are many times lousy, it's strange, and yet shift so often. As an ale-house in the country is beholden to a wild schoolmaster, so an whore-house to some of these, for they both spend all they get. Well, I like them well, if when they act vice they will leave it, and when virtue they will follow. I speak no more of them, but when I please I will come and see them.

DONALD LUPTON, *London and the Countrey carbonadoed* 1632

THE THEATRE

English and Italian theatres compared
An Englishman in Venice

I was at one of their play-houses, where I saw a comedy acted. The house is very beggarly and base in comparison of our stately play-houses in England : neither can their actors compare with us for apparel, shews and music. Here I observed certain things that I never saw before. For I saw women act, a thing that I never saw before, though I have heard that it hath been sometimes used in London ; and they performed it with as good a grace, action, gesture and whatsoever convenient for a player, as ever I saw any masculine actor. Also their noble and favourite courtezans came to this comedy, but so disguised, that a man cannot perceive them. For they wore double masks upon their faces, to the end they might not be seen ; one reaching from the top of their forehead to their chin, and under their neck ; another with twisks of downy or woolly stuff covering their noses. And as for their necks round about, they were so covered and wrapped with cobweb lawn and other things, that no part of their skin could be discerned. Upon their heads they wore little black felt caps very like to those of the clarissimoes that I will hereafter speak of. Also each of them wore a black short taffeta cloak. They were so graced, that they sat on high alone by themselves, in the best room of all the play-house. If any man should be so resolute to unmask one of them but in merriment only to see their faces, it is said that—were he never so noble or worthy a personage—he should be cut in pieces before he should come forth of the room, especially if he were a stranger. I saw some men also in the play-house, disguised in the same manner with double vizards : those were said to be the favourites of the same courtezans. They sit not here in galleries as we do in London; for there is but one or two little galleries in the house, wherein the courtezans only sit. But all the men do sit beneath in the yard or court, every man upon his several stool, for the which he payeth a gazet.

THOMAS CORYAT, *Crudities* 1611

PLAYHOUSES AND BEAR-GARDENS

Paris-Garden

York. Call hither to the stake my two brave bears,
That with the very shaking of their chains
They may astonish these fell-lurking curs.

      *   *   *   *   *

Clifford. Are these thy bears? we'll bait thy bears to death
And manacle the bear-ward in their chains,
If thou dar'st bring them to the baiting-place.

Richard. Oft have I seen a hot o'er-weening cur
Run back and bite, because he was withheld;
Who, being suffer'd with the bear's fell paw,
Hath clapp'd his tail between his legs, and cried.

2 Henry VI., v. i. 144—154

This may better be termed a foul den than a fair garden. It's pity so good a piece of ground is no better employed. Here are cruel beasts in it, and as badly used; here are foul beasts come to it, and as bad or worse keep it; they are fitter for a wilderness than a city. Idle base persons (most commonly) that want employment, or else will not be otherwise employed, frequent this place; and that money which was got basely here, to maintain as bad as themselves, or spent lewdly. Here come few that either regard their credit or loss of time: the swaggering roarer, the cunning cheater, the rotten bawd, the swearing drunkard and the bloody butcher have their rendezvous here, and are of chief place and respect. There are as many civil religious men here, as they're saints in hell. Here these are made to fight by art which would agree by nature. They thrive most when the poor beasts fight oftenest: their employment is all upon quarrels as unlawful as unseemly. They cause the beasts first to fight, and then they put in first to part them. It's pity such beastly fellows should be so well maintained; they torment poor creatures, and make a gains and game of it. The beasts come forth with as ill a will, as bears to the stake. A bear-ward and an attorney are not much unlike; the attorney seems the more cruel, for these bait but beasts, but these men—their clients; the bear-ward strives to recover the hurts of his beasts, but the attorney regards not the damages of any, and they both follow the trade for profit. Well, I leave the place, and when I intend to spend an hour or two to see an ass and an ape to loss and charges, I may perhaps come hither: but as long as I can have any employment elsewhere, I will not come to see such a great company so ill occupied, in so bad a place.

DONALD LUPTON, *London and the Countrey carbonadoed* 1632

§ 3. The Audience

If the tag-rag people did not clap him and hiss him, according as he pleased and displeased them, as they use to do the players in the theatre, I am no true man. *Julius Caesar*, I. ii. 260—264

These are the youths that thunder at a playhouse, and fight for bitten apples. *Henry VIII.*, v. iv. 65

General behaviour

In our assemblies at plays in London, you shall see such heaving, and shoving, such itching and shouldering to sit by women : such care for their garments, that they be not trod on : such eyes to their laps, that no chips light in them : such pillows to their backs, that they take no hurt : such masking in their ears, I know not what : such giving them pippins to pass the time : such playing at foot-saunt without cards : such tickling, such toying, such smiling, such winking, and such manning them home, when the sports are ended, that it is a right comedy to mark their behaviour, to watch their conceits, as the cat for the mouse, and as good as a course at the game itself, to dog them a little, or follow aloof by the print of their feet, and so discover by slot where the deer taketh soil. If this were as well noted as ill seen, or as openly punished as secretly practised, I have no doubt but the cause would be seared to dry up the effect, and these pretty rabbits very cunningly ferreted from their burrows. For they that lack customers all the week, either because their haunt is unknown, or the constables and officers of their parish watch them so narrowly that they dare not quetch, to celebrate the sabbath flock to theatres, and there keep a general market of bawdry. Not that any filthiness in deed is committed within the compass of that ground, as was done in Rome, but that every wanton and his paramour, every man and his mistress, every John and his Joan, every knave and his quean, are there first acquainted and cheapen the merchandise in that place, which they pay for elsewhere as they can agree.

STEPHEN GOSSON, *The Schoole of Abuse* 1579

THE AUDIENCE

In Rome it was the fashion of wanton young men to place themselves as nigh as they could to the courtezans, to present them pomegranates, to play with their garments, and wait on them home, when the sport was done. In the playhouses at London it is the fashion of youths to go first into the yard, and to carry their eye through every gallery, then like unto ravens where they spy the carrion thither they fly, and press as near to the fairest as they can. Instead of pomegranates they give them pippins, they dally with their garments to pass the time, they minister talk upon all occasions, and either bring them home to their houses on small acquaintance, or slip into taverns when the plays are done. He thinketh best of his painted sheath, and taketh himself for a jolly fellow, that is noted of most to be busiest with women in all such places. This open corruption is a prick in the eyes of them that see it, and a thorn in the sides of the godly, when they hear it. This is a poison to beholders, and a nursery of idleness to the players.

STEPHEN GOSSON, *Playes Confuted in five Actions* 1582

How a gallant should behave himself in a play-house

The theatre is your poets' Royal Exchange, upon which their muses (that are now turned to merchants) meeting, barter away that light commodity of words for a lighter ware than words—plaudities and the breath of the great beast, which, like the threatenings of two cowards, vanish all into air. Players and their factors, who put away the stuff, and make the best of it they possibly can (as indeed 'tis their parts so to do) your gallant, your courtier and your captain had wont to be the soundest paymasters, and, I think, are still the surest chapmen : and these, by means that their heads are well stocked, deal upon this comical freight by the gross ; when your groundling and gallery-commoner buys his sport by the penny ; and, like a haggler, is glad to utter it again by retailing.

Sithence then the place is so free in entertainment, allowing a stool as well to the farmer's son as to your Templar ; that your stinkard has the selfsame liberty to be there in his tobacco-fumes, which your sweet courtier hath ; and that your carman and tinker claim as strong a voice in their suffrage, and sit to give judgment on the play's life and death, as well as the proudest Momus among the tribe of critic : it is fit that

167

he, whom the most tailors' bills do make room for, when he comes should not be basely (like a viol) cased up in a corner.

Whether therefore the gatherers of the public or private play-house stand to receive the afternoon's rent, let our gallant, having paid it, presently advance himself up to the throne of the stage. I mean not into the lords' room, which is now but the stage's suburbs—no, those boxes, by the iniquity of custom, conspiracy of waiting-women and gentlemen-ushers that there sweat together, and the covetousness of sharers, are contemptibly thrust into the rear ; and much new satin is there damned, by being smothered to death in darkness—but on the very rushes where the comedy is to dance, yea, and under the state of Cambyses himself, must our feathered ostrich, like a piece of ordnance, be planted valiantly, because impudently, beating down the mews and hisses of the opposed rascality.

For do but cast up a reckoning ; what large comings-in are pursed up by sitting on the stage ? First a conspicuous eminence is gotten, by which means the best and most essential parts of a gallant (good clothes, a proportionable leg, white hand, the Persian lock and a tolerable beard) are perfectly revealed.

By sitting on the stage you have a signed patent to engross the whole commodity of censure, may lawfully presume to be a girder, and stand at the helm to steer the passage of scenes ; yet no man shall once offer to hinder you from obtaining the title of an insolent overweening coxcomb.

By sitting on the stage you may, without travelling for it, at the very next door ask whose play it is ; and by that quest of inquiry the law warrants you to avoid much mistaking. If you know not the author, you may rail against him, and peradventure so behave yourself, that you may enforce the author to know you.

By sitting on the stage, if you be a knight, you may happily get you a mistress ; if a mere Fleet-street gentleman, a wife : but assure yourself, by continual residence, you are the first and principal man in election to begin the number of "We three."

By spreading your body on the stage, and by being a justice in examining of plays, you shall put yourself into such true scenical authority, that some poet shall not dare to present his muse rudely upon your eyes, without having first unmasked her, rifled her, and discovered all her bare and most mystical parts before you at a tavern; when you most knightly shall, for his pains, pay for both their suppers.

By sitting on the stage you may, with small cost, purchase the dear acquaintance of the boys; have a good stool for six-pence; at any time know what particular part any of the infants present; get your match lighted; examine the play-suits' lace, and perhaps win wagers upon laying it is copper, &c. And to conclude, whether you be a fool or a justice of peace; a cuckold or a captain; a lord-mayor's son or a dawcock; a knave or an undersheriff; of what stamp soever you be, current or counterfeit, the stage, like time, will bring you to most perfect light, and lay you open. Neither are you to be hunted from thence, though the scarecrows in the yard hoot at you, hiss at you, spit at you, yea throw dirt even in your teeth: 'tis most gentlemanlike patience to endure all this and to laugh at the silly animals. But if the rabble with a full throat cry: "Away with the fool!" you were worse than a madman to tarry by it; for the gentleman and the fool should never sit on the stage together.

Marry; let this observation go hand in hand with the rest; or rather like a country serving-man some five yards before them. Present not yourself on the stage, especially at a new play, until the quaking Prologue hath by rubbing got colour into his cheeks, and is ready to give the trumpets their cue that he is upon point to enter; for then it is time, as though you were one of the properties, or that you dropped out of the hang-ings, to creep from behind the arras, with your tripos or three-footed stool in one hand and a teston mounted between a fore-finger and a thumb in the other; for, if you should bestow your person upon the vulgar, when the belly of the house is but half full, your apparel is quite eaten up, the fashion lost, and the proportion of your body in more danger to be devoured than if it were served up in the Counter amongst the poultry: avoid that as you would the bastone. It shall crown you with rich commendation to laugh aloud in the midst of the most serious and saddest scene of the terriblest tragedy; and to let that clapper, your tongue, be tossed so high, that all the house may ring of it. Your lords use it; your knights are apes to the lords, and do so too; your Inn-a-court man is zany to the knights, and (many very scurvily) comes likewise limping after it. Be thou a beagle to them all, and never lin snuffing till you have scented them : for by talking and laughing, like a ploughman in a morris, you heap Pelion upon Ossa, glory upon glory. As first, all the eyes in the galleries will leave walking after the players, and only follow you; the simplest dolt in the house snatches up your name, and, when he meets you in the streets, or that you fall into his hands in the middle of a watch, his word shall be taken for you; he'll cry "He's such a gallant," and you pass. Secondly, you publish your temperance to the world, in that you seem not to resort thither to taste vain pleasures with a hungry appetite, but only as a gentleman to spend a foolish hour or two, because you can do nothing else. Thirdly, you mightily disrelish the audience, and disgrace the author : marry, you take up, though it be at the worst hand, a strong opinion of your own judgment, and enforce the poet to take pity of your weakness, and by some dedicated sonnet to bring you into a better paradise, only to stop your mouth.

If you can either for love or money, provide yourself a lodging by the water-side; for, above the convenience it brings to shun shoulder-clapping, and to ship away your cockatrice betimes in the morning, it adds a kind of state unto you to be carried from thence to the stairs of your playhouse. Hate a sculler, remember that, worse than to be acquainted with one o' th' scullery. No, your oars are your only sea-crabs, board them, and take heed you never go twice together with one pair ; often shifting is a great credit to gentlemen, and that dividing of your fare will make the poor water-snakes be ready to pull you in pieces to enjoy your custom. No matter whether, upon landing, you have money, or no; you may swim in twenty of their boats over the river upon ticket : marry, when silver comes in, remember to pay treble their fare ; and it will make your flounder-catchers to send more thanks after you when you do not draw, than when you do : for they know it will be their own another day.

Before the play begins, fall to cards; you may win or lose, as fencers do in a prize, and beat one another by confederacy, yet share the money when you meet at supper. Notwithstanding, to gull the ragamuffins that stand aloof gaping at you, throw the cards, having first torn four or five of them, round about the stage, just upon the third sound, as though you had lost. It skills not if the four knaves lie on their backs, and outface the audience ; there's none such fools as dare take exceptions at them, because, ere the play go off, better knaves than they will fall into the company.

Now, sir ; if the writer be a fellow that hath either epigrammed you, or hath had a flirt at your mistress, or hath brought either your feather, or your red beard, or your little legs, &c., on the stage ; you shall disgrace him worse than by tossing him in a blanket, or giving him the bastinado in a tavern, if, in the middle of his play, be it pastoral or comedy, moral or tragedy, you rise with a screwed and discontented face from your stool to be gone. No matter whether the scenes be good, or no; the better they are, the worse do you distaste them. And, being on your feet, sneak not away like a coward ; but salute all your gentle acquaintance, that are spread either on the rushes, or on stools about you; and draw what troop you can from the stage after you. The mimics are beholden to you for allowing them elbow-room : their poet cries perhaps, "A pox go with you "; but care not for that ; there's no music without frets.

Marry ; if either the company or indisposition of the weather bind you to sit it out, my counsel is then that you turn plain ape. Take up a rush, and tickle the earnest ears of your fellow gallants, to make other fools fall a laughing ; mew at passionate speeches ; blare at merry ; find fault with the music ; whew at the children's action ; whistle at the songs ; and, above all, curse the sharers, that whereas the same day you had bestowed forty shillings on an embroidered felt and feather, Scotch fashion, for your mistress in the court, or your punk in the city, within two hours after you encounter with the very same block on the stage, when the haberdasher swore to you the impression was extant but that morning.

To conclude. Hoard up the finest play-scraps you can get ; upon which your lean wit may most savourly feed, for want of other stuff, when the Arcadian and Euphuized gentlewomen have their tongues sharpened to set upon you : that quality (next to your shuttlecock) is the only furniture to a courtier that's but a new beginner, and is but in his A B C of compliment.

The next places that are filled, after the play-houses be emptied, are, or ought to be, taverns; into a tavern then let us next march, where the brains of one hogshead must be beaten out to make up another.

THOMAS DEKKER, *The Gulls Horne-booke* 1609

§ 4. The Actor and his craft

> ...A strutting player, whose conceit
> Lies in his hamstring, and doth think it rich
> To hear the wooden dialogue and sound
> 'Twixt his stretch'd footing and the scaffoldage.
>
> *Troilus and Cressida,* I. iii. 153—156

Shakespeare's opinion

Hamlet. Speak the speech, I pray you, as I pronounced it to you, trippingly on the tongue; but if you mouth it, as many of your players do, I had as lief the town-crier spoke my lines. Nor do not saw the air too much with your hand, thus; but use all gently: for in the very torrent, tempest, and—as I may say—whirlwind of passion, you must acquire and beget a temperance, that may give it smoothness. O! it offends me to the soul to hear a robustious periwig-pated fellow tear a passion to tatters, to very rags, to split the ears of the groundlings, who for the most part are capable of nothing but inexplicable dumb-shows and noise: I would have such a fellow whipped for o'er-doing Termagant; it out-herods Herod: pray you, avoid it.

First Player. I warrant your honour.

Hamlet. Be not too tame neither, but let your own discretion be your tutor: suit the action to the word, the word to the action; with this special observance, that you o'erstep not the modesty of nature; for anything so overdone is from the purpose of playing, whose end, both at the first and now, was and is, to hold, as 'twere, the mirror up to nature; to show virtue her own feature, scorn her own image, and the very age and body of the time his form and pressure. Now, this overdone, or come tardy off, though it make the unskilful laugh, cannot but make the judicious grieve; the censure of which one must in your allowance o'erweigh a whole theatre of others. O! there be players that I have seen play, and heard

172

others praise, and that highly, not to speak it profanely, that, neither having the accent of Christians nor the gait of Christian, pagan, nor man, have so strutted and bellowed that I have thought some of nature's journeymen had made men and not made them well, they imitated humanity so abominably.

First Player. I hope we have reformed that indifferently with us.

Hamlet. O! reform it altogether. And let those that play your clowns speak no more than is set down for them; for there be of them that will themselves laugh, to set on some quantity of barren spectators to laugh too, though in the mean time some necessary question of the play be then to be considered; that's villanous, and shows a most pitiful ambition in the fool that uses it.

Hamlet, III. ii. 1—50

The character of a player (two views)

The best in this kind are but shadows, and the worst are no worse, if imagination amend them. *A Midsummer Night's Dream,* v. i. 215

Whatsoever is commendable to the grave orator, is most exquisitely perfect in him; for by a full and significant action of body, he charms our attention: sit in a full theatre, and you will think you see so many lines drawn from the circumference of so many ears, whiles the actor is the centre. He doth not strive to make nature monstrous; she is often seen in the same scene with him, but neither on stilts nor crutches; and for his voice, 'tis not lower than the prompter, nor louder than the foil and target. By his action he fortifies moral precepts with examples; for what we see him personate, we think truly done before us: a man of a deep thought might apprehend the ghost of our ancient heroes walked again, and take him (at several times) for many of them. He is much affected to painting, and 'tis a question whether that make him an excellent player, or his playing an excellent painter. He adds grace to the poet's labours: for what in the poet is but ditty, in him is both ditty and music. He entertains us in the best leisure of our life, that is between meals, the most unfit time either for study or bodily exercise. The flight of hawks and chase of wild beasts, either of them are delights noble: but some think this sport of men the worthier, despite all calumny. All men have been of his occupation: and indeed, what he doth feignedly, that do others essentially: this day one plays a monarch, the next a private person. Here one acts a tyrant, on the morrow an exile: a parasite this man to-night, to-morrow a precisian, and so of divers others. I observe, of all men living, a worthy actor in one kind is the strongest motive of affection that can be: for when he dies, we cannot be persuaded any man can do his parts like him. But to conclude, I value a worthy actor by the corruption of some few of the quality, as I would do gold in the ore; I should not mind the dross, but the purity of the metal.

Sir Thomas Overbury, Characters 1614—16

Players are discredited in the very subject of their profession, which is only scratching the itching humours of scabbed minds with pleasing content and profane jests; and how can he be well reputed, that employs all his time in vanity and lies, counterfeiting and practising nothing else.

Player is afraid of the plague, as much as a coward of a musket: for as death is formidable to the one, so is poverty and wants to the other.

Player is afraid of the statute, for if he have no better supportation than his profession, he is neither admitted in public, nor if he be a roamer dares justify himself in private, being a flat rogue by the statute.

Player's practices can hardly be warranted in religion: for a man to put on woman's apparel, and a woman a man's, is plain prohibition; I speak not of execrable oaths, artificial lies, discoveries of cozenage, scurrilous words, obscene discourses, corrupt courtings, licentious motions, lascivious actions, and lewd jestures: for all these are incident to other men. But here is the difference: in these they come by imperfection, in them by profession.

Player is a great spender, and indeed may resemble strumpets, who get their money filthily, and spend it profusely.

Player is much out of countenance, if fools do not laugh at them, boys clap their hands, peasants ope their throats, and the rude rascal rabble cry "excellent, excellent": the knaves have acted their parts in print.

THE ACTOR AND HIS CRAFT

Player hath many times many excellent qualities : as dancing, activity, music, song, elocution, ability of body, memory, vigilancy, skill of weapon, pregnancy of wit, and such like : in all which he resembleth an excellent spring of water, which grows the more sweeter and the more plentiful by the often drawing out of it: so are all these the more perfect and plausible by the often practice.

Player is at the first very bashful, as stricken with amaze at the multitude, which being of various dispositions, will censure him accordingly: but custom maketh perfectness, and emboldeneth him sometimes to be shameless.

Player must take heed of wrested and enforced action : for if there be not a facility in his deliverance, and as it were a natural dexterity, it must needs sound harsh to the auditor, and procure his distaste and displeasure.

Player is like a garment which the tailor maketh at the direction of the owner ; so they frame their action at the disposing of the poet : so that in truth they are reciprocal helps to one another ; for the one writes for money, and the other plays for money, and the spectator pays his money.

T. G., *The Rich Cabinet* 1616

The magnificence of players' dress

Overlashing in apparel is so common a fault, that the very hirelings of some of our players, which stand at reversion of six shillings by the week, jet it under gentlemen's noses in suits of silk, exercising themselves to prating on the stage, and common scoffing when they come abroad, where they look askance over the shoulder at every man, of whom the Sunday before they begged an alms. I speak not this, as though every one that professeth the quality so abused himself, for it is well known that some of them are sober, discreet, properly learned, honest householders and citizens, well thought on amongst their neighbours at home, though the pride of their shadows (I mean those hangbys whom they succour with stipend) cause them to be somewhat ill talked of abroad.

STEPHEN GOSSON, *The Schoole of Abuse* 1579

175

THE THEATRE

A story of the Queen's players touring in the provinces

[see also p. 20]

Amongst other choleric wise justices he was one, that having a play presented before him and his township by Tarlton and the rest of his fellows, her Majesty's servants, and they were now entering into their first merriment (as they call it), the people began exceedingly to laugh when Tarlton first peeped out his head. Whereat the justice, not a little moved, and seeing with his becks and nods he could not make them cease, he went with his staff, and beat them round about unmercifully on the bare pates, in that they, being but farmers and poor country hinds, would presume to laugh at the Queen's men, and make no more account of her cloth in his presence.

THOMAS NASHE, *Pierce Penilesse* 1592

A royal licence for Shakespeare's company,
"The King's Players," May 19, 1603

James by the grace of God etc. To all justices, mayors, sheriffs, constables, headboroughs and other our officers and loving subjects greeting. Know ye that We of our special grace, certain knowledge and mere motion, have licensed and authorised and by these presents do license and authorise these our servants Lawrence Fletcher, William Shakespeare, Richard Burbage, Augustine Phillipps, John Heming, Henry Condell, William Sly, Robert Armin, Richard Cowley, and the rest of their associates freely to use and exercise the art and faculty of playing comedies, tragedies, histories, interludes, morals, pastorals, stage-plays, and such others like as they have already studied or hereafter shall use or study, as well for the recreation of our loving subjects as for our solace and pleasure when we shall think good to see them during our pleasure. And the said comedies, tragedies, histories, interludes, morals, pastorals, stage-plays and such like to shew and exercise publicly to their best commodity, when the infection of the plague shall decrease, as well within their now usual house, called the Globe, within our county of Surrey, as also within any town-halls or moot-halls or other convenient places within the liberties and freedom of any other city, university town or borough what-soever within our said realms and dominions. Willing and commanding you and every of you as you tender our pleasure not only to permit and suffer them herein without any your lets and hindrances or molestations during our said pleasure, but also to be aiding and assisting to them if any wrong be to them offered. And to allow them such former courtesies as hath been given to men of their place and quality, and also what further favour you shall show to these our servants, for our sake, we shall take kindly at your hands. In witness whereof etc. witness ourself at Westminster the nineteenth day of May.

§ 5. Puritan opposition to the theatre

[From the erection of the theatres in 1576 to their suppression at the outbreak of the Civil War, the Puritan party waged an unceasing warfare against the stage. But for the protection of the court the Elizabethan drama would have come to an untimely end before Shakespeare reached London. The tracts on either side of the controversy tell us a good deal about the theatrical and dramatic conditions of the day.]

Puritan denunciation from Paul's Cross

Look but upon the common plays in London, and see the multitude that flocketh to them and followeth them. Behold the sumptuous theatre houses, a continual monument of London's prodigality and folly. But I understand they are now forbidden because of the plague. I like the policy well if it hold still, for a disease is but lodged or patched up that is not cured in the cause, and the cause of plagues is sin, if you look to it well : and the cause of sin are plays : therefore the cause of plagues are plays.

THOMAS WHITE, *A Sermon Preached at Pawles Crosse* 1578

Will not a filthy play, with the blast of a trumpet, sooner call thither a thousand, than an hour's tolling of a bell bring to the sermon a hundred ? Nay even here in the city, without it be at this place and some other certain ordinary audience, where shall you find a reasonable company ? Whereas if you resort to the Theater, the Curtain, and other places of plays in the city, you shall on the Lord's day have those places, with many other that I cannot reckon, so full as possible they can throng, besides a great number of other lets to pull from the hearing of the word of which I will speak hereafter...What should I speak of beastly plays, against which out of this place every man crieth out? Have we not houses of purpose built with great charges for the maintenance of them; and that without the liberties, as who would say: "There, let them say what they will, we will play." I know not how I might with the godly learned especially more discommend the gorgeous playing-place erected in the fields than to term it, as they please to have it called, a Theater, that is even after the manner of the old heathenish theatre at Rome, a shew-place of all beastly and filthy matters, to the which it cannot be chosen that men should resort without learning thence much corruption....For reckoning with the least, the gain that is reaped of eight ordinary places in the city, which I know, by playing but once a week (whereas many times they play twice or sometimes thrice) it amounteth to two thousand pounds by the year.

JOHN STOCKWOOD, *A Sermon Preached at Paules Crosse* 1578

A sweeping condemnation of plays

Do they not maintain bawdry, insinuate foolery, and renew the remembrance of heathen idolatry? Do they not induce whoredom and uncleanness? Nay, are they not rather plain devourers of maidenly virginity and chastity? For proof whereof but mark the flocking and running to Theaters and Curtains, daily and hourly, night and day, time and tide, to see plays and interludes, where such wanton gestures, such bawdy speeches, such laughing and fleering, such kissing and bussing, such clipping and culling, such winking and glancing of wanton eyes, and the like is used, as is wonderful to behold. Then these goodly pageants being ended, every mate sorts to his mate, every one brings another homeward of their way very friendly, and in their secret conclaves (covertly) they play the sodomites, or worse. And these be the fruits of plays and interludes, for the most part. And whereas, you say, there are good examples to be learnt in them: truly so there are; if you will learn falsehood; if you will learn cozenage; if you will learn to deceive; if you will learn to play the hypocrite, to cog, to lie and falsify; if

178

you will learn to jest, laugh and fleer, to grin, to nod and mow ; if you will learn to play the Vice, to swear, tear and blaspheme both heaven and earth ; if you will learn to become a bawd, unclean, and to devirginate maids, to deflower honest wives ; if you will learn to murder, flay, kill, pick, steal, rob and rove ; if you will learn to rebel against princes, to commit treasons, to consume treasures, to practise idleness, to sing and talk of bawdy love and venery ; if you will learn to deride, scoff, mock and flout, to flatter and smooth ; if you will learn to play the whoremaster, the glutton, drunkard, or incestuous person ; if you will learn to become proud, haughty and arrogant ; and finally, if you will learn to contemn God and all His laws, to care neither for Heaven nor Hell, and to commit all kinds of sin and mischief, you need to go to no other school, for all these good examples may you see painted before your eyes in interludes and plays.

PHILIP STUBBES, *The Anatomie of Abuses* 1583

What the authorities of the city thought of the theatre

To the Lords against Stage Plays. Our humble duties remembered to your good Lords and the rest. We have signified to your Honours many times heretofore the great inconvenience which we find to grow by the common exercise of stage-plays. We presumed to do [so], as well in respect of the duty we bear towards her Highness for the good government of this her city, as for conscience sake, being persuaded (under correction of your Honours' judgment) that neither in polity nor in religion they are to be suffered in a Christian commonwealth, specially being of that frame and matter as usually they are, containing nothing but profane fables, lascivious matters, cozening devices, and scurrilous behaviours, which are so set forth as that they move wholly to imitation and not to the avoiding of those faults and vices which they represent. Among other inconveniences it is not the least that they give opportunity to the refuse sort of evil-disposed and ungodly people that are within and about this city to assemble themselves and to make their matches for all their lewd and ungodly practices ; being as heretofore we have found by the examination of divers apprentices and other servants who have confessed unto us that the said stage-plays were the very places of their rendezvous, appointed by them to meet with such other as were to join with them in their designs and mutinous attempts, being also the ordinary places for masterless men to come together and to recreate themselves. For avoiding whereof we are now again most humble and earnest suitors to your honours to direct your letters as well to ourselves as to the justices of peace of Surrey and Middlesex for the present stay and final suppressing of the said stage-plays, as well at the Theater, Curtain and Bankside as in all other places in and about the city; whereby we doubt not but the opportunity and the very cause of many disorders being taken away, we shall be more able to keep the worse sort of such evil and disordered people in better order than heretofore we have been. And so most humbly we take our leaves. From London the 28th of July 1597.

The incon- 1. They are a special cause of corrupting
veniences that their youth, containing nothing but unchaste
grow by stage-
plays about matters, lascivious devices, shifts of cozenage,
the city of and other lewd and ungodly practices, being so
London. as that they impress the very quality and corrup-
tion of manners which they represent, contrary to the rules and art prescribed for the making of comedies even among the heathen, who used them seldom and at certain set times, and not all the year long as our manner is. Whereby such as frequent them, being of the base and refuse sort of people or such young gentlemen as have small regard of credit or conscience, draw the same into imitation and not to the avoiding the like vices which they represent.

2. They are the ordinary places for vagrant persons, masterless men, thieves, horse-stealers, whoremongers, cozeners, coney-catchers, contrivers of treason and other idle and dangerous persons to meet together and to make their matches to the great displeasure of Almighty God and the hurt and annoyance of her Majesty's people; which cannot be prevented nor discovered by the governors of the city for that they are out of the city's jurisdiction.

3. They maintain idleness in such persons as have no vocation, and draw apprentices and other servants from their ordinary works and all sorts of people from the resort unto sermons and other Christian exercises to the great hindrance of

trades and profanation of religion established by her Highness within this realm.

4. In the time of sickness it is found by experience that many, having sores and yet not heart-sick, take occasion hereby to walk abroad and to recreate themselves by hearing a play. Whereby others are infected, and themselves also many things miscarry.

A letter from the Lord Mayor and Aldermen to the Privy Council,
July 28, 1597

A dramatist's reply to the puritans

Good my lord, will you see the players well bestowed? Do you hear, let them be well used; for they are the abstracts and brief chronicles of the time: after your death you were better have a bad epitaph than their ill report while you live. *Hamlet*, ii. ii. 553—557

That state or kingdom that is in league with all the world and hath no foreign sword to vex it, is not half so strong or confirmed to endure, as that which lives every hour in fear of invasion. There is a certain waste of the people for whom there is no use but war: and these men must have some employment still to cut them off. *Nam si foras hostem non habent, domi invenient.* If they have no service abroad, they will make mutinies at home. Or if the affairs of the state be such, as cannot exhale all these corrupt excrements, it is very expedient they have some light toys to busy their heads withal, cast before them as bones to gnaw upon, which may keep them from having leisure to intermeddle with higher matters.

To this effect, the policy of plays is very necessary, howsoever some shallow-brained censurers (not the deepest searchers into the secrets of government) mightily oppugn them. For whereas the afternoon, being the idlest time of the day, wherein men that are their own masters (as gentlemen of the court, the Inns of the Court, and the number of captains and soldiers about London) do wholly bestow themselves upon pleasure, and that pleasure they divide (how virtuously it skills not) either into gaming, following of harlots, drinking, or seeing a play: is it not then better (since of four extremes all the world cannot keep them but they will choose one) that they should betake them to the least, which is plays? Nay, what if I prove plays to be no extreme, but a rare exercise of virtue? First, for the subject of them (for the most part) it is borrowed out of our English chronicles, wherein our forefathers' valiant acts (that have lain long buried in rusty brass and worm-eaten books) are revived, and they themselves raised from the grave of oblivion, and brought to plead their aged honours in open presence: than which, what can be a sharper reproof to these degenerate effeminate days of ours?

How would it have joyed brave Talbot (the terror of the French) to think that after he had lain two hundred years in his tomb, he should triumph again on the stage, and have his bones new embalmed with the tears of ten thousand spectators at least (at several times), who in the tragedian that represents his person imagine they behold him fresh bleeding.

I will defend it against any cullion or club-fisted usurer of them all, there is no immortality can be given a man on earth like unto plays. What talk I to them of immortality, that are the only underminers of honour, and do envy any man that is not sprung up by base brokery like themselves? They care not if all the ancient houses were rooted out, so that, like the burgomasters of the Low-countries, they might share the government amongst them as states, and be quarter-masters of our monarchy. All arts to them are vanity: and, if you tell them what a glorious thing it is to have Henry V represented on the stage, leading the French king prisoner, and forcing both him and the Dauphin to swear fealty, "Aye but" (will they say) "what do we get by it?" Respecting neither the right of fame that is due to true nobility deceased, nor what hopes of eternity are to be proposed to adventurous minds, to encourage them forward, but only their execrable lucre and filthy unquenchable avarice.

They know when they are dead they shall not be brought upon the stage for any goodness, but in a merriment of the Usurer and the Devil, or buying arms of the herald, who gives them the lion, without tongue, tail, or talons, because his master whom he must serve is a townsman and a man of peace, and must not keep any quarrelling beasts to annoy his honest neighbours.

In plays, all cozenages, all cunning drifts over-gilded with outward holiness, all stratagems of war, all the cankerworms that breed on the rust of peace are most lively anatomized. They shew the ill-success of treason, the fall of hasty climbers, the wretched end of usurpers, the misery of civil dissension, and how just God is evermore in punishing of murder. And to prove every one of these allegations, could I propound the circumstances of this play and that play, if I meant to handle this theme otherwise than *obiter*. What should I say more? They are sour pills of reprehension, wrapped up in sweet words. Whereas some petitioners of the Council against them object they corrupt the youth of the city, and withdraw prentices from their work, they heartily wish they might be troubled with none of their youth nor their prentices; for some of them (I mean the ruder handicrafts' servants) never come abroad, but they are in danger of undoing. And as for corrupting them when they come, that's false; for no play they have encourageth any man to tumults or rebellion, but lays before such the halter and the gallows; or praiseth or approveth pride, lust, whoredom, prodigality or drunkenness, but beats them down utterly. As for the hindrance of trades and traders of the city by them, that is an article foisted in by the vintners, alewives, and victuallers, who surmise, if there were no plays, they should have all the company that resort to them lie boozing and beer-bathing in their houses every afternoon. Nor so, nor so, good Brother Bottle-ale, for there are other places besides where money can bestow itself. The sign of the smock will wipe your mouth clean: and yet I have heard ye have made her a tenant to your tap-houses. But what shall he do that hath spent himself? Where shall he haunt? Faith, when dice, lust, and drunkenness and all have dealt upon him, if there be never a play for him to go to for his penny, he sits melancholy in his chamber, devising upon felony or treason, and how he may best exalt himself by mischief.

In Augustus' time (who was the patron of all witty sports) there happened a great fray in Rome about a player, insomuch as all the city was in an uproar: whereupon the emperor (after the broil was somewhat overblown) called the player before him, and asked what was the reason that a man of his quality durst presume to make such a brawl about nothing. He smilingly replied, " It is good for thee, O Caesar, that the people's heads are troubled with brawls and quarrels about us and our light matters : for otherwise they would look into thee and thy matters." Read Lipsius or any profane or Christian politician, and you shall find him of this opinion. Our players are not as the players beyond sea, a sort of squirting bawdy comedians, that have whores and common courtezans to play women's parts, and forbear no immodest speech or unchaste action that may procure laughter ; but our scene is more stately furnished than ever it was in the time of Roscius, our representations honourable and full of gallant resolution, not consisting, like theirs, of a pantaloon, a whore, and a zany, but of emperors, kings and princes, whose true tragedies (*Sophocleo cothurno*) they do vaunt.

Not Roscius nor Æsop, those admired tragedians that have lived ever since before Christ was born, could ever perform more in action than famous Ned Alleyn. I must accuse our poets of sloth and partiality, that they will not boast in large impressions what worthy men (above all nations) England affords. Other countries cannot have a fiddler break a string but they will put it in print, and the old Romans in the writings they published thought scorn to use any but domestical examples of their own home-bred actors, scholars and champions, and them they would extol to the third and fourth generation : cobblers, tinkers, fencers, none escaped them, but they mingled them all in one gallimaufry of glory.

Here I have used a like method, not of tying myself to mine own country, but by insisting in the experience of our time : and, if I ever write anything in Latin (as I hope one day I shall), not a man of any desert here amongst us but I will have up. Tarlton, Ned Alleyn, Knell, Bently, shall be made known to France, Spain, and Italy : and not a part that they surmounted in, more than other, but I will there note and set down, with the manner of their habits and attire.

THOMAS NASHE, *Pierce Penilesse* 1592

PURITAN OPPOSITION

Qui s'excuse, s'accuse

[By the ordinance of Sept. 2nd, 1642, Parliament closed all the theatres in London, which remained shut until the Restoration. The following amusing little pamphlet, protesting against the ordinance or pretending to, gives us a very curious insight into the theatrical life of the time. It is here printed entire.]

Oppressed with many calamities and languishing to death under the burden of a long and (for aught we know) an ever-lasting restraint, we the comedians, tragedians and actors of all sorts and sizes belonging to the famous private and public houses within the city of London and the suburbs thereof, to you great Phoebus and your sacred Sisters, the sole patronesses of our distressed calling, do we in all humility present this our humble and lamentable complaint, by whose intercession to those powers who confined us to silence we hope to be restored to our pristine honour and employment.

First, it is not unknown to all the audience that have frequented the private houses of Black-friars, the Cock-pit and Salisbury-court, without austerity we have purged our stages from all obscene and scurrilous jests, such as might either be guilty of corrupting the manners, or defaming the persons of any men of note in the city or kingdom ; that we have en-deavoured, as much as in us lies, to instruct one another in the true and genuine art of acting, to repress bawling and railing, formerly in great request, and for to suit our language and action to the more gentle and natural garb of the times; that we have left off for our own parts, and so have commanded our servants, to forget that ancient custom which formerly rendered men of our quality infamous, namely the inveigling in young gentlemen, merchants' factors and prentices to spend their patrimonies and masters' estates upon us and our harlots in taverns ; we have clean and quite given over the borrowing money at first sight of puny gallants or praising their swords, belts and beavers, so to invite them to bestow them upon us ; and to our praise be it spoken, we were for the most part very well reformed, few of us keeping, or being rather kept by, our mistresses, betook ourselves wholly to our wives, observing the matrimonial vow of chastity. Yet for all these conformities and

185

reformations we were by authority (to which we in all humility submit) restrained from the practice of our profession; that profession which had before maintained us in comely and convenient equipage, some of us by it merely being enabled to keep horses (though not whores) is now condemned to a perpetual, at least a very long temporary, silence, and we left to live upon our shifts or the expense of our former gettings, to the great impoverishment and utter undoing of ourselves, wives, children and dependants, besides which it is of all other our extremest grievance, that plays being put down under the name of public recreations, other public recreations of far more harmful consequences [are] permitted still to stand *in statu quo prius*, namely that nurse of barbarism and beastliness, the Bear-Garden, where upon their usual days those demi-monsters are baited by bandogs; the gentlemen of stave and tail, namely boisterous butchers, cutting cobblers, hard-handed masons and the like rioting companions, resorting thither with as much freedom as formerly, making with their sweat and crowding a far worse stink than the ill-formed beasts they persecute with their dogs and whips; pick-pockets, which in an age are not heard of in any of our houses, repairing thither, and other disturbers of the public peace which dare not be seen in our civil and well-governed theatres, where none use to come but the best of the nobility and gentry; and though some have taxed our houses unjustly for being the receptacles of harlots, the exchanges where they meet and make their bargains with their frank chapmen of the country and city, yet we may justly excuse ourselves of either knowledge or consent in these lewd practices, we having no prophetic souls to know women's honesty by instinct, nor commission to examine them; and if we had, worthy were these wretches of Bridewell, that out of their own mouths would convince themselves of lasciviousness. Puppet-plays, which are not so much valuable as the very music between each act at ours, are still up with uncontrolled allowance, witness the famous motion of *Bell and the Dragon*, so frequently visited at Holborn Bridge these past Christmas holidays, whither citizens of all sorts repair with far more detriment to themselves than [they] ever did to plays, comedies and tragedies, being the lively representations of men's actions in which vice is always sharply glanced at and punished, and virtue rewarded and encouraged, the most exact and natural eloquence of our English language expressed and daily amplified. And yet for all this we suffer and are enforced, ourselves and our dependants, to tender our complaint in doleful manner to you great Phoebus and you inspired Heliconian Virgins. First our house-keepers that grew wealthy by our endeavours complain that they are enforced to pay the grand landlords rents during this long vacation out of their former gettings ; instead of ten, twenty, nay thirty shillings shares which used nightly to adorn and comfort with their harmonious music their large and well-stuffed pockets, they have shares in nothing with us now but our misfortunes, living merely out of the stock, out of the interest and principal of their former gotten moneys, which daily is exhausted by the maintenance of themselves and families.

For ourselves, such as were sharers are so impoverished that, were it not for some slender helps afforded us in this time of calamity by our former providence, we might be enforced to act our tragedies. Our hired-men are dispersed, some turned soldiers and trumpeters, others destin'd to meaner courses, or depending upon us, whom in courtesy we cannot see want for old acquaintance sakes. Their friends, young gentlemen that used to feast and frolick with them at taverns, having either quitted the kin in these times of distraction, or their money having quitted them, they are ashamed to look upon their old expensive friends. Nay, their very mistresses, those buxom and bountiful lasses that usually were enamoured on the persons of the younger sort of actors, for the good clothes they wore upon the stage, believing them really to be the persons they did only represent, are quite out of sorts themselves and so disabled for supplying their poor friends' necessities. Our fools who had wont to allure and excite laughter with their very countenances, at their first appearance on the stage (hard shifts are better than none) are enforced, some of them at least, to maintain themselves by virtue of their baubles. Our boys, ere we shall have liberty to act again, will be grown out of use, like cracked organ-pipes, and have faces as old as our flags.

Nay our very door-keepers, men and women, most grievously complain that by this cessation they are robbed of the privilege of stealing from us with licence : they cannot now, as in King Agamemnon's days, seem to scratch their heads where they itch

187

not, and drop shillings and half-crown-pieces in at their collars. Our music that was held so delectable and precious, that they scorned to come to a tavern under twenty shillings' salary for two hours, now wander with their instruments under their cloaks, I mean such as have any, into all houses of good fellowship, saluting every room where there is company with, "Will you have any music, gentlemen?" For our tire-men, and others that belonged formerly to our ward-robe, with the rest, they are out of service : our stock of clothes, such as are not in tribulation for the general use, being a sacrifice to moths. The tobacco-men, that used to walk up and down, selling for a penny-pipe, that which was not worth twelve pence an horse-load, being now bound under tapsters in inns and tippling-houses. Nay such a terrible distress and dissolution hath befallen us and all those that had dependence on the stage, that it hath quite unmade our hopes of future recovery; for some of our ablest ordinary poets instead of their annual stipends and beneficial second-days, being for mere necessity compelled to get a living by writing contemptible penny-pamphlets in which they have not so much as poetical licence to use any attribute of their profession but that of *Quid libet audiendi?* and feigning miraculous stories and relations of unheard of battles. Nay, it is to be feared that shortly some of them (if they have not been enforced to do it already) will be incited to enter themselves into Martin Parker's society, and write ballads. And what a shame this is, great Phoebus and you sacred Sisters, for your own priests thus to be degraded of their ancient dignities. Be yourselves righteous judges, when those who formerly have sung with such elegance the acts of kings and potentates, charming like Orpheus the dull and brutish multitude, scarce a degree above stones and forests, into admiration though not into understanding with their divine raptures, shall be by that tyrant Necessity reduced to such abject exigents, wandering like grand-children of old Erra Paters, those learned almanac-makers, without any Maecenas to cherish their lofty conceptions, prostituted by the misfortune of our silence to inexplicable miseries, having no heavenly Castalian sack to actuate and inform their spirits almost confounded with stupidity and coldness by their frequent drinking (and glad too they can get it) of fulsome ale and heretical beer as their usual beverage.

PURITAN OPPOSITION

To conclude this our humble complaint, great Phoebus and you nine sacred Sisters, the patronesses of wit and protectresses of us poor disrespected comedians, if for the present by your powerful intercessions we may be reinvested in our former houses, and settled in our former calling, we shall for the future promise never to admit into our sixpenny-rooms those unwholesome enticing harlots that sit there merely to be taken up by prentices or lawyers' clerks, nor any female of what degree soever, except they come lawfully with their husbands or near allies. The abuses in tobacco shall be reformed, none vended, nor so much as in threepenny galleries, unless of the pure Spanish leaf. For ribaldry or any such paltry stuff as may scandal the pious and provoke the wicked to looseness, we will utterly expel it, with the bawdy and ungracious poets the authors, to the Antipodes. Finally we shall hereafter so demean ourselves as none shall esteem us of the ungodly, or have cause to repine at our action or interludes : we will not entertain any comedian that shall speak his part in a tone, as if he did it in derision of some of the pious, but reform all our disorders, and amend all our amisses, so prosper us Phoebus and the nine Muses, and be propitious to this our complaint.

The Actors Remonstrance 1643

CHAPTER VIII

THE COURT

What infinite heart's ease
Must kings neglect that private men enjoy!
And what have kings that privates have not too,
Save ceremony, save general ceremony?
And what art thou, thou idle ceremony?
What kind of god art thou, that suffer'st more
Of mortal griefs than do thy worshippers?
What are thy rents? what are thy comings-in?

*   *   *   *   *   *

'Tis not the balm, the sceptre and the ball,
The sword, the mace, the crown imperial,
The intertissued robe of gold and pearl,
The farced title running 'fore the king,
The throne he sits on, nor the tide of pomp
That beats upon the high shore of this world,
No, not all these, thrice-gorgeous ceremony,
Not all these, laid in bed majestical,
Can sleep so soundly as the wretched slave,
Who with a body fill'd and vacant mind
Gets him to rest, cramm'd with distressful bread.

Henry V., IV. i. 256—290

About, about!
Search Windsor castle, elves, within and out:
Strew good luck, ouphs, on every sacred room,
That it may stand till the perpetual doom,
In seat as wholesome as in state 'tis fit,
Worthy the owner, and the owner it.
The several chairs of order look you scour
With juice of balm and every precious flower:
Each fair instalment, coat, and several crest,
With loyal blazon, ever more be blest!

QUEEN ELIZABETH AT GREENWICH

And nightly, meadow-fairies, look you sing,
Like to the Garter's compass, in a ring:
The expressure that it bears, green let it be,
More fertile-fresh than all the field to see;
And, *Honi soit qui mal y pense* write
In emerald tufts, flowers purple, blue, and white;
Like sapphire, pearl, and rich embroidery,
Buckled below fair knighthood's bending knee.

The Merry Wives of Windsor, v. v. 61—78

[At Christmas 1594 Shakespeare acted before Elizabeth at Greenwich. Under James I. he ranked as a Groom of the Chamber.]

§ 1. Queen Elizabeth at Greenwich

Elizabeth, the reigning Queen of England, was born at the royal palace of Greenwich, and here she generally resides, particularly in summer, for the delightfulness of its situation. We were admitted by an order, which Mr Rogers had procured from the Lord Chamberlain, into the presence-chamber hung with rich tapestry, and the floor, after the English fashion, strewed with hay, through which the Queen commonly passes in her way to chapel. At the door stood a gentleman dressed in velvet, with a gold chain, whose office was to introduce to the Queen any person of distinction that came to wait on her. It was Sunday, when there is usually the greatest attendance of nobility. In the same hall were the Archbishop of Canterbury, the Bishop of London, a great number of counsellors of state, officers of the crown, and gentlemen, who waited the Queen's coming out, which she did from her own apartment when it was time to go to prayers, attended in the following manner :—

First went gentlemen, barons, earls, knights of the Garter, all richly dressed and bareheaded ; next came the Lord High Chancellor of England, bearing the seals in a red silk purse, between two, one of whom carried the royal sceptre, the other the sword of state in a red scabbard, studded with golden fleur-de-lis, the point upwards ; next came the Queen, in the 65th year of her age (as we were told), very majestic ; her face oblong, fair but wrinkled ; her eyes small, yet black and pleasant ; her nose a little hooked, her lips narrow, and her teeth black (a defect the English seem subject to, from their too great use of sugar); she had in her ears two pearls with very rich drops; her hair was of an auburn colour, but false; upon her head she had a small crown, reported to be made of some of the gold of the celebrated Luneburg table; her bosom was uncovered, as all the English ladies have it till they marry; and she had on a necklace of exceeding fine jewels; her hands were slender, her fingers rather long, and her stature neither tall nor low; her air was stately, her manner of speaking mild and obliging. That day she was dressed in white silk, bordered with pearls of the size of beans, and over it a mantle of black silk shot with silver threads; her train was very long, the end of it borne by a marchioness; instead of a chain, she had an oblong collar of gold and jewels. As she went along in all this state and magnificence, she spoke very graciously, first to one, then to another (whether foreign ministers, or those who attend for different reasons), in English, French and Italian; for besides being well skilled in Greek, Latin and the languages I have mentioned, she is mistress of Spanish, Scotch and Dutch. Whoever speaks to her, it is kneeling; now and then she raises some with her hand. While we were there, William Slawata, a Bohemian baron, had letters to present to her; and she, after pulling off her glove, gave him her right hand to kiss, sparkling with rings and jewels—a mark of particular favour. Wherever she turned her face as she was going along, everybody fell down on their knees. The ladies of the court followed next to her, very handsome and well-shaped, and for the most part dressed in .white. She was guarded on each side by the gentlemen pensioners, fifty in number, with gilt halberds. In the ante-chapel, next the hall where we were, petitions were presented to her, and she received them most graciously, which occasioned the acclamation of *God save the Quene Elizabeth!* She answered it with *I thancke you myn good peupel.* In the chapel was excellent music; as soon as it and the service were over, which scarcely exceeded half-an-hour, the Queen returned in the same state and order, and prepared to go to dinner. But while she was still at prayers, we saw her table set out with the following solemnity :—

A gentleman entered the room bearing a rod, and along with him another who had a table-cloth, which after they had both knelt three times, with the utmost veneration, he spread upon the table, and after kneeling again they both retired. Then came two others, one with the rod again, the other with a salt-cellar, a plate and bread; when they had knelt as the others had done, and placed what was brought upon the table, they too retired with the same ceremonies performed by the first. At last came an unmarried lady of extraordinary beauty (we were told that she was a countess) and along with her a married one, bearing a tasting-knife; the former was dressed in white silk, who, when she had prostrated herself three times, in the most graceful manner, approached the table and rubbed the plates with bread and salt with as much awe as if the Queen had been present. When they had waited there a little while, the yeomen of the guard entered, bareheaded, clothed in scarlet, with a golden rose upon their backs, bringing in at each turn a course of twenty-four dishes, served in silver most of it gilt; these dishes were received by a gentleman in the same order as they were brought and placed upon the table, while the lady-taster gave to each of the guard a mouthful to eat of the particular dish he had brought, for fear of any poison. During the time that this guard, which consists of the tallest and stoutest men that can be found in all England, 100 in number, being carefully selected for this service, were bringing dinner, twelve trumpets and two kettle-drums made the hall ring for half-an-hour together. At the end of all this cere-monial, a number of unmarried ladies appeared, who with particular solemnity lifted the meat off the table, and conveyed it into the Queen's inner and more private chamber, where after she had chosen for herself, the rest goes to the ladies of the court. The Queen dines and sups alone with very few attend-ants; and it is very seldom that any body, foreigner or native, is admitted at that time, and then only at the intercession of some distinguished personage.

PAUL HENTZNER, *Travels in England* 1598 [Rye]

THE COURT

§ 2. The Courtier

The ideal

> The courtier's, soldier's, scholar's eye, tongue, sword,
> The expectancy and rose of the fair state,
> The glass of fashion and the mould of form,
> The observed of all observers. *Hamlet*, III. i. 160—163

To ride comely, to run fair at the tilt or ring, to play at all weapons, to shoot fair in bow or surely in gun, to vault lustily, to run, to leap, to wrestle, to swim, to dance comely, to sing and play of instruments cunningly, to hawk, to hunt, to play at tennis and all pastimes generally which be joined with labour, used in open place and on the daylight, containing either some fit exercise for war or some pleasant pastime for peace, be not only comely and decent, but also very necessary, for a courtly gentleman to use....

To join learning with comely exercises Conto Baldassare Castiglione in his book, *Cortegiano*, doth timely teach : which book, advisedly read and diligently followed but one year at home in England, would do a young gentleman more good, I wiss, than three years travel abroad spent in Italy....And besides good precepts in books, in all kinds of tongues, this court also never lacked many fair examples for young gentlemen to follow. And, surely, one example is more valuable, both to good and ill, than twenty precepts written in books....Present examples of this present time, I list not to touch, yet there is one example for all the gentlemen of this court to follow, that may well satisfy them, or nothing will serve them, nor no example move them to goodness and learning.

It is your shame (I speak to you all, you young gentlemen of England), that one maid should go beyond you all, in excellency of learning and knowledge of divers tongues. Point forth six of the best given gentlemen of this court, and all they together shew not so much good will, spend not so much time, bestow not so many hours, daily, orderly and constantly, for the increase of learning and knowledge, as doth the Queen's Majesty herself. Yea I believe that, beside her perfect readiness in Latin, Italian, French and Spanish, she readeth here now at Windsor more Greek every day than some prebendary of this church doth read Latin in a whole week. And that which is most praiseworthy of all, within the walls of her privy chamber she hath obtained that excellence of learning, to understand, speak and write, both wittily with head and fair with hand, as scarce one or two rare wits in both the universities have in many years reached unto. Amongst all the benefits that God hath blessed me withal, next the knowledge of Christ's true religion, I count this the greatest, that it pleased God to call me to be one poor minister in setting forward these excellent gifts of learning in this most excellent Prince. Whose only example if the rest of our nobility would follow, then might England be, for learning and wisdom in nobility, a spectacle to all the world beside. But see the mishap of men: the best examples have never such force to move to any goodness, as the bad, vain, light and fond, have to all illness....

Take heed therefore, ye great ones in the court, yea, though ye be the greatest of all, take heed what ye do, take heed how ye live. For as you great ones use to do, so all mean men love to do. You be indeed makers or marrers of all men's manners within the realm. For though God hath placed you to be chief in making of laws, to bear greatest authority, to command all others, yet God doth order that all your laws, all your authority, all your commandments, do not half so much with mean men, as doth your example and manner of living. And for example even in the greatest matter, if you yourselves do serve God gladly and orderly for conscience sake, not coldly and sometime for manner sake, you carry all the court with you, and the whole realm beside, earnestly and orderly to do the same. If you do otherwise, you be the only authors of all misorders in religion, not only to the court, but to all England beside. Infinite shall be made cold in religion by your example that never were hurt by reading of books.

And in meaner matters, if three or four great ones in court will needs outrage in apparel, in huge hose, in monstrous hats, in garish colours, let the Prince proclaim, make laws, order, punish, command every gate in London daily to be watched, let all good men beside do everywhere what they can, surely the misorder of apparel in mean men abroad shall never be amended, except the greatest in court will order and mend themselves first.

ROGER ASCHAM, *The Scholemaster* 1570

THE COURT

The other side of the picture

Hamlet. Dost know this water-fly?

Horatio. No, my good lord.

Hamlet. Thy state is the more gracious; for 'tis a vice to know him.
He hath much land, and fertile: let a beast be lord of beasts, and his crib
shall stand at the king's mess: 'tis a chough; but, as I say, spacious in
the possession of dirt.

    *   *   *   *   *   *   *

Osric. Sir, here is newly come to court Laertes; believe me, an
absolute gentleman, full of most excellent differences, of very soft society
and great showing: indeed to speak feelingly of him, he is the card or
calendar of gentry, for you shall find in him the continent of what part
a gentleman would see.   *Hamlet,* v. ii. 84—117

Hotspur.   When the fight was done,
When I was dry with rage and extreme toil,
Breathless and faint, leaning upon my sword,
Came there a certain lord, neat, and trimly dress'd,
Fresh as a bridegroom; and his chin, new reap'd,
Show'd like a stubble-land at harvest-home:
He was perfumed like a milliner,
And 'twixt his finger and his thumb he held
A pouncet-box, which ever and anon
He gave his nose and took't away again;
Who therewith angry when it next came there,
Took it in snuff: and still he smiled and talk'd;
And as the soldiers bore dead bodies by,
He call'd them untaught knaves, unmannerly,
To bring a slovenly unhandsome corpse
Betwixt the wind and his nobility.
                  1 *Henry IV.,* i. iii. 30—45

The courtier's hands are perfumed with civet.
                As You Like It, iii. ii. 67

A courtier to all men's thinking is a man, and to most men
the finest: all things else are defined by the understanding, but
this by the senses: but his surest mark is, that he is to be found
only about princes. He smells; and putteth away much of his
judgment about the situation of his clothes. He knows no man
that is not generally known. His wit, like the marigold, openeth
with the sun, and therefore he riseth not before ten of the
clock. He puts more confidence in his words than meaning,

196

and more in his pronunciation than his words. Occasion is his Cupid, and he hath but one receipt of making love. He follows nothing but inconstancy, admires nothing but beauty, honours nothing but fortune, loves nothing. The sustenance of his discourse is news, and his censure, like a shot, depends upon the charging. He is not, if he be out of court; but fish-like breathes destruction, if out of his own element. Neither his motion nor aspect are regular, but he moves by the upper spheres, and is the reflection of higher substances.

If you find him not here, you shall in Paul's, with a pick-tooth in his hat, a cape-cloak and a long stocking.

Sir Thomas Overbury, Characters 1614

Touchstone as a Courtier

Jaques. Good my lord, bid him welcome. This is the motley-minded gentleman that I have so often met in the forest: he hath been a courtier, he swears.

Touchstone. If any man doubt that, let him put me to my purgation. I have trod a measure; I have flattered a lady; I have been politic with my friend, smooth with mine enemy; I have undone three tailors; I have had four quarrels, and like to have fought one.

Jaques. And how was that ta'en up?

Touchstone. Faith, we met, and found the quarrel was upon the seventh cause.

Jaques. How seventh cause?...How did you find the quarrel on the seventh cause?

Touchstone. Upon a lie seven times removed...as thus, sir. I did dislike the cut of a certain courtier's beard: he sent me word, if I said his beard was not cut well, he was in the mind it was: this is called "the retort courteous." If I sent him word again, it was not well cut, he would send me word, he cut it to please himself: this is called "the quip modest." If again, it was not well cut, he disabled my judgment: this is called the "reply churlish." If again, it was not cut well, he would answer, I spake not true: this is called the "reproof valiant": if again, it was not well cut, he would say, I lie: this is called the "countercheck quarrel-some": and so to the "lie circumstantial" and the "lie direct."

Jaques. And how oft did you say his beard was not well cut?

Touchstone. I durst go no further than the "lie circumstantial," nor he durst not give me the "lie direct"; and so we measured swords and parted.

Jaques. Can you nominate in order now the degrees of the lie?

Touchstone. O sir, we quarrel in print; by the book, as you have books for good manners: I will name you the degrees. The first, the "retort courteous"; the second, the "quip modest"; the third, the "reply churlish"; the fourth, the "reproof valiant"; the fifth, the "countercheck quarrelsome"; the sixth, the "lie with circumstance"; the seventh, the "lie direct." All these you may avoid but the lie direct; and you may avoid that too with an "if." I knew when seven justices could not take up a quarrel; but when the parties were met themselves, one of them thought but of an "if," as "If you said so, then I said so"; and they shook hands, and swore brothers. Your "if" is the only peacemaker; much virtue in "if."

As You Like It, **v.** iv. 40—109

§ 3. Masques at Court

Duke Theseus. Come now; what masques, what dances shall we have,
To wear away this long age of three hours
Between our after-supper and bed-time?
Where is our usual manager of mirth?
What revels are in hand? Is there no play,
To ease the anguish of a torturing hour?
Call Philostrate.

Philostrate. Here, mighty Theseus.

Duke Theseus. Say, what abridgment have you for this evening?
What masque? what music? How shall we beguile
The lazy time, if not with some delight?

Philostrate. There is a brief how many sports are ripe:
Make choice of which your highness will see first.

A Midsummer Night's Dream, v. i. 32—43

Masques in honour of the marriage of Princess Elizabeth, daughter of James I., Feb. 11—16, 1613

And that night, in honour of this joyful nuptial, there was a very stately masque of lords and ladies, with many ingenious speeches, delicate devices, melodious music, pleasant dances, with other princely entertainments of time, all which were singularly well performed in the Banqueting-house. The four honourable Inns of Court, as well the elders and grave benchers of each house as the towardly young active gallant gentlemen of the same houses, being of infinite desire to express their singular love and duteous affection to his Majesty, and to perform some memorable and acceptable service worthy their own reputation, in honour of this nuptial, and thereupon with great expedition they jointly and severally consulted and agreed amongst themselves to set out two several rich and stately masques, and to perform them bravely, without respect of charge or expenses, and from amongst themselves they selected the most pregnant and active gentlemen to be their masquers, who, to the lasting honour of themselves and their societies, performed all things as worthily. They employed the best wits and skilfullest artisans in devising, composing and erecting their several strange properties, excellent speeches, pleasant devices and delicate music, brave in habit, rich in ornaments, in demeanour courtly, in their going by land and water very stately and orderly: all which, with their rare inventions and variable entertainments of time, were such as the like was never performed in England by any society, and was now as graciously accepted of by his Majesty, the Queen, the Prince, the bride and bridegroom, from whom they received all princely thanks and encouragement. Concerning which two masques, with the multiplicity of devices, depending upon those entertainments of time, though I may not set down the particulars, nor say all I ought in their deserving commendations, by reason it would require a very large discourse, yet for distinction sake I will briefly set down their several times and order of going to the court.

Upon Shrove Monday at night, the gentlemen of the Middle Temple and Lincoln's Inn, with their train for this business, assembled in Chancery Lane, at the house of Sir Edward Philips, Master of the Rolls, and about eight of the clock they marched thence through the Strand, to the court at Whitehall, in this manner. First rode fifty choice gentlemen richly attired, and as gallantly mounted, with every one his footman to attend him; these rode very stately like a vanguard. Next after, with fit distance, marched an antic or mock-masque of baboons, attired like fantastic travellers in very strange and confused manner, riding upon asses or dwarf jades, using all apish and mocking tricks to the people, moving much laughter as they passed with torches on either side to shew their state to be as ridiculous as the rest was noble. After them came two chariots triumphal, very pleasant and full of state, wherein rode the choice musicians of this kingdom, in robes like to the Virginian priests, with sundry devices, all pleasant and significant, with two ranks of torches. Then came the chief masquers with great state in white Indian habit or like the great princes of Barbary, richly embroidered with the golden sun, with suitable ornaments in all points; about their necks were ruffs of feathers, spangled and beset with pearl and silver, and upon their heads lofty coronets suitable to the rest. They wore long silk stockings, curiously embroidered with gold to the mid-leg. Their buskins were likewise embroidered, and in their hands, as they rode, they brandished cane darts of the finest gold: their vizards were of olive colour, their hair long and black, down to their shoulders. The horses for rich shew equalled the masquers: their caparisons were enchased with suns of gold and ornamental jewels, with silver, scarfing over the whole caparison and about their heads, which made such a strange and glorious show, that it dazzled the eyes of the beholders with great admiration. Every of these horses had two Moors to attend them, attired like Indian slaves, with wreaths of gold and watshod about their heads, being about an hundred in number. The torch-bearers carried torches of virgin wax, the staves whereof were great canes gilded all over, and their habits were likewise of the Indian garb, but more extravagant than those of the masquers. The masquers rode single, and had every man his torch-bearer riding before him. All which, with the last triumphal chariot, wherein sat many strange attired personages, with their emblems, conceitful and variable devices, made a wondrous pleasing show. And thus they marched through the Strand to Whitehall, where the King, the Prince, the bride and bridegroom, and the chief nobility stood in the gallery before the tilt-yard to behold their approach; and because there should be a full view had of their state and train, the King caused them to march one turn about the list; and being dismounted, they were honourably attended through the gallery to a chamber, in which they were to make them ready for performance of their scene in the hall; in which place were erected their sundry properties and devices, formerly mentioned, where they performed all things answerable to the best of expectation, and received as royal thanks and commendations.

The next day being Shrove Tuesday, the gentlemen of the Inner Temple and Gray's Inn, with their train and many other gallant young gentlemen of both these houses as their convoy, assembled themselves at Winchester House, being the appointed place for their rendezvous. This night's entertainment consisted of three several masques, viz. an antimasque of a strange and different fashion from others, both in habit and manners, and very delectable; a rural or country masque consisting of many persons, men and women, being all in sundry habits, being likewise as strange, variable and delightful; the third, which they called the main masque, was a masque of knights, attired in arming doublets of carnation satin, richly embroidered with stars of silver plate beset with smaller stars, spangles and silver lace, between gorgets of silver mail, with long Venetian hose embroidered suitable to the rest, silk carnation stockings embroidered all over, their garters and roses answerable. Their hats were of the same stuff and embroidered, cut before like a helmet and the hinder part like a scallop, answering the skirts of their doublets; their hat-bands were wreaths of silver, in form of garlands of wild olives; their feathers white and carnation; their belts embroidered, silver swords, little Italian falling-bands and cuffs embroidered; their hair fair and long; their vizards fair and young; and concerning their sundry ingenious properties and devices already erected in the court hall, they were all excellent, fraught with art, state and delights, having all their actors correspondent. These masquers, with their whole train in all triumphant manner and good order, took barge at Winchester stairs, about seven of the clock that night, and rowed to Whitehall against the tide. The chief masquers went in the King's barge royally adorned, and plenteously furnished with a great number of great war-lights, that they alone made a glorious show. Other gentlemen went in the Prince's barge, and certain other went in other fair barges, and were led by two admirals. Besides all these, they had four lusty warlike galleys to convoy and attend them. Each barge and galley, being replenished with store of torch-lights, made so rare and brave a show upon the water as the like was never seen upon the

Thames. They had three peals of great ordnance in three several places upon the shore, viz. when they embarked, as they past by the Temple, and at Strangate when they arrived at court, where the King, Prince Charles, the bride and bridegroom, stood in the upper gallery to behold them upon the water and to view them in particular at their arrival. They landed at the privy stairs, and were received by the Lord Chamberlain and conducted to the vestry, for the hall wherein they should perform their scene was by this time filled with company: who although they were of very good fashion, yet were there many principal ladies and other noble personages, besides ambassadors and other strangers of account, not come, so as when they should be placed, the room would be so scanted, as it would prove very inconvenient; whereupon his Majesty was most graciously pleased, with consent of the gentlemen masquers, to put it off until the next Saturday, and that then they should perform all their present intended entertainments in the great Banqueting-house, adding this favour withal, that this deferring should be no impediment unto the outward ceremony of magnificence until that day. And upon Saturday, at seven of the clock at night, they came privately in troop, and were brought to their places by the Earl of Northampton, and a choice room was reserved for the gentlemen of both these houses; and that night they bravely performed their scene, to the great delight, and full satisfaction of all the beholders; and from his Majesty they received as kingly thanks, and gracious acceptation.

EDMOND HOWES, *Annales* 1615

§ 4. The Death of Queen Elizabeth

Within the hollow crown
That rounds the mortal temples of a king
Keeps Death his court; and there the antick sits,
Scoffing his state and grinning at his pomp;
Allowing him a breath, a little scene,
To monarchize, be fear'd and kill with looks:
Infusing him with self and vain conceit,
As if this flesh, which walls about our life,
Were brass impregnable; and humour'd thus,
Comes at the last, and with a little pin
Bores through his castle-wall, and farewell, king!

Richard II., III. ii. 160—170

THE DEATH OF QUEEN ELIZABETH

Le roi est mort, vive le roi!

[The events here described took place in March, 1603 at Richmond Palace.]

When I came to court, I found the Queen ill disposed, and she kept her inner lodging; yet she, hearing of my arrival, sent for me. I found her in one of her withdrawing chambers, sitting low upon her cushions. She called me to her; I kissed her hand, and told her, it was my chiefest happiness to see her in safety and in health, which I wished might long continue. She took me by the hand, and wrung it hard; and said "No, Robin, I am not well!" and then discoursed with me of her indisposition, and that her heart had been sad and heavy for ten or twelve days; and, in her discourse, she fetched not so few as forty or fifty great sighs. I was grieved, at the first, to see her in this plight: for, in all my lifetime before, I never knew her fetch a sigh, but when the Queen of Scots was beheaded; then, upon my knowledge, she shed many tears and sighs, manifesting her innocence that she never gave consent to the death of that Queen. I used the best words I could to persuade her from this melancholy humour; but I found by her it was too deep rooted in her heart, and hardly to be removed. This was upon a Saturday night: and she gave command that the great closet should be prepared for her to go to chapel the next morning.

The next day, all things being in a readiness, we long expected her coming. After eleven o'clock, one of the grooms came out, and bade make ready for the private closet; she would not go to the great. There we stayed long for her coming: but at last she had cushions laid for her in the privy chamber, hard by the closet door; and there she heard service. From that day forwards she grew worse and worse. She remained upon her cushions four days and nights, at the least. All about her could not persuade her, either to take any sustenance or go to bed. I, hearing that neither the physicians, nor none about her, could persuade her to take any course for her safety, feared her death would soon after ensue. I could not but think in what a wretched estate I should be left, most of my livelihood depending on her life. And hereupon I bethought myself with what grace and favour I was ever received by the King of Scots, whensoever I was sent to him. I did assure myself it was neither unjust nor unhonest for me to do for myself, if God at that time should call her to his mercy. Hereupon I wrote to the King of Scots, knowing him to be the right heir to the crown of England, and certified him in what state her Majesty was. I desired him not to stir from Edinburgh: if of that sickness she should die, I would be the first man that should bring him news of it.

The Queen grew worse and worse, because she would be so: none about her being able to persuade her to go to bed. My Lord Admiral was sent for, who, by reason of my sister's death that was his wife, had absented himself some fortnight from court. What by fair means, what by force, he gat her to bed. There was no hope of her recovery, because she refused all remedies. On Wednesday, the 23rd of March, she grew speechless. That afternoon, by signs, she called for her Council: and by putting her hand to her head, when the King of Scots was named to succeed her, they all knew he was the man she desired should reign after her. About six at night, she made signs for the Archbishop, and her chaplains to come to her; at which time, I went in with them, and sat upon my knees full of tears to see that heavy sight. Her Majesty lay upon her back, with one hand in the bed and the other without. The bishop kneeled down by her, and examined her first of her faith: and she so punctually answered all his several questions by lifting up her eyes and holding up her hand, as it was a comfort to all beholders. Then the good man told her plainly, what she was and what she was to come to, and though she had been long a great Queen here upon earth, yet shortly she was to yield an accompt of her stewardship to the King of Kings. After this he began to pray, and all that were by did answer him. After he had continued long in prayer, till the old man's knees were weary, he blessed her, and meant to rise and leave her. The Queen made a sign with her hand. My sister Scroop, knowing her meaning, told the bishop, the Queen desired he would pray still. He did so for a long half-hour after, and then thought to leave her. The second time she made sign to have him continue in prayer. He did so for half an hour more, with earnest cries to God for her soul's health, which he uttered with that fervency of spirit as the Queen, to all our sight, much rejoiced thereat, and gave testimony to us all of her Christian and comfortable end. By this time, it grew late, and every one departed, all but her women that attended her. This that I heard with my ears and did see with my eyes, I thought it my duty to set down, and to affirm it for a truth upon the faith of a Christian; because I know there have been many false lies reported of the end and death of that good lady.

I went to my lodging, and left word with one in the cofferer's chamber to call me, if that night it was thought she would die; and gave the porter an angel to let me in at any time, when I called. Between one and two of the clock on Thursday morning, he that I left in the cofferer's chamber, brought me word the Queen was dead. I rose and made all haste to the gate, to get in. There I was answered, I could not enter: the Lords of the Council having been with him and commanded him that none should go in or out, but by warrant from them. At the very instant, one of the Council, the Comptroller, asked whether I was at the gate. I said " Yes." He said, if I pleased, he would let me in. I desired to know how the Queen was. He answered, " Pretty well." I bade him good-night. He replied and said, " Sir, if you will come in, I will give you my word and credit you shall go out again at your own pleasure." Upon his word, I entered the gate, and came up to the cofferer's chamber: where I found all the ladies weeping bitterly. He led me from thence to the privy chamber, where all the Council was assembled. There I was caught hold of; and assured I should not go for Scotland till their pleasures were further known. I told them I came of purpose to that end. From thence, they all went to the secretary's chamber: and, as they went, they gave a special command to the porters, that none should go out at the gates but such servants as they should send to prepare their coaches and horses for London.

There was I left, in the midst of the court, to think my own thoughts till they had done counsel. I went to my brother's chamber, who was in bed, having been overwatched many nights before. I got him up with all speed; and when the Council's men were going out of the gate, my brother thrust to the gate. The porter, knowing him to be a great officer, let him out. I pressed after him, and was stayed by the porter. My brother said angrily to the porter, " Let him out, I will answer for him ! " Whereupon I was suffered to pass: which I was not a little glad of. I got to horse, and rode to the Knight Marshal's lodging by Charing Cross; and there stayed till the Lords came to Whitehall Garden. I stayed there till it was nine o'clock in the morning; and hearing that all the Lords were in the old orchard at Whitehall, I sent the Marshal to tell them, that I had stayed all that while to know their pleasures; and that I would attend them, if they would command me any service. They were very glad when they heard I was not gone: and desired the Marshal to send for me; and I should, with all speed, be despatched for Scotland. The Marshal believed them; and sent Sir Arthur Savage for me. I made haste to them. One of the Council, my Lord of Banbury that now is, whispered the Marshal in the ear, and told him, if I came they would stay me and send some other in my stead. The Marshal got from them and met me coming to them, between the two gates. He bade me be gone, for he had learned, for certain, that if I came to them, they would betray me.

I returned, and took horse between nine and ten o'clock; and that night rode to Doncaster. The Friday night I came to my own house at Witherington, and presently took order with my deputies to see the Borders kept in quiet; which they had much to do: and gave order, the next morning, the King of Scotland should be proclaimed King of England, and at Morpeth and Alnwick. Very early, on Saturday, I took horse for Edinburgh, and came to Norham about twelve at noon, so that I might well have been with the King at supper time. But I got a great fall by the way; and my horse, with one of his heels, gave me a great blow on the head, that made me shed much blood. It made me so weak, that I was forced to ride a soft pace after: so that the King was newly gone to bed by the time I knocked at the gate. I was quickly let in; and carried up to the King's Chamber. I kneeled by him, and saluted him by his title of " England, Scotland, France, and Ireland." He gave me his hand to kiss, and bade me welcome. After he had long discoursed of the manner of the Queen's sickness, and of her death, he asked what letters I had from the Council. I told him, none: and acquainted him how narrowly I escaped from them. And yet I brought him a blue ring from a fair lady, that I hoped would give him assurance of the truth that I had reported. He took it, and looked upon it, and said, "It is enough. I know by this you are a true messenger." Then he committed me to the charge of my Lord Hume, and gave straight command that I should want nothing. He sent for his chirurgeons to attend me; and when I kissed his hand, at my departure, he said to me these gracious words: "I know you have lost a near kinswoman and a loving mistress: but take here my hand, I will be as good a master to you, and will requite you this service with honour and reward." So I left him that night, and went with my Lord Hume to my lodging: where I had all things fitting for so weary a man as I was. After my head was dressed, I took leave of my Lord and many others that attended me, and went to my rest.

The next morning, by ten o'clock, my Lord Hume was sent to me from the King, to know how I had rested: and withal said, that his Majesty commanded him to know of me, what it was that I desired most that he should do for me; bade me ask, and it should be granted. I desired my Lord to say to his Majesty from me, that I had no reason to importune him for any suit; for that I had not, as yet, done him any service: but my humble request to his Majesty was to admit me a gentleman of his bedchamber; and hereafter, I knew, if his Majesty saw me worthy, I should not want to taste his bounty. My Lord returned this answer, that he sent me word back, "With all his heart, I should have my request." And the next time I came to court, which was some four days after at night, I was called into his bedchamber: and there, by my Lord of Richmond, in his presence, I was sworn one of the gentlemen of his bedchamber; and presently I helped to take off his clothes, and stayed till he was in bed. After this, there came, daily, gentlemen and noblemen from our court; and the King set down a fixed day for his departure towards London.

SIR ROBERT CAREY, *Memoirs*, pub. 1759, written before 1627

CHAPTER IX

HOUSE AND HOME

"Fast bind, fast find,"
A proverb never stale in thrifty mind.
The Merchant of Venice, II. v. 54—55

§ 1.   Houses and Furniture

My house within the city
Is richly furnished with plate and gold:
Basins and ewers to lave her dainty hands;
My hangings all of Tyrian tapestry;
In ivory coffers I have stuff'd my crowns;
In cypress chests my arras counterpoints,
Costly apparel, tents, and canopies,
Fine linen, Turkey cushions boss'd with pearl,
Valance of Venice gold in needle-work,
Pewter and brass, and all things that belong
To house or housekeeping: then at my farm
I have a hundred milch-kine to the pail,
Six score fat oxen standing in my stalls,
And all things answerable to this portion.
Taming of the Shrew, II. i 340—353

[May 4, 1597, Shakespeare buys New Place, Stratford-on-Avon. He takes up his residence there in 1608, and dies there April 23, 1616.]

The greatest part of our building in the cities and good towns of England consisteth only of timber, for as yet few of the houses of the communalty (except here and there in the west-country towns) are made of stone, although they may in my opinion in divers other places be builded so good cheap of the one as of the other. In old time the houses of the Britons were slightly set up with a few posts and many raddles,

208

Charlecote Hall near Stratford

the home of Sir Thomas Lucy, who is said to have been the original of Justice Shallow

with stable and all offices under one roof, the like whereof almost is to be seen in the fenny countries and northern parts unto this day, where for lack of wood they are enforced to continue this ancient manner of building....

Certes this rude kind of building made the Spaniards in Queen Mary's days to wonder, but chiefly when they saw what large diet was used in many of these so homely cottages; insomuch that one of no small reputation amongst them said after this manner—"These English," quoth he, "have their houses made of sticks and dirt, but they fare commonly so well as the king." Whereby it appeareth that he liked better of our good fare in such coarse cabins than of their own thin diet in their prince-like habitations and palaces. In like sort as every country house is thus apparelled on the outside, so is it inwardly divided into sundry rooms above and beneath; and, where plenty of wood is, they cover them with tiles, otherwise with straw, sedge or reed, except some quarry of slate be near hand, from whence they have for their money much as may suffice them. The clay wherewith our houses are impanelled is either white, red or blue; and of these the first doth participate very much of the nature of our chalk, the second is called loam, but the third eftsoons changeth colour as soon as it is wrought, notwithstanding that it looks blue when it is thrown out of the pit....

The walls of our houses on the inner sides in like sort be either hanged with tapestry, arras work, or painted cloths, wherein either divers histories, or herbs, beasts, knots and such like are stained, or else they are ceiled with oak of our own, or wainscot brought hither out of the east countries, whereby the rooms are not a little commended, made warm and much more close than otherwise they would be. As for stoves, we have not hitherto used them greatly, yet do they now begin to be made in divers houses of the gentry and wealthy citizens, who build them not to work and feed in, as in Germany and elsewhere, but now and then to sweat in, as occasion and need shall require it.

This also hath been common in England, contrary to the customs of all other nations, and yet to be seen (for example, in most streets of London), that many of our greatest houses have outwardly been very simple and plain to sight, which inwardly have been able to receive a duke with his whole train, and lodge them at their ease. Hereby, moreover, it is come to pass that the fronts of our streets have not been so uniform and orderly builded as those of foreign cities, where (to say truth) the outer side of their mansions and dwellings have oft more cost bestowed upon them than all the rest of the house, which are often very simple and uneasy within, as experience doth confirm. Of old time, our country houses, instead of glass, did use much lattice, and that made either of wicker or fine rifts of oak in chequerwise. I read also that some of the better sort, in and before the times of the Saxons (who notwithstanding used some glass also since the time of Benedict Biscop, the monk that brought the feat of glazing first into the land), did make panels of horn instead of glass, and fix them in wooden calms. But as horn in windows is now quite laid down in every place, so our lattices are also grown into less use, because glass is come to be so plentiful and within a very little so good cheap, if not better than the other....

The furniture of our houses also exceedeth, and is grown in manner even to passing delicacy: and herein I do not speak of the nobility and gentry only, but likewise of the lowest sort in most places of our south country that have anything at all to take to. Certes in noblemen's houses it is not rare to see abundance of arras, rich hangings of tapestry, silver vessel, and so much other plate as may furnish sundry cupboards to the sum oftentimes of a thousand or two thousand pounds at the least, whereby the value of this and the rest of their stuff doth grow to be almost inestimable. Likewise in the houses of knights, gentlemen, merchantmen, and some other wealthy citizens, it is not geason to behold generally their great provision of tapestry, Turkey work, pewter, brass, fine linen, and thereto costly cupboards of plate, worth five or six hundred or a thousand pounds to be deemed by estimation. But, as herein all these sorts do far exceed their elders and predecessors, and in neatness and curiosity the merchant all other, so in time past the costly furniture stayed there, whereas now it is descended yet lower even unto the inferior artificers and many farmers, who, by virtue of their old and not of their new leases, have for the most part learned also to garnish their cupboards with plate, their joined beds with tapestry and silk hangings, and their tables with carpets and fine napery, whereby the wealth of our country (God be praised therefore, and give us grace to employ it well) doth infinitely appear. Neither do I speak this in reproach of any man, God is my judge, but to shew that I do rejoice rather to see how God hath blessed us with his good gifts; and whilst I behold how that, in a time wherein all things are grown to most excessive prices, and what commodity so ever is to be had is daily plucked from the communalty by such as look into every trade, we do yet find the means to obtain and achieve such furniture as heretofore hath been unpossible.

There are old men yet dwelling in the village where I remain which have noted three things to be marvellously altered in England within their sound remembrance, and other three things too too much increased.

One is the multitude of chimneys lately erected, whereas in their young days there were not above two or three, if so many, in most uplandish towns of the realm (the religious houses and manor places of their lords always excepted, and peradventure some great personages), but each one made his fire against a reredos in the hall, where he dined and dressed his meat.

The second is the great (although not general) amendment of lodging; for, said they, our fathers, yea and we ourselves also, have lain full oft upon straw pallets, on rough mats covered only with a sheet, under coverlets made of dagswain or hopharlots (I use their own terms), and a good round log under their heads instead of a bolster or pillow. If it were so that our fathers or the goodman of the house had within seven years after his marriage purchased a mattress or flock bed, and thereto a sack of chaff to rest his head upon, he thought himself to be as well lodged as the lord of the town, that peradventure lay seldom in a bed of down or whole feathers, so well were they contented, and with such base kind of furniture : which also is not very much amended as yet in some parts of Bedfordshire, and elsewhere, further off from our southern parts. Pillows (said they) were thought meet only for women in childbed. As for servants, if they had any sheet above them, it was well, for seldom had they any under their bodies to keep them from the pricking straws that ran oft through the canvas of the pallet and rased their hardened hides.

The third thing they tell of is the exchange of vessel, as of treen platters into pewter, and wooden spoons into silver or tin. For so common were all sorts of treen stuff in old time that a man

should hardly find four pieces of pewter (of which one was peradventure a salt) in a good farmer's house, and yet for all this
frugality (if it may so be justly called) they were scarce able to
live and pay their rents at their days without selling of a
cow or a horse or more, although they paid but four pounds at
the uttermost by the year. Such also was their poverty that, if
some one odd farmer or husbandman had been at the ale-house,
a thing greatly used in those days, amongst six or seven of his
neighbours, and there in a bravery, to shew what store he had,
did cast down his purse, and therein a noble or six shillings in
silver, unto them (for few such men then cared for gold, because
it was not so ready payment, and they were oft enforced to give
a penny for the exchange of an angel), it was very likely that
all the rest could not lay down so much against it; whereas in
my time, although peradventure four pounds of old rent be im-
proved to forty, fifty or a hundred pounds, yet will the farmer,
as another palm or date tree, think his gains very small towards
the end of his term if he have not six or seven years' rent lying
by him, therewith to purchase a new lease, beside a fair garnish
of pewter on his cupboard, with so much more in odd vessel
going about the house, three or four feather beds, so many
coverlets and carpets of tapestry, a silver salt, a bowl for wine (if
not a whole nest), and a dozen of spoons to furnish up the suit.

WILLIAM HARRISON, *Description of England* 1587 (2nd ed.)

§ 2.   Gardens and Orchards

Justice Shallow. Nay, you shall see mine orchard, where, in an arbour,
we will eat a last year's pippin of my own graffing, with a dish of caraways,
and so forth ; come, cousin Silence ; and then to bed.
Sir John Falstaff. 'Fore God, you have here a goodly dwelling and
a rich.   2 *Henry IV.*, v. iii. 1—6

> Lord ! who would live turmoiled in the court
> And may enjoy such quiet walks as these ?
>   2 *Henry VI.*, IV. x. 18—19

If you look into our gardens annexed to our houses, how
wonderfully is their beauty increased, not only with flowers
...and variety of curious and costly workmanship, but also
with rare and medicinable herbs sought up in the land within

these forty years: so that, in comparison of this present, the ancient gardens were but dunghills and laystows to such as did possess them. How art also helpeth nature in the daily colouring, doubling and enlarging the proportion of our flowers, it is incredible to report: for so curious and cunning are our gardeners now in these days that they presume to do in manner what they list with nature, and moderate her course in things as if they were her superiors. It is a world also to see how many strange herbs, plants and annual fruits are daily brought unto us from the Indies, Americans, Taprobane, Canary Isles, and all parts of the world: the which, albeit that in respect of the constitutions of our bodies they do not grow for us, because that God hath bestowed sufficient commodities upon every country for her own necessity, yet, for delectation sake unto the eye and their odoriferous savours unto the nose, they are to be cherished, and God to be glorified also in them, because they are his good gifts, and created to do man help and service. There is not almost one nobleman, gentleman or merchant that hath not great store of these flowers, which now also do begin to wax so well acquainted with our soils that we may almost account of them as parcel of our own commodities. They have no less regard in like sort to cherish medicinable herbs fetched out of other regions nearer hand, insomuch that I have seen in some one garden to the number of three hundred or four hundred of them, if not more, of the half of whose names within forty years past we had no manner knowledge. But herein I find some cause of just complaint, for that we extol their uses so far that we fall into contempt of our own, which are in truth more beneficial and apt for us than such as grow elsewhere, sith (as I said before) every region hath abundantly within her own limits whatsoever is needful and most convenient for them that dwell therein....

And even as it fareth with our gardens, so doth it with our orchards, which were never furnished with so good fruit nor with such variety as at this present. For, beside that we have most delicate apples, plums, pears, walnuts, filberts, etc., and those of sundry sorts, planted within forty years past, in comparison of which most of the old trees are nothing worth, so have we no less store of strange fruit, as apricots, almonds, peaches, figs, corn-trees in noblemen's orchards. I have seen capers, oranges and lemons, and heard of wild olives growing here, beside other strange trees brought from far, whose names I know not. So that England for these commodities was never better furnished, neither any nation under their clime more plentifully endued with these and other blessings from the most high God, who grant us grace withal to use the same to his honour and glory, and not as instruments and provocations unto further excess and vanity, wherewith his displeasure may be kindled, lest these his benefits do turn unto thorns and briers unto us for our annoyance and punishment, which he hath bestowed upon us for our consolation and comfort.

WILLIAM HARRISON, *Description of England* 1587 (2nd ed.)

§ 3. Housekeeping and the table

Lady Capulet. Hold, take these keys, and fetch more spices, nurse.
Nurse. They call for dates and quinces in the pastry.
Capulet. Come, stir, stir, stir! the second cock hath crow'd
 The curfew bell hath rung, 'tis three o'clock:
 Look to the bak'd meats, good Angelica:
 Spare not for cost. *Romeo and Juliet*, IV. iv. 1—5

 Let me see; what am I to buy for our sheep-shearing feast? "Three pound of sugar; five pound of currants; rice," what will this sister of mine do with rice?...I must have saffron, to colour the warden pies; mace, dates,—none; that's out of my note: nutmegs seven; a race or two of ginger,—but that I may beg,—four pound of prunes, and as many of raisins o' the sun. *The Winter's Tale*, IV. ii. 38—53

An English Housewife

 A woman mov'd is like a fountain troubled,
 Muddy, ill-seeming, thick, bereft of beauty;
 *   *   *   *   *
 Such duty as the subject owes the prince,
 Even such a woman oweth to her husband;
 And when she's froward, peevish, sullen, sour,
 And not obedient to his honest will,
 What is she but a foul contending rebel,
 And graceless traitor to her loving lord?
 The Taming of the Shrew, V. ii. 137—161

It is now meet that we descend in as orderly a method as we can, to the office of our English housewife, who is the mother and mistress of the family, and hath her most general employments within the house; where from the general example of her virtues, and the most approved skill of her knowledges, those of her family may both learn to serve God, and sustain man in that godly and profitable sort which is required of every true Christian.

First then to speak of the inward virtues of her mind; she ought, above all things, to be of an upright and sincere religion, and in the same both zealous and constant; giving by her example, an incitement and spur unto all her family to pursue the same steps, and to utter forth by the instruction of her life, those virtuous fruits of good living, which shall be pleasing both to God and his creatures; I do not mean that herein she should utter forth that violence of spirit which many of our (vainly accounted pure*) women do, drawing a contempt upon the ordinary ministry, and thinking nothing lawful but the fantasies of their own inventions, usurping to themselves a power of preaching and interpreting the holy word, to which only they ought to be but hearers and believers, or at the most but modest persuaders; this is not the office either of good housewife or good woman. But let our English housewife be a godly, constant and religious woman, learning from the worthy preacher and her husband those good examples which she shall with all careful diligence see exercised amongst her servants.

In which practice of hers, what particular rules are to be observed, I leave her to learn of them who are professed divines, and have purposely written of this argument; only thus much will I say, which each one's experience will teach him to be true, that the more careful the master and mistress are to bring up their servants in the daily exercises of religion toward God, the more faithful they shall find them in all their businesses towards men, and procure God's favour the more plentifully on all the household: and therefore a small time morning and evening bestowed in prayers, and other exercises of religion, will prove no lost time at the week's end.

Next unto this sanctity and holiness of life, it is meet that our English housewife be a woman of great modesty and temperance as well inwardly as outwardly. Inwardly, as in her behaviour and carriage towards her husband, wherein she shall

* i.e. puritan.

shun all violence of rage, passion and humour, coveting less to direct than to be directed, appearing ever unto him pleasant, amiable and delightful; and though occasion, mishaps or the misgovernment of his will may induce her to contrary thoughts, yet virtuously to suppress them, and with a mild sufferance rather to call him home from his error, than with the strength of anger to abate the least spark of his evil, calling into her mind that evil and uncomely language is deformed though uttered even to servants, but most monstrous and ugly when it appears before the presence of a husband. Outwardly, as in her apparel and diet, both which she shall proportion according to the competency of her husband's estate and calling, making her circle rather strait than large, for it is a rule if we extend to the uttermost we take away increase, if we go a hair breadth beyond we enter into consumption, but if we preserve any part, we build strong forts against the adversaries of fortune, provided that such preservation be honest and conscionable: for as lavish prodigality is brutish, so miserable covetousness is hellish. Let therefore the housewife's garments be comely, cleanly and strong, made as well to preserve the health, as adorn the person, altogether without toyish garnishes or the gloss of light colours, and as far from the vanity of new and fantastic fashions, as near to the comely imitations of modest matrons. Let her diet be wholesome and cleanly, prepared at due hours, and cooked with care and diligence; let it be rather to satisfy nature than our affections, and apter to kill hunger than revive new appetites; let it proceed more from the provision of her own yard, than the furniture of the markets; and let it be rather esteemed for the familiar acquaintance she hath with it, than for the strangeness and rarity it bringeth from other countries.

To conclude, our English housewife must be of chaste thought, stout courage, patient, untired, watchful, diligent, witty, pleasant, constant in friendship, full of good neighbourhood, wise in discourse, but not frequent therein, sharp and quick of speech, but not bitter or talkative, secret in her affairs, comfortable in her counsels, and generally skilful in all the worthy knowledges which do belong to her vocation.

GERVASE MARKHAM, The English Hus-wife 1615

HOUSEKEEPING AND THE TABLE

The Table

Clearing away

First Servant. Where's Potpan, that he helps not to take away? he shift a trencher! he scrape a trencher!

Second Servant. When good manners shall lie all in one or two men's hands and they unwashed too, 'tis a foul thing.

First Servant. Away with the joint-stools, remove the court-cupboard, look to the plate. Good thou, save me a piece of marchpane; and, as thou lovest me, let the porter let in Susan Grindstone and Nell. Antony! and Potpan!

Second Servant. Ay, boy; ready.

First Servant. You are looked for and called for, asked for and sought for in the great chamber.

Third Servant. We cannot be here and there too.

Romeo and Juliet, I. v. 1—17

Meals

The Italian Sansovino is much deceived, writing, that in general the English eat and cover the table at least four times in the day; for howsoever those that journey and some sickly men staying at home may perhaps take a small breakfast, yet in general the English eat but two meals (of dinner and supper) each day, and I could never see him that useth to eat four times in the day. And I will profess for myself and other Englishmen, passing through Italy so famous for temperance, that we often observed, that howsoever we might have a pullet and some flesh prepared for us, eating it with a moderate proportion of bread, the Italians at the same time, with a charger full of herbs for a sallad, and with roots, and like meats of small price, would each of them eat two or three penny-worth of bread. And since all fulness is ill, and that of bread worst, I think we were more temperate in our diet, though eating more flesh, than they eating so much more bread than we did. It is true that the English prepare largely for ordinary diet for themselves and their friends coming by chance, and at feasts for invited friends are so excessive in the number of dishes, as the table is not thought well-furnished, except they stand one upon another. Neither use they to set drink on the table, for which no room is left, but the cups and glasses are served in upon a side table, drink being offered to none, till they call for it.

FYNES MORYSON, *Itinerary* 1617

217

HOUSE AND HOME

Of the food and diet of the English

The situation of our region, lying near unto the north, doth cause the heat of our stomachs to be of somewhat greater force: therefore our bodies do crave a little more ample nourishment than the inhabitants of the hotter regions are accustomed withal, whose digestive force is not altogether so vehement, because their internal heat is not so strong as ours, which is kept in by the coldness of the air that from time to time (especially in winter) doth environ our bodies.

It is no marvel therefore that our tables are oftentimes more plentifully garnished than those of other nations, and this trade hath continued with us even since the very beginning....

In number of dishes and change of meat the nobility of England (whose cooks are for the most part musical-headed Frenchmen and strangers) do most exceed, sith there is no day in manner that passeth over their heads wherein they have not only beef, mutton, veal, lamb, kid, pork, cony, capon, pig or so many of these as the season yieldeth, but also some portion of the red or fallow deer, beside great variety of fish and wild-fowl, and thereto sundry other delicates wherein the sweet hand of the seafaring Portingal is not wanting: so that for a man to dine with one of them, and to taste of every dish that standeth before him (which few use to do, but each one feedeth upon that meat him best liketh for the time, the beginning of every dish not-withstanding being reserved unto the greatest personage that sitteth at the table, to whom it is drawn up still by the waiters as order requireth, and from whom it descendeth again even to the lower end, whereby each one may taste thereof), is rather to yield unto a conspiracy with a great deal of meat for the speedy suppression of natural health, than the use of a necessary mean to satisfy himself with a competent repast to sustain his body withal. But as this large feeding is not seen in their guests no more is it in their own persons, for sith they have daily much resort unto their tables (and many times unlooked for) and thereto retain great numbers of servants, it is very requisite and expedient for them to be somewhat plentiful in this behalf.

The chief part likewise of their daily provision is brought in before them (commonly in silver vessel, if they be of the degree of barons, bishops and upwards) and placed on their tables, whereof, when they have taken what it pleaseth them, the rest is reserved and afterward sent down to their serving men and waiters, who feed thereon in like sort with convenient moderation, their reversion also being bestowed upon the poor which lie ready at their gates in great numbers to receive the same. This is spoken of the principal tables whereat the nobleman, his lady and guests are accustomed to sit; besides which they have a certain ordinary allowance daily appointed for their halls, where the chief officers and household servants (for all are not permitted by custom to wait upon their master), and with them such inferior guests do feed as are not of calling to associate the nobleman himself; so that, besides those aforementioned, which are called to the principal table, there are commonly forty or three score persons fed in those halls, to the great relief of such poor suitors and strangers also, as oft be partakers thereof and otherwise like to dine hardly.   As for drink it is usually filled in pots, goblets, jugs, bowls of silver, in noblemen's houses; also in fine Venice glasses of all forms; and, for want of these elsewhere, in pots of earth of sundry colours and moulds, whereof many are garnished with silver, or at the leastwise in pewter, all which notwithstanding are seldom set on the table, but each one, as necessity urgeth, calleth for a cup of such drink as him listeth to have, so that, when he hath tasted of it, he delivereth the cup again to some one of the standers by, who, making it clean by pouring out the drink that remaineth, restoreth it to the cupboard from whence he fetched the same....

It is a world to see in these our days, wherein gold and silver most aboundeth, how that our gentility, as loathing those metals (because of the plenty) do now generally choose rather the Venice glasses, both for our wine and beer, than any of those metals or stone wherein before time we have been accustomed to drink; but such is the nature of man generally that it most coveteth things difficult to be attained; and such is the estimation of this stuff that many become rich only with their new trade unto Murano (a town near to Venice, situate on the Adriatic Sea), from whence the very best are daily to be had, and such as for beauty do well near match the crystal or the ancient *Murrhina vasa* whereof now no man hath knowledge.   And as this is seen in the gentility, so in the wealthy communalty the like desire of glass is not neglected, whereby the gain gotten by their purchase is yet much more increased to the benefit of the merchant. The poorest also will have glass if they may; but, sith the Venetian is somewhat too dear for them, they content themselves with such as are made at home of fern and burnt stone; but in fine all go one way— that is, to shards at the last, so that our great expenses in glasses (besides that they breed much strife toward such as have the charge of them) are worst of all bestowed in mine opinion, because their pieces do turn unto no profit....

At such time as the merchants do make their ordinary or voluntary feasts, it is a world to see what great provision is made of all manner of delicate meats, from every quarter of the country, wherein, beside that they are often comparable herein to the nobility of the land, they will seldom regard anything that the butcher usually killeth, but reject the same as not worthy to come in place. In such cases also gellifs of all colours, mixed with a variety in the representation of sundry flowers, herbs, trees, forms of beasts, fish, fowls and fruits, and thereunto marchpane wrought with no small curiosity, tarts of divers hues and sundry denominations, conserves of old fruits, foreign and home-bred, suckets, codiniacs, marmalades, march-pane, sugar-bread, gingerbread, florentines, wild-fowl, venison of all sorts, and sundry outlandish confections, altogether seasoned with sugar (which Pliny called *mel ex arundinibus*, a device not common nor greatly used in old time at the table, but only in medicine, although it grew in Arabia, India, and Sicilia), do generally bear the sway, besides infinite devices of our own not possible for me to remember. Of the potato, and such venerous roots as are brought out of Spain, Portingal, and the Indies to furnish up our banquets, I speak not, wherein our mures of no less force, and to be had about Crosby-Ravenswath, do now begin to have place....

I might here talk somewhat of the great silence that is used at the tables of the honourable and wiser sort generally over all the realm (albeit that too much deserveth no commendation, for it belongeth to guests neither to be *muti* nor *loquaces*), likewise of the moderate eating and drinking that is daily seen, and finally of the regard that each one hath to keep himself from the note of surfeiting and drunkenness (for which cause salt meat, except beef, bacon and pork, are not any whit esteemed, and yet these three may not be much powdered); but, as in rehearsal thereof I should commend the nobleman, merchant and frugal artificer, so I could not clear the meaner sort of husbandmen and country inhabitants of very much babbling (except it be here and there some odd yeoman), with whom he is thought to be the merriest that talketh of most ribaldry or the wisest man that speaketh fastest among them, and now and then surfeiting and drunkenness which they rather fall into for want of heed-taking than wilfully following or delighting in those errors of set mind and purpose. It may be that divers of them living at home, with hard and pinching diet, small drink, and some of them having scarce enough of that, are soonest overtaken when they come into such banquets; howbeit they take it generally as no small disgrace if they happen to be cupshotten, so that it is a grief unto them, though now sans remedy, sith the thing is done and past. If the friends also of the wealthier sort come to their houses from far, they are commonly so welcome till they depart as upon the first day of their coming; whereas in good towns and cities, as London, etc., men oftentimes complain of little room, and, in reward of a fat capon or plenty of beef and mutton bestowed upon them in the country, a cup of wine or beer with a napkin to wipe their lips and an " You are heartily welcome ! " is thought to be a great entertainment...

Heretofore there hath been much more time spent in eating and drinking than commonly is in these days; for whereas of old we had breakfasts in the forenoon, beverages or nunchions after dinner, and thereto rear-suppers generally when it was time to go to rest...now these odd repasts, thanked be God, are very well left, and each one in manner (except here and there some young hungry stomach that cannot fast till dinnertime) contenteth himself with dinner and supper only....

With us the nobility, gentry and students do ordinarily go to dinner at eleven before noon, and to supper at five or between five and six at afternoon. The merchants dine and sup seldom before twelve at noon, and six at night, especially in London. The husbandmen dine also at high noon as they call it, and sup at seven or eight; but out of the term in our universities the scholars dine at ten. As for the poorest sort they generally dine and sup when they may, so that to talk of their order of repast it were but a needless matter. I might here take occasion also to set down the variety used by antiquity in their beginnings of their diets, wherein almost every nation had a several fashion, some beginning of custom (as we do in summer time) with salads at supper, and some ending with lettuce, some making their entry with eggs, and shutting up their tables with mulberries, as we do with fruit and conceits of all sorts. Divers (as the old Romans) began with a few crops of rue, as the Venetians did with the fish called *gobius*, the Belgies with butter, or (as we do yet also) with butter and eggs upon fish days. But whereas we commonly begin with the most gross food, and end with the most delicate, the Scot, thinking much to leave the best for his menial servants, maketh his entrance at the best, so that he is sure thereby to leave the worst. We use also our wines by degrees, so that the hottest cometh last to the table: but to stand upon such toys would spend much time and turn to small profit. Wherefore I will deal with other things more necessary for this turn.

WILLIAM HARRISON, *Description of England* 1587 (2nd ed.)

A servant's duties at table

When your master will go to his meat, take a towel about your neck, then take a cupboard cloth, a basin and an ewer, and a towel to array your cupboard, then cover your table, and set on salt, bread, and trenchers, the salt before the bread, and trenchers before the salt, and set your napkins and spoons on the cupboard ready, and lay every man a trencher, and napkin, and a spoon. And if ye have more messes than one at your master's table, consider what degree the persons are of, and thereafter you may serve them: and then set down everything at that mess as before, except your carving knives. If there be many gentlemen or yeomen, then set on bread, salt, trenchers, spoons, after they be set, or else after the custom of the house. And some do use to set before every man a loaf of bread and his cup, and some use the contrary. · Thus must you have respect to the custom of your house. And in some places it is used to set drink and a loaf or two. Also you shall understand that in some places the carver doth use to show and set down, and goeth before the course, and beareth no dish, and in some places he beareth the first dish, and maketh obeisance to his master, and setteth it down covered before the degree of a knight, or else not used, and take off the covers and set them by. Also the carver hath authority to carve to all at his master's mess in special, and also unto other that sit joining by them if he list. Also see ye have voiders in a readiness for to avoid the morsels that they do leave on their trenchers. Then with your trencher knife take off such fragments, and put them in your voider, and set them clean again. And whether your sovereign move trenchers or bread, void them once or twice, specially when they are wet, or give him clean, and as ye see men leave eating of the first and second dish, so avoid them from the table. And then if so be ye have any more courses than one or two, ye may make the more haste in voiding, and ever let one dish or two stand till the next course, and then take up all, and set down fresh and clean voiders withal, and let them not be too full before ye empty them, and then set clean again. And look what sauce is ordained for any meat, void the sauce thereof when ye take away the meat; and at the degree of a knight ye may set down your cup covered, and lift off the cover and set it on again, and when he listeth to drink and taketh off the cover, take the cover in thy hand and set it on again. And when he hath drunken, look the cup of wine or ale be not empty, but oft renewed. Also the carver shall break his dish before his master, or at a side cupboard, with clean knives, and see there be no lack of bread nor ale; and when men have well eaten, and do begin to wax weary of eating, or if ye perceive by the countenance of your master when ye shall take up the meat and void the table, begin at the lowest mess, take away your spoons, if there be any, howbeit ye may avoid them, after broths and bake meats are past. Then take away your voiders and then your dishes of meat, as they were set down, so take them up in order. And then set down cheese or fruits, and that ended, avoid your cheese or fruits, and cover your cup, ale or wine: first avoid the ale, and then the wine: then set on a broad voider and put therein the small pieces of bread, and small crumbs, with trenchers and napkins, and with your trencher knife or napkin make clean the table, then set away your bread whole, and also your voider, then take up the salt, and make obeisance: mark if your master use to wash at the table or standing: if he be at the table, cast a clean towel upon your tablecloth, and set down your basin and ewer before your sovereign, and take the ewer in your hand, and give them water. Then avoid your basin and ewer, and fold the board cloth together with your towel therein, and so take them off the board. And when your sovereign shall wash, set your towel on the left hand of him, and the water before you at dinner or supper; if it be to bedward, set up your basin and towel on the board again. And if your master will have any conceits after dinner, as apples, nuts or cream, then lay forth a towel on the board, and set thereon a loaf or two, see that ye have your trenchers and spoons in a readiness if need require, then serve forth your master well, and so take it up again with a voider.

Hugh Rhodes, The Booke of Nurture 1568

Forks

Here I will mention a thing that might have been spoken of before, in discourse of the first Italian town. I observed a custom in all those Italian cities and towns through the which I passed, that is not used in any other country that I saw in my travels, neither do I think that any other nation of Christendom doth use it, but only Italy. The Italians, and also most strangers that are commorant in Italy, do always at their meals use a little fork when they cut their meat. For while with their knife, which they hold in one hand, they cut the meat out of the dish, they fasten their fork which they hold in their other hand upon the same dish, so that whatsoever he be that, sitting in the company of any others at meal, should unadvisedly touch the dish of meat with his fingers from which all at the table do cut, he will give occasion of offence unto the company, as having transgressed the laws of good manners, in so much that for his error he shall be at the least brow-beaten if not reprehended in words. This form of feeding I understand is generally used in all places of Italy, their forks being for the most part made of iron or steel, and some of silver, but those are used only by gentlemen. The reason of this their curiosity is, because the Italian cannot by any means endure to have his dish touched with fingers, seeing all men's fingers are not alike clean. Hereupon I myself thought good to imitate the Italian fashion by this forked cutting of meat, not only while I was in Italy, but also in Germany, and oftentimes in England since I came home: being once quipped for that frequent using of my fork by a certain learned gentleman, a familiar friend of mine, one Mr Laurence Whitaker, who in his merry humour doubted not to call me at table *furcifer*, only for using a fork at feeding, but for no other cause.

THOMAS CORYAT, *Crudities* 1611

Hospitality

For time is like a fashionable host,
That slightly shakes his parting guest by the hand,
And with his arms outstretch'd, as he would fly,
Grasps in the comer : welcome ever smiles,
And farewell goes out sighing.

Troilus and Cressida, III. iii. 165—169

This true noble hearted fellow is to be dignified and honoured, wheresoever he keeps house. It's thought that pride, puritans, coaches and covetousness hath caused him to leave our land. There are six upstart tricks come up in great houses of late which he cannot brook: peeping windows for the ladies to view what doings there are in the hall, a buttery hatch that's kept locked, clean tables and a French cook in the kitchen, a porter that locks the gates in dinner time, the decay of black-jacks in the cellar and blue-coats in the hall. He always kept his greatness by his charity: he loved three things, an open cellar, a full hall and a sweating cook: he always provided for three dinners, one for himself, another for his servants, the third for the poor. Any one may know where he kept house, either by the chimney's smoke, by the freedom at gate, by want of whirligig-jacks in the kitchen, by the fire in the hall or by the full furnished tables. He affects not London, Lent, lackeys or bailiffs. There are four sorts that pray for him, the poor, the passenger, his tenants, and servants. He is one that will not hoard up all nor lavishly spend all, he neither racks nor rakes his neighbours (they are sure of his company at church as well as at home),and gives his bounty as well to the preacher as to others whom he loves for his good life and doctrine. He had his wine came to him by full butts, but this age keeps her wine-cellar in little bottles. Lusty able men well maintained were his delight, with whom he would be familiar. His tenants knew

when they saw him, for he kept the old fashion, good, commendable, plain. The poor about him wore upon their backs; but
now since his death, landlords wear and waste their tenants
upon their backs in French or Spanish fashions. Well, we can
say that once such a charitable practitioner there was, but now
he's dead, to the grief of all England: and 'tis shrewdly suspected
that he will never rise again in our climate.

DONALD LUPTON, *London and the Countrey carbonadoed* 1632

The Kitchen

Capulet. Sirrah, go hire me twenty cunning cooks.
Servant. You shall have none ill, sir; for I'll try if they can lick
their fingers.
Capulet. How canst thou try them so?
Servant. Marry, sir, 'tis an ill cook that cannot lick his own fingers:
therefore he that cannot lick his fingers goes not with me.

Romeo and Juliet, IV. ii. 2—8

Marry, sir, she's the kitchen-wench, and all grease; and I know not
what use to put her to but to make a lamp of her and run from her by
her own light. I warrant her rags and the tallow in them will burn a
Poland winter; if she lives till doomsday, she'll burn a week longer than
the whole world. *The Comedy of Errors*, III. ii. 97—103

The Ideal Cook

It resteth now that I proceed unto cookery itself, which is
the dressing and ordering of meat in good and wholesome
manner; to which, when our housewife shall address herself,
she shall well understand, that these qualities must ever accom-
pany it: first, she must be cleanly both in body and garments,
she must have a quick eye, a curious nose, a perfect taste and a
ready ear. She must not be butter-fingered, sweet-toothed nor
faint-hearted; for the first will let everything fall, the second
will consume what it should increase, and the last will lose time
with too much niceness.

GERVASE MARKHAM, *The English Hus-wife* 1615

A Cook

The kitchen is his hell, and he the devil in it, where his
meat and he fry together. His revenues are showered down
from the fat of the land, and he interlards his own grease among

to help the drippings. Choleric he is, not by nature so much as his art, and it is a shrewd temptation that the chopping knife is so near. His weapons ofter offensive are a mess of hot broth and scalding water, and woe be to him that comes in his way. In the kitchen he will domineer and rule the roast, in spite of his master, and curses is the very dialect of his calling. His labour is mere blustering and fury, and his speech like that of sailors in a storm, a thousand businesses at once; yet in all this tumult he does not love combustion, but will be the first man that shall go and quench it. He is never good Christian till a hissing pot of ale has slaked him, like water cast on a firebrand, and for that time he is tame and dispossessed. His cunning is not small in architecture, for he builds strange fabrics in paste, towers and castles, which are offered to the assault of valiant teeth, and like Darius his palace, in one banquet demolished. He is a pitiless murderer of innocents, and he mangles poor fowls with unheard of tortures, and it is thought the martyrs' persecutions were devised from hence; sure we are Saint Lawrence his gridiron came out of his kitchen. His best faculty is at the dresser, where he seems to have great skill in the tactics, ranging his dishes in order military and placing with great discretion in the fore-front meats more strong and hardy, and the more cold and cowardly in the rear, as quaking tarts, and quivering custards, and such milk-sop dishes which scape many times the fury of the encounter. But now the second course is gone up, and he down into the cellar, where he drinks and sleeps till four o'clock in the afternoon, and then returns again to his regiment.

JOHN EARLE, *Micro-cosmographie* 1628

An Elizabethan mince-pie

Take a leg of mutton, and cut the best of the best flesh from the bone, and parboil it well: then put to it three pound of the best mutton suet, and shred it very small: then spread it abroad, and season it with pepper and salt, cloves and mace: then put in good store of currants, great raisins and prunes, clean washed and picked, a few dates sliced, and some orange-pills sliced: then being all well mixed together, put it into a coffin, or into divers coffins, and so bake them: and when they are served up, open the lids, and strew store of sugar on the top of the meat, and upon the lid. And in this sort you may also bake beef or veal; only the beef would not be parboiled, and the veal will ask a double quantity of suet.

GERVASE MARKHAM, The English Hus-wife 1623 (2nd ed.)

The Dairy

Your cream being neatly and sweet kept, you shall churm or churn it on those usual days which are fittest either for your use in the house or the markets adjoining near unto you, according to the purpose for which you keep your dairy. Now the days most accustomably held amongst ordinary housewives, are Tuesday and Friday: Tuesday in the afternoon, to serve Wednesday morning market, and Friday morning to serve Saturday market; for Wednesday and Saturday are the most general market days of this kingdom, and Wednesday, Friday, and Saturday, the usual fasting days of the week and so meetest for the use of butter. Now for churming, take your cream and through a strong and clean cloth strain it into the churn ; and then covering the churn close, and setting it in a place fit for the action in which you are employed (as in the summer in the coolest place of your dairy), and exceeding early in the morning or very late in the evening, and in the winter in the warmest place of your dairy, and in the most temperate hours, as about noon or a little before or after, and so churn it, with swift strokes, marking the noise of the same which will be solid, heavy and entire, until you hear it alter, and the sound is light, sharp and more spirity : and then you shall say that your butter breaks, which perceived both by this sound, the lightness of the churn-staff, and the sparks and drops which will appear yellow about the lip of the churn, and cleanse with your hand both the lid and inward sides of the churn, and having put all together you shall cover the churn again, and then with easy strokes round, and not to the bottom, gather the butter together into one entire lump and body, leaving no pieces thereof several or unjoined.

GERVASE MARKHAM, The English Hus-wife 1615

§ 4. Sleep and Health

The Bedroom

The innocent sleep,
Sleep that knits up the ravell'd sleave of care,
The death of each day's life, sore labour's bath,
Balm of hurt minds, great nature's second course,
Chief nourisher in life's feast. *Macbeth*, II. ii. 37—41

The Valet's Duties

When your master intendeth to bedward, see that ye have fire and candle sufficient and see ye have clean water in at night and in the morning: and if your master lie in fresh sheets, dry off the dankness by the fire. If he lie in a strange place, see his sheets be clean and sweet, and then fold down his bed, and warm his night kerchief, and see his house ot office be clean, help off his clothing, and draw the curtains, and make sure the fire and candle, and avoid the dogs, and shut all the doors. And in the evening or in the morning, your master being alone, if ye have anything to say to him, then is good leisure and time to know his pleasure. In the morning if it be cold, make a fire, and have in clean water, bring him his petticoat warm, with his doublet, and all his apparel clean brushed, and his shoes made clean, and help to array him, truss his points, strike up his hosen clean, and set all thing clean and cleanly about him ; give him good attendance, and in especial among strangers, for attendance doth please masters very well. Thus doing with diligence, God will prefer you to honour and good fortune.

HUGH RHODES, *The Booke of Nurture* 1568

The Care of the Body (a *physician's advice*)

To bedward be you merry or have merry company about you, so that to bedward no anger nor heaviness, sorrow nor pensivefulness, do trouble or disquiet you. To bedward and also in the morning, use to have a fire in your chamber, to waste and consume the evil vapours within the chamber, for the breath of man may putrify the air within the chamber : I do advertise you not to stand nor to sit by the fire, but stand or sit a good way off from the fire, taking the flavour of it, for fire doth arify and doth dry up a man's blood, and doth make stark the sinews and joints of man. In the night let the windows of

229

your house, specially of your chamber, be closed. When you be in your bed, lie a little while on your left side, and sleep on your right side....

Let your nightcap be of scarlet, and this, I do advertise you, to cause to be made a good thick quilt of cotton, or else of pure flocks or of clean wool, and let the covering of it be of white fustian, and lay it on the featherbed that you do lie on ; and in your bed lie not too hot nor too cold, but in a temperance. Old ancient doctors of physic saith eight hours of sleep in summer and nine in winter is sufficient for any man ; but I do think the sleep ought to be taken as the complexion of man is. When you do rise in the morning, rise with mirth and remember God. Let your hosen be brushed within and without, and flavour the inside of them against the fire ; use linen socks, or linen hosen next your legs : when you be out of your bed, stretch forth your legs and arms and your body, cough and spit....

After you have evacuated your body and trussed your points, comb your head oft, and so do divers times in the day. And wash your hands and wrists, your face and eyes and your teeth, with cold water ; and after that you be apparelled, walk in your garden or park, a thousand pace or two. And then great and noble men do use to hear mass, and other men that cannot do so, but must apply their business, doth serve God with some prayers, surrendering thanks to him for his manifold goodness, with asking mercy for their offences. And before you go to your refection, moderately exercise your body with some labour, or playing at the tennis, or casting a bowl, or poising weights or plummets of lead in your hands, or some other thing, to open your pores, and to augment natural heat. At dinner and supper use not to drink sundry drinks, and eat not of divers meats : but feed of two or three dishes at the most. After that you have dined and supped, labour not by-and-by after, but make a pause, sitting or standing upright the space of an hour or more with some pastime : drink not much after dinner. At your supper, use light meats of digestion, and refrain from gross meats ; go not to bed with a full nor an empty stomach. And after your supper make a pause ere you go to bed ; and go to bed, as I said, with mirth.

ANDREW BOORDE, *A Compendyous Regyment or a Dietary of helth* 1542

SLEEP AND HEALTH

The Physician

Macbeth. Canst thou not minister to a mind diseas'd,
           Pluck from the memory a rooted sorrow,
           Raze out the written troubles of the brain,
           And with some sweet oblivious antidote
           Cleanse the stuff'd bosom of that perilous stuff
           Which weighs upon the heart?
Doctor.   Therein the patient
           Must minister to himself.
Macbeth. Throw physic to the dogs; I'll none of it.
               ...If thou couldst, doctor, cast
           The water of my land, find her disease,
           And purge it to a sound and pristine health,
           I would applaud thee to the very echo,
           That should applaud again....
           What rhubarb, senna, or what purgative drug
           Would scour these English hence?

Macbeth, v. iii. 40—55

[In 1607 Shakespeare's eldest daughter Susanna married the physician, John Hall.]

A worthy physician is the enemy of sickness, in purging nature from corruption. His action is most in feeling of pulses, and his discourses chiefly of the nature of diseases. He is a great searcher out of simples, and accordingly makes his composition. He persuades abstinence and patience, for the benefit of health, while purging and bleeding are the chief courses of his counsel. The apothecary and the chirurgeon are his two chief attendants, with whom conferring upon time, [he] grows temperate in his cures. Surfeits and wantonness are great agents for his employment, when by the secret of his skill out of others' weakness he gathers his own strength. In sum, he is a necessary member for an unnecessary malady, to find a disease and to cure the diseased.

An unlearned and so unworthy physician is a kind of horseleech, whose cure is most in drawing of blood, and a desperate purge, either to cure or kill, as it hits. His discourse is most of the cures that he hath done, and them afar off; and not a receipt under a hundred pounds, though it be not worth three halfpence. Upon the market-day he is much haunted

231

with urinals, where if he find anything (though he know nothing), yet he will say somewhat, which if it hit to some purpose with a few fustian words, he will seem a piece of strange stuff. He is never without old merry tales and stale jests to make old folks laugh, and comfits or plums in his pocket to please little children ; yea, and he will be talking of complexions, though he know nothing of their dispositions ; and if his medicine do a feat, he is a made man among fools ; but being wholly unlearned, and ofttimes unhonest, let me thus briefly describe him : he is a plain kind of mountebank and a true quacksalver, a danger for the sick to deal withal, and a dizard in the world to talk withal.

NICHOLAS BRETON, *The Good and the Badde* 1616

Death

It is therefore Death alone that can suddenly make man to know himself. He tells the proud and insolent that they are but abjects and humbles them at the instant; makes them cry, complain and repent, yea, even to hate their forepassed happiness. He takes the account of the rich and proves him a beggar, a naked beggar, which hath interest in nothing but in the gravel that fills his mouth. He holds a glass before the eyes of the most beautiful and makes them see therein their deformity and rottenness, and they acknowledge it. Oh eloquent, just and mighty Death! whom none could advise thou hast persuaded, what none hath dared thou hast done, and whom all the world hath flattered thou only hast cast out of the world and despised. Thou hast drawn together all the far-stretched greatness, all the pride, cruelty and ambition of man, and covered it all over with those two narrow words, *Hic jacet.*

SIR WALTER RALEGH, *The Historie of the World* 1614

CHAPTER X

ROGUES AND VAGABONDS

There are cozeners abroad; therefore it behoves men to be wary.
The Winter's Tale, IV. iii. 256

My traffic is sheets; when the kite builds, look to lesser linen. My father named me Autolycus; who being, as I am, littered under Mercury, was likewise a snapper-up of unconsidered trifles. With die and drab I purchased this caparison, and my revenue is the silly cheat. Gallows and knock are too powerful in the highway: beating and hanging are terrors to me: for the life to come, I sleep out the thought of it.
Ibid. IV. ii. 23—31

To have an open ear, a quick eye, and a nimble hand, is necessary for a cut-purse: a good nose is requisite also, to smell out work for the other senses. I see this is the time that the unjust man doth thrive....Every lane's end, every shop, church, session, hanging, yields a careful man work.
Ibid. IV. iii. 686—704

Rogues and the law

[The law referred to below is the famous statute of 1572. It will be noticed that it includes players among other classes of vagrants, and the passage was constantly quoted with glee by puritan opponents of the theatre. But the law was directed against wandering actors not attached to a nobleman's company such as that of the Lord Chamberlain, to which Shakespeare belonged.]

With us the poor is commonly divided into three sorts, so that some are poor by impotency, as the fatherless child, the aged, blind and lame, and the diseased person that is judged to be incurable: the second are poor by casualty, as the wounded soldier, the decayed householder, and the sick person visited with grievous and painful diseases: the third consisteth of thriftless poor, as the rioter that hath consumed all, the

233

vagabond that will abide nowhere but runneth up and down from place to place, and finally the rogue and the strumpet.... Such as are idle beggars through their own default are of two sorts, and continue their estates either by casual or mere voluntary means. Those that are such by casual means are in the beginning justly to be referred either to the first or second sort of poor aforementioned, but, degenerating into the thriftless sort, they do what they can to continue their misery, and, with such impediments as they have, to stray and wander about, as creatures abhorring all labour and every honest exercise. Certes I call these casual means, not in the respect of the original of their poverty, but of the continuance of the same, from whence they will not be delivered, such is their own ungracious lewdness and froward disposition. The voluntary means proceed from outward causes, as by making of corrosives and applying the same to the more fleshy parts of their bodies, and also laying of ratsbane, spearwort, crowfoot and such like unto their whole members, thereby to raise pitiful and odious sores and move the hearts of the goers by such places where they lie, to yearn at their misery, and thereupon bestow large alms upon them. How artificially they beg, what forcible speech, and how they select and choose out words of vehemency, whereby they do in manner conjure or adjure the goer-by to pity their cases, I pass over to remember, as judging the name of God and Christ to be more conversant in the mouths of none and yet the presence of the heavenly Majesty further off from no men than from this ungracious company. Which maketh me to think that punishment is far meeter for them than liberality or alms, and sith Christ willeth us chiefly to have a regard to himself and his poor members.

Unto this nest is another sort to be referred, more sturdy than the rest, which, having sound and perfect limbs, do yet notwithstanding sometime counterfeit the possession of all sorts of diseases. Divers times in their apparel also they will be like serving-men or labourers: oftentimes they can play the mariners and seek for ships which they never lost. But in fine they are all thieves and caterpillars in the commonwealth, and by the word of God not permitted to eat, sith they do but lick the sweat from the true labourer's brows, and bereave the godly poor of that which is due unto them, to maintain their excess, consuming the charity of well-disposed people bestowed upon them, after a most wicked and detestable manner.

It is not yet full threescore years since this trade began : but how it hath prospered since that time it is easy to judge, for they are now supposed, of one sex and another, to amount unto above 10,000 persons, as I have heard reported. Moreover, in counterfeiting the Egyptian rogues, they have devised a language among themselves, which they name " canting," but others "pedlar's French," a speech compact thirty years since of English and a great number of odd words of their own devising, without all order or reason, and yet such is it as none but themselves are able to understand. The first deviser thereof was hanged by the neck—a just reward, no doubt, for his deserts, and a common end to all of that profession.

A gentleman [Thomas Harman] also of late hath taken great pains to search out the secret practices of this ungracious rabble. And among other things he setteth down and describeth three and twenty sorts of them whose names it shall not be amiss to remember whereby each one may take occasion to read and know as also by his industry what wicked people they are, and what villainy remaineth in them.

The several disorders and degrees amongst our idle vagabonds*.

1.	Rufflers.	2.	Uprightmen.
3.	Hookers or anglers.	4.	Rogues.
5.	Wild rogues.	6.	Priggers of prancers.
7.	Palliards.	8.	Fraters.
9.	Abrams.	10.	Freshwater mariners or whipjacks.
11.	Dummerers.	12.	Drunken tinkers.
13.	Swadders or pedlars.	14.	Jarkmen or patricoes.

Of the women kind.

1.	Demanders for glimmer or fire.	2.	Bawdy-baskets.
3.	Morts.	4.	Autem morts.
5.	Walking morts.	6.	Doxies.
7.	Dells.	8.	Kinching morts.
	9.	Kinching coes.	

* See glossary under "Rogues."

The punishment that is ordained for this kind of people is very sharp, and yet it cannot restrain them from their gadding: wherefore the end must needs be martial law, to be exercised upon them, as upon thieves, robbers, despisers of all laws, and enemies to the commonwealth and welfare of the land. What notable robberies, pilferies, murders, rapes and stealings of young children, burning, breaking and disfiguring their limbs to make them pitiful in the sight of the people, I need not to rehearse. But for their idle roguing about the country the law ordaineth this manner of correction. The rogue being apprehended, committed to prison, and tried in the next assizes (whether they be of gaol delivery or sessions of the peace), if he happen to be convicted for a vagabond, either by inquest of office or the testimony of two honest and credible witnesses upon their oaths, he is then immediately adjudged to be grievously whipped and burned through the gristle of the right ear with an hot iron of the compass of an inch about, as a manifestation of his wicked life, and due punishment received for the same. And this judgment is to be executed upon him except some honest person worth five pounds in the Queen's books in goods, or twenty shillings in land, or some rich householder to be allowed by the justices, will be bound in recognisance to retain him in his service for one whole year. If he be taken the second time, and proved to have forsaken his said service, he shall then be whipped again, bored likewise through the other ear, and set to service: from whence if he depart before a year be expired and happen afterward to be attached again, he is condemned to suffer pains of death as a felon (except before excepted) without benefit of clergy or sanctuary, as by the statute doth appear. Among rogues and idle persons, finally, we find to be comprised all proctors that go up and down with counterfeit licences, cozeners and such as gad about the country using unlawful games, practisers of physiognomy and palmistry, tellers of fortune, fencers, players, minstrels, jugglers, pedlars, tinkers, pretended scholars, shipmen, prisoners gathering for fees, and others, so oft as they be taken without sufficient licence. From among which company our bearwards are not excepted, and just cause: for I have read that they have, either voluntarily or for want of power to master their savage beasts, been occasion of the death and devouration of many children in sundry countries by which they have passed, whose parents never knew what was become of them. And for that cause there is and have been many sharp laws made for bearwards in Germany, whereof you may read in other. But to our rogues. Each one also that harboureth or aideth them with meat or money is taxed and compelled to fine with the queen's majesty for every time that he doth succour them as it shall please the justices of peace to assign, so that the taxation exceed not twenty shillings, as I have been informed.

WILLIAM HARRISON, *The Description of England* 1587 (2nd ed.)

A Courtesy Man

A courtesy man is one that walketh about the back lanes in London in the day time, and sometime in the broad streets in the night season, and when he meeteth some handsome young man cleanly apparelled or some other honest citizen, he maketh humble salutations and low courtesy, and sheweth him that he hath a word or two to speak with his mastership. This child can behave himself mannerly, for he will desire him that he talketh withal to take the upper hand, and shew him much reverence, and at last like his familiar acquaintance will put on his cap, and walk side by side and talk on this fashion: " Oh sir, you seem to be a man and one that favoureth men, and therefore I am the more bolder to break my mind unto your good mastership. Thus it is sir, there is a certain of us (though I say it, both tall and handsome men of their hands) which have come lately from the wars, and as God knoweth have nothing to take to, being both masterless and moneyless, and knowing no way whereby to earn one penny. And further, whereas we have been wealthily brought up and we also have been had in good estimation, we are ashamed now to declare our misery and to fall a-craving as common beggars, and as for to steal and rob (God is our record) it striketh us to the heart to think of such a mischief, that ever any handsome man should fall into such a danger for this worldly trash. Which if we had to suffice our want and necessity, we should never seek thus shamefastly to crave on such good pitiful men as you seem to be, neither yet so dangerously to hazard our lives for so vile a thing. Therefore good sir, as you seem to be a handsome

237

man yourself, and also such a one as pitieth the miserable case of handsome men, as now your eyes and countenance sheweth to have some pity upon this my miserable complaint, so in God's cause I require your mastership, and in the behalf of my poor afflicted fellows, which though here in sight they cry not with me to you, yet wheresoever they be, I am sure they cry unto God to move the hearts of some good men to shew forth their liberality in this behalf; all which, and I with them, crave now the same request at your good mastership's hand." With these or such like words he frameth his talk. Now if the party (which he thus talketh withal) profereth him a penny or twopence he taketh it, but very scornfully, and at last speaketh on this sort : "Well sir, your good will is not to be refused. But yet you shall understand, good sir, that this is nothing for them, for whom I do thus shamefastly entreat. Alas sir, it is not a groat or twelvepence I speak for, being such a company of servitors as we have been : yet nevertheless God forbid I should not receive your gentle offer at this time, hoping hereafter through your good motions to some such like good gentleman as you be, that I or some of my fellows in my place, shall find the more liberality." These kind of idle vagabonds will go commonly well-apparelled, without any weapon, and in place where they meet together, as at their hostelries or other places, they will bear the port of right good gentlemen, and some are the more trusted, but commonly they pay them with stealing a pair of sheets or coverlet, and so take their farewell early in the morning, before the master or dame be stirring.

JOHN AWDELEY, *The Fraternitye of Vacabondes* 1575 (1st ed. 1561)

Abraham Men

Edgar.   My face I'll grime with filth,
Blanket my loins, elf all my hair in knots,
And with presented nakedness out-face
The winds and persecutions of the sky.
The country gives me proof and precedent
Of Bedlam beggars, who, with roaring voices,
Strike in their numb'd and mortified bare arms
Pins, wooden pricks, nails, sprigs of rosemary;

ROGUES AND VAGABONDS

And with this horrible object, from low farms,
Poor pelting villages, sheep-cotes, and mills,
Sometime with lunatic bans, sometime with prayers,
Enforce their charity.   Poor Turlygood! poor Tom!

King Lear, II. iii. 9—20

These Abraham men be those that feign themselves to
have been mad and have been kept either in Bethlehem or
in some other prison a good time, and not amongst twenty
that ever came in prison for any such cause: yet will they
say how piteously and most extremely they have been beaten
and dealt withal.   Some of these be merry and very pleasant,
they will dance and sing; some others be as cold and reasonable
to talk withal.   These beg money, either when they come at
farmer's houses they will demand bacon either cheese or wool
or anything that is worth money.   And if they espy small
company within, they will with fierce countenance demand
somewhat, where for fear the maids will give them largely
to be rid of them.

Rufflers on Shooter's Hill

[The story below, it has been observed, is quite in the manner of
Falstaff's escapades.]

The ruffler, because he is first in degree of this odious
order, and is so called in a statute made for the punishment of
vagabonds in the xxvii. year of King Henry VIII, late of most
famous memory, he shall be first placed, as the worthiest of this
unruly rabblement.   And he is so called when he goeth first
abroad ; either he hath served in the wars, or else he hath been
a serving-man, and, weary of well doing, shaking off all pain,
doth choose him this idle life, and wretchedly wanders about
the most shires of this realm.   And with stout audacity he
demandeth where he thinketh he may be bold, and circumspect
enough, as he seeth cause to ask charity, ruefully and lamentably, that it would make a flinty heart to relent and pity his
miserable estate, how he hath been maimed and bruised in the
wars ; and, peradventure, some will shew you some outward
wound which he got at some drunken fray, either halting of
some privy wound festered with a filthy fiery flankard.   For be
well assured that the hardiest soldiers be either slain or maimed,

239

either and* they escape all hazards and return home again, if they be without relief of their friends, they will surely desperately rob and steal, and either shortly be hanged or miserably die in prison; for they be so much ashamed and disdain to beg or ask charity, that rather they will as desperately fight for to live and maintain themselves, as manfully and valiantly they ventured themselves in the prince's quarrel. Now these rufflers, the outcasts of serving-men, when begging or craving fails, then they pick and pilfer from other inferior beggars that they meet by the way, as rogues, palliards, morts and doxies. Yea, if they meet with a woman alone riding to the market either old man or boy that he well knoweth will not resist, such they filch and spoil. These rufflers, after a year or two at the farthest, become uprightmen, unless they be prevented by twined hemp.

I had of late years an old man to my tenant, who customably a great time went twice in the week to London, either with fruit or with peascods, when time served therefore. And as he was coming homewards on Blackheath, at the end thereof next to Shooter's Hill, he overtook two rufflers, the one mannerly waiting on the other, as one had been the master, and the other the man or servant carrying his master's cloak. This old man was very glad that he might have their company over the hill, because that day he had made a good market; for he had seven shillings in his purse, and an old angel, which this poor man had thought had not been in his purse, for he willed his wife over night to take out the same angel and lay it up until his coming home again. And he verily thought that his wife had so done, which indeed forgot to do it. Thus after salutations had, this master ruffler entered into communication with this simple old man, who, riding softly beside them, communed of many matters. Thus feeding this old man with pleasant talk, until they were on the top of the hill, where these rufflers might well behold the coast about them clear, quickly steps unto this poor man, and taketh hold of his horse bridle, and leadeth him into the wood, and demandeth of him what and how much money he had in his purse. "Now, by my troth," quoth this old man; "you are a merry gentleman. I know you mean not to take away anything from me, but rather

* or if.

to give me some if I should ask it of you." By and by, this servant thief casteth the cloak that he carried on his arm about this poor man's face, that he should not mark or view them, with sharp words to deliver quickly that he had, and to confess truly what was in his purse. This poor man, then all abashed, yielded and confessed that he had but just seven shillings in his purse ; and the truth is he knew of no more. This old angel was fallen out of a little purse into the bottom of a great purse. Now, this seven shillings in white money they quickly found, thinking indeed that there had been no more ; yet farther groping and searching found this old angel. And with great admiration, this gentleman thief began to bless him, saying, " Good Lord, what a world is this ! how may," quoth he, " a man believe or trust in the same ? See you not," quoth he, " this old knave told me that he had but seven shillings, and here is more by an angel : what an old knave and a false knave have we here !" quoth this ruffler, " Our Lord have mercy on us, will this world never be better ? "—and therewith went their way, and left the old man in the wood, doing him no more harm. But sorrowfully sighing, this old man, returning home, declared his misadventure, with all the words and circumstances above shewed. Whereat for the time was great laughing, and this poor man for his losses among his loving neighbours well considered in the end.

A Hooker or Angler

These hookers, or anglers, be perilous and most wicked knaves, and be derived or proceed forth from the upright-men. They commonly go in frieze jerkins and gally-slops, pointed beneath the knee. These when they practise their pilfering, it is all by night ; for, as they walk a-day-times from house to house, to demand charity, they vigilantly mark where or in what place they may attain to their prey, casting their eyes up to every window, well noting what they see there, whether apparel or linen, hanging near unto the said windows, and that will they be sure to have the next night following. For they customably carry with them a staff of five or six foot long, in which, within one inch of the top thereof, is a little hole bored through, in which hole they put an iron hook, and with the same they will pluck unto them quickly anything that they may reach therewith, which hook in the daytime they covertly carry about them, and is never seen or taken out till they come to the place where they work their feat. Such have I seen at my house, and have oft talked with them and have handled their staves, not then understanding to what use or intent they served, although I had and perceived, by their talk and behaviour, great likelihood of evil suspicion in them. They will either lean upon their staff, to hide the hole thereof, when they talk with you, or hold their hand upon the hole; and what stuff, either woollen or linen, they thus hook out, they never carry the same forthwith to their stauling-kens, but hide the same a three days in some secret corner, and after convey the same to their houses abovesaid, where their host or hostess giveth them money for the same, but half the value that it is worth, or else their doxies shall afar off sell the same at the like houses. I was credibly informed that a hooker came to a farmer's house in the dead of the night, and putting back a draw-window of a low chamber, the bed standing hard by the said window, in which lay three persons (a man and two big boys), this hooker with his staff plucked off their garments which lay upon them to keep them warm, with the coverlet and sheet, and left them lying asleep naked saving their shirts, and had away all clean, and never could understand where it became. I verily suppose that when they were well waked with cold, they surely thought that Robin Goodfellow (according to the old saying) had been with them that night.

Two Rogues and a Parson

There was not long since two rogues that always did associate themselves together, and would never separate themselves, unless it were for some especial causes, for they were sworn brothers, and were both of one age, and much like of favour. These two, travelling into east Kent, resorted unto an alehouse there, being wearied with travelling, saluting with short courtesy, when they came into the house, such as they saw sitting there, in which company was the parson of the parish, and calling for a pot of the best ale, sat down at the table's end. The liquor liked them so well, that they had pot upon pot, and sometime, for a little good manner, would drink and offer the cup to such as they best fancied; and to be short, they sat out all the company, for each man departed home about their business. When they had well refreshed themselves, then these rousy rogues requested the good man of the house with his wife to sit down and drink with them, of whom they enquired what priest the same was and where he dwelt. Then they feigning that they had an uncle a priest, and that he should dwell in these parts, which by all presumptions it should be he, and that they came of purpose to speak with him, but because they had not seen him since they were six years old, they durst not be bold to take acquaintance of him until they were farther instructed of the truth, and began to enquire of his name, and how long he had dwelt there, and how far his house was off from the place they were in. The good wife of the house, thinking them honest men without deceit, because [what] they so far enquired of their kinsman was but of a good zealous natural intent, shewed them cheerfully that he was an honest man and well-beloved in the parish, and of good wealth, and had been there resident fifteen years at the least. "But," saith she, "are you both brothers?" "Yea, surely," said they, "we have been both in one belly, and were twins." "Mercy, God!" quoth this foolish woman; "it may well be, for ye be not much unlike,"—and went unto her hall window, calling these young men unto her, and looking out thereat, pointed with her finger and shewed them the house standing alone, no house near the same by almost a quarter of a mile. "That," said she, "is your uncle's house." "Nay," saith one of them, "he is not only my uncle, but also my godfather." "It may well be," quoth she, "nature will bind him to be the better unto you." "Well," quoth they, "we be weary, and mean not to trouble our uncle to-night; but to-morrow, God willing, we will see him and do our duty: but, I pray you, doth our uncle occupy husbandry? what company hath he in his house?" "Alas!" saith she, "but one old woman and a boy, he hath no occupying at all. Tush!" quoth this good wife, "you be madmen; go to him this night, for he hath better lodging for you than I have, and yet I speak foolishly against my own profit, for by your tarrying here I should gain the more by you." "Now, by my troth," quoth one of them, "we thank you, good hostess, for your wholesome counsel, and we mean to do as you will us: we will pause awhile, and by that time it will be almost night; and I pray you give us a reckoning."

So, mannerly paying for that they took, bade their host and hostess farewell with taking leave of the cup, marched merely out of the doors towards this parson's house, viewed the same well round about, and passed by two bowshots off into a young wood, where they lay consulting what they should do until midnight. Quoth one of them, of sharper wit and subtler than the other, to his fellow, "Thou seest that this house is stone-walled about, and that we cannot well break in, in any part thereof; thou seest also that the windows be thick of mullions, that there is no creeping in between: wherefore we must of necessity use some policy when strength will not serve. I have a horse-lock here about me," saith he; "and this I hope shall serve our turn." So when it was about twelve of the clock, they came to the house and lurked near unto his chamber window. The dog of the house barked a good [deal], that with the noise, this priest waketh out of his sleep, and began to cough and hem: then one of these rogues steps forth nearer the window and maketh a rueful and pitiful noise, requiring for Christ sake some relief, that was both hungry and thirsty and was like to lie without the doors all night and starve for cold, unless he were relieved by him with some small piece of money. "Where dwellest thou?" quoth this parson. "Alas! sir," saith this rogue, "I have small dwelling, and have come out of my way; and should I now," saith he, "go to any town now at this time of night, they would set me in the stocks and punish me." "Well," quoth this pitiful parson, "away from my house either lie in some of my outhouses until the morning, and hold, here is a couple of pence for thee." "Ah God reward you," quoth this rogue; "and in heaven may you find it." The parson openeth his window, and thrusteth out his arm to give his alms to this rogue that came whining to receive it, and quickly taketh hold of his hand, and calleth his fellow to him, which was ready at hand with the horse-lock, and clappeth the same about the wrist of his arm, that the mullions standing so close together for strength, that for his life he could not pluck in his arm again, and made him believe, unless he would at the least give them £3, they would smite off his arm from the body. So

244

that poor parson, in fear to lose his hand, called up his old woman that lay in the loft over him, and willed her to take out all the money he had, which was four marks, which he said was all the money in his house, for he had lent £6 to one of his neighbours not four days before. "Well," quoth they, "master parson, if you have no more, upon this condition we will take off the lock, that you will drink twelve pence for our sakes to-morrow at the alehouse where we found you, and thank the good wife for the cheer she made us." He promised faithfully that he would do so ; so they took off the lock, and went their way so far ere it was day, that the parson could never have any understanding more of them.

Now this parson, sorrowfully slumbering that night between fear and hope, thought it was but folly to make two sorrows of one. He used contentation for his remedy, not forgetting in the morning to perform his promise, but went betimes to his neighbour that kept tippling, and asked angerly where the same two men were that drank with her yesterday. "Which two men?" quoth this good wife. "The strangers that came in when I was at your house with my neighbours yesterday." "What ! your nephews?" quoth she. "My nephews ?" quoth this parson; "I trow thou art mad." "Nay, by God ! " quoth this good wife, "as sober as you ; for they told me faithfully that you were their uncle : but, in faith, are you not so indeed ? for, by my troth, they are strangers to me. I never saw them before." "O, out upon them ! " quoth the parson ; "they be false thieves, and this night they compelled me to give them all the money in my house." "Benedicite ! " quoth this good wife, "and have they so indeed ? as I shall answer before God, one of them told me besides that you were godfather to him, and that he trusted to have your blessing before he departed." "What ! did he ?" quoth this parson ; "a halter bless him for me ! " "Me thinketh, by the mass, by your countenance you looked so wildly when you came in," quoth this good wife, "that something was amiss." "I use not to jest," quoth this parson, "when I speak so earnestly." "Why, all your sorrows go with it," quoth this good wife, "and sit down here, and I will fill a fresh pot of ale shall make you merry again." "Yea," saith this parson, "fill in and give me some meat ; for they made me swear and promise them faithfully that I should drink twelve pence with you this day." "What! did they?" quoth she; "now, by the Mary mass, they be merry knaves. I warrant you they mean to buy no land with your money; but how could they come into you in the night, your doors being shut fast? your house is very strong." Then this parson shewed her all the whole circumstance, how he gave them his alms out at the window, they made such lamentable cry that it pitied him at the heart; for he saw but one when he put out his hand at the window. "Be ruled by me," quoth this good wife. "Wherein?" quoth this parson. "By my troth, never speak more of it: when they shall understand of it in the parish, they will but laugh you to scorn." "Why, then," quoth this parson, "the devil go with it,"—and there an end.

A Counterfeit Crank (and a printer in pursuit of copy)

Upon All-hallows-day in the morning last *anno domini* 1566, ere my book was half printed, I mean the first impression, there came early in the morning a counterfeit crank under my lodging at the White Friars, within the cloister, in a little yard or court, whereabouts lay two or three great ladies, being without the liberties of London, whereby he hoped for the greater gain. This crank there lamentably lamenting and pitifully crying to be relieved, declared to divers there his painful and miserable disease. I being risen and not half ready, heard his doleful words and rueful mournings, hearing him name the falling sickness, thought assuredly to myself that he was a deep dissembler. So, coming out at a sudden, and beholding his ugly and irksome attire, his loathsome and horrible countenance, it made me in a marvellous perplexity what to think of him, whether it were feigned or truth. For after this manner went he: he was naked from the waist upward, saving he had an old jerkin of leather patched, and that was loose about him, that all his body lay out bare; a filthy foul cloth he ware on his head, being cut for the purpose, having a narrow place to put out his face, with a beaver made to truss up his beard, and a string that tied the same down close about his neck; with an old felt hat which he still carried in his hand to receive the charity and devotion of the people, for that would he hold out from him; having his face, from the eyes downward, all smeared with fresh blood, as though he had new fallen, and

246

been tormented with his painful pangs,—his jerkin being all berayed with dirt and mire : surely the sight was monstrous and terrible. I called him unto me, and demanded of him what he ailed. "Ah, good master," quoth he, "I have the grievous and painful disease called the falling sickness." "Why," quoth I, "how cometh thy jerkin, hose, and hat so berayed with dirt and mire, and thy skin also ?" "Ah, good master, I fell down on the backside here in the foul lane hard by the waterside ; and there I lay almost all night, and have bled almost all the blood out in my body." It rained that morning very fast ; and while I was thus talking with him, a honest poor woman that dwelt thereby brought him a fair linen cloth, and bid him wipe his face therewith ; and there being a tub standing full of rain water, offered to give him some in a dish that he might make himself clean : he refuseth the same. "Why dost thou so ?" quoth I. "Ah, sir," saith he, "if I should wash myself, I should fall to bleeding afresh again, and then I should not stop myself." These words made me the more to suspect him.

Then I asked of him where he was born, what his name was, how long he had this disease, and what time he had been here about London, and in what place. "Sir," saith he, "I was born at Leicester, my name is Nicholas Genings, and I have had this falling sickness eight years, and can get no remedy for the same ; for I have it by kind, my father had it and my friends before me ; and I have been these two years here about London, and a year and a half in Bethlehem." "Why, wast thou out of thy wits?" quoth I. "Yea, sir, that I was." "What is the keeper's name of the house ?" "His name is," quoth he, "John Smith." "Then," quoth I, "he must understand of thy disease; if thou haddest the same for the time thou wast there, he knoweth it well." "Yea, not only he, but all the house beside," quoth this crank ; "for I came thence but within this fortnight."

I had stood so long reasoning the matter with him that I was a cold, and went into my chamber and made me ready, and commanded my servant to repair to Bethlehem, and bring me true word from the keeper there whether any such man hath been with him as a prisoner having the disease aforesaid, and gave him a note of his name and the

247

keeper's also. My servant, returning to my lodging, did assure me that neither was there ever any such man there, neither yet any keeper of any such name; but he that was there keeper, he sent me his name in writing, affirming that he letteth no man depart from him unless he be fetched away by his friends, and that none that came from him begged about the city. Then I sent for the printer of this book, and shewed him of this dissembling crank, and how I had sent to Bethlehem to understand the truth, and what answer I received again, requiring him that I might have some servant of his to watch him faithfully that day, that I might understand trustily to what place he would repair at night unto, and thither I promised to go myself to see their order, and that I would have him to associate me thither. He gladly granted to my request, and sent two boys, that both diligently and vigilantly accomplished the charge given them, and found the same crank about the Temple, whereabout the most part of the day he begged, unless it were about twelve of the clock he went on the backside of Clement's Inn without Temple-bar, there is a lane that goeth into the fields; there he renewed his face again with fresh blood, which he carried about him in a bladder, and daubed on fresh dirt upon his jerkin, hat and hosen. And so came back again unto the Temple, and sometime to the waterside, and begged of all that passed by. The boys beheld how some gave groats, some sixpence, some gave more; for he looked so ugly and irksomely, that everyone pitied his miserable case that beheld him. To be short, there he passed all the day till night approached; and when it began to be somewhat dark, he went to the waterside and took a sculler, and was set over the water into Saint George's fields, contrary to my expectation; for I had thought he would have gone into Holborn or to Saint Giles in the field. But these boys, with Argus's and lynx's eyes, set sure watch upon him, and the one took a boat and followed him and the other went back to tell his master.

The boy that so followed him by water, had no money to pay for his boat hire, but laid his penner and his inkhorn to gage for a penny; and by that time the boy was set over, his master, with all celerity, had taken a boat and followed him apace. Now had they still a sight of the crank, which crossed over the fields towards Newington, and thither he went, and by that time they came thither it was very dark. The printer had there no acquaintance, neither any kind of weapon about him, neither knew he how far the crank would go, because he then suspected that they dogged him of purpose. He there stayed him, and called for the constable, which came forth diligently to enquire what the matter was. This zealous printer charged this officer with him as a malefactor and a dissembling vagabond. The constable would have laid him all night in the cage that stood in the street. "Nay," saith this pitiful printer, "I pray you have him into your house; for this is like to be a cold night, and he is naked: you keep a victualling house; let him be well cherished this night, for he is well able to pay for the same. I know well his gains hath been great to-day, and your house is a sufficient prison for the time, and we will there search him." The constable agreed thereunto: they had him in, and caused him to wash himself: that done, they demanded what money he had about him. Saith this crank, "So God help me, I have but twelve pence," and plucked out the same of a little purse. "Why, have you no more?" quoth they. "No," saith this crank, "as God shall save my soul at the day of judgment." "We must see more," quoth they, and began to strip him. Then he plucked out another purse, wherein was forty pence. "Tush," saith this printer, "I must see more." Saith this crank, "I pray God I be damned both body and soul if I have any more." "No," saith this printer, "thou false knave, here is my boy that did watch thee all this day, and saw when such men gave thee pieces of six pence, groats, and other money; and yet thou hast shewed us none but small money." When this crank heard this, and the boy vowing it to his face, he relented, and plucked out another purse, wherein was eight shillings and odd money; so had they in the whole that he had begged that day thirteen shillings threepence halfpenny. Then they stripped him stark naked, and as many as saw him said they never saw handsomer man, with a yellow flaxen beard, and fair skinned, without any spot or grief. Then the good wife of the house fetched her goodman's old cloak, and caused the same to be cast about him, because the sight should not abash her shamefast maidens, neither loth her squeamish sight.

Thus he set down at the chimney's end, and called for a pot of beer, and drank off a quart at a draught, and called for another, and so the third, that one had been sufficient for any reasonable man, the drink was so strong; I myself, the next morning, tasted thereof. But let the reader judge what and how much he would have drunk and he had been out of fear. Then when they had thus wrung water out of a flint in spoiling him of his evil gotten goods, his passing pence, and fleeting trash, the printer with this officer were in jolly jollity, and devised to search a barn for some rogues and uprightmen, a quarter of a mile from the house, that stood alone in the fields, and went out about their business, leaving this crank alone with his wife and maidens. This crafty crank, espying all gone, requested the good wife that he might go out on the backside to make water, and to exonerate his paunch. She bad him draw the latch of the door and go out, neither thinking or mistrusting he would have gone away naked. But, to conclude, when he was out, he cast away the cloak, and, as naked as ever he was born, he ran away, that he could never be heard of again. Now the next morning betimes, I went unto Newington, to understand what was done, because I had word or it was day that there my printer was. And at my coming thither, I heard the whole circumstance, as I above have written; and I, seeing the matter so fall out, took order with the chief of the parish that this thirteen shillings and threepence halfpenny might the next day be equally distributed, by their good discretions, to the poverty of the same parish, and so it was done.

[The counterfeit crank was eventually captured, as Harman relates in a subsequent edition of his book.]

THOMAS HARMAN, *A Caveat or Warening for Commen Cursetors* 1567

CHAPTER XI

THE SEA

Boatswain. Heigh, my hearts! cheerly, cheerly, my hearts! yare, yare! Take in the topsail! Tend to the master's whistle!—Blow, till thou burst thy wind, if room enough!

* * * * * * *

Gonzalo. Now would I give a thousand furlongs of sea for an acre of barren ground; long heath, brown furze, any thing. The wills above be done! but I would fain die a dry death. *The Tempest,* I. i.

Yet his means are in supposition: he hath an argosy bound to Tripolis, another to the Indies; I understand moreover upon the Rialto, he hath a third at Mexico, a fourth for England, and other ventures he hath, squandered abroad. But ships are but boards, sailors but men: there be land-rats and water-rats, land-thieves and water-thieves,—I mean pirates,—and then there is the peril of waters, winds and rocks.

The Merchant of Venice, I. iii. 17—25.

Hakluyt extols England's Greatness at Sea

He does smile his face into more lines than are in the new map with the augmentation of the Indies. *Twelfth Night,* III. ii. 87.

To the Right Honourable Sir Francis Walsingham Knight. Right Honourable, I do remember that being a youth, and one of her Majesty's scholars at Westminster that fruitful nursery, it was my hap to visit the chamber of Mr Richard Hakluyt my cousin, a gentleman of the Middle Temple, well known unto you, at a time when I found lying open upon his board certain books of cosmography, with an universal map. He seeing me somewhat curious in the view thereof, began to instruct my ignorance, by showing me the division of the earth into three parts after the old account, and then according to the latter and better distribution, into more: he pointed with his wand to all the known seas, gulfs, bays, straits, capes, rivers, empires, kingdoms, dukedoms, and territories of each part, with declaration also of their special commodities and particular wants, which, by the benefit of traffic and intercourse of merchants, are plentifully supplied. From the map he brought me to the Bible, and turning to the 107 Psalm, directed me to the 23 and 24 verses, where I read, that they which go down to the sea in ships, and occupy by the great waters, they see the works of the Lord, and his wonders in the deep, etc. Which words of the prophet together with my cousin's discourse (things of high and rare delight to my young nature) took in me so deep an impression, that I constantly resolved, if ever I were preferred to the university, where better time and more convenient place might be ministered for these studies, I would by God's assistance prosecute that knowledge and kind of literature, the doors whereof (after a sort) were so happily opened before me.

According to which my resolution, when, not long after, I was removed to Christ Church in Oxford, my exercises of duty first performed, I fell to my intended course, and by degrees read over whatsoever printed or written discoveries and voyages, I found extant either in the Greek, Latin, Italian, Spanish, Portugal, French or English languages, and in my public lectures was the first, that produced and showed both the old imperfectly composed, and the new lately reformed maps, globes, spheres and other instruments of this art for demonstration in the common schools, to the singular pleasure and general contentment of my auditory. In continuance of time, and by reason principally of my insight in this study, I grew familiarly acquainted with the chiefest captains at sea, the greatest merchants and the best mariners of our nation : by which means having gotten somewhat more than common knowledge, I passed at length the narrow seas into France with Sir Edward Stafford, her Majesty's careful and discreet leger, where during my five years' abode with him in his dangerous and chargeable residency in her Highness's service, I both heard in speech, and read in books other nations miraculously extolled for their discoveries and notable enterprises by sea, but the English of all others, for their sluggish security and continual neglect of the like attempts especially in so long and happy a time of peace, either ignominiously reported or exceedingly condemned.......
Thus both hearing, and reading the obloquy of our nation, and finding few or none of our own men able to reply herein,

and further, not seeing any man to have care to recommend to the world the industrious labours and painful travels of our countrymen : for stopping the mouths of the reproachers, myself being the last winter returned from France with the honourable the Lady Sheffield, for her passing good behaviour highly esteemed in all the French court, determined notwithstanding all difficulties to undertake the burden of that work wherein all others pretended either ignorance, or lack of leisure, or want of sufficient argument, whereas (to speak truly) the huge toil, and the small profit to ensue, were the chief causes of the refusal......

To harp no longer upon this string, and to speak a word of that just commendation which our nation do indeed deserve : it cannot be denied, but as in all former ages, they have been men full of activity, stirrers abroad, and searchers of the remote parts of the world, so in this most famous and peerless government of her most excellent Majesty, her subjects through the special assistance and blessing of God, in searching the most opposite corners and quarters of the world, and to speak plainly, in compassing the vast globe of the earth more than once, have excelled all the nations and people of the earth. For, which of the kings of this land before her Majesty, had their banners ever seen in the Caspian Sea? which of them hath ever dealt with the Emperor of Persia, as her Majesty hath done, and obtained for her merchants large and loving privileges? who ever saw, before this regiment, an English leger in the stately porch of the Grand Signor at Constantinople? who ever found English consuls and agents at Tripolis, in Syria, at Aleppo, at Babylon, at Balsara, and which is more, who ever heard of Englishmen at Goa before now? what English ships did heretofore ever anchor in the mighty river of Plate? pass and repass the unpassable (in former opinion) straits of Magellan, range along the coast of Chili, Peru and all the backside of Nova Hispania further than any Christian ever passed, traverse the mighty breadth of the South Sea, land upon the Luzones in despite of the enemy, enter into alliance, amity and traffic with the princes of the Moluccas and the Isle of Java, double the famous Cape of Bona Speranza, arrive at the Isle of Santa Helena, and last of all return home most richly laden with the commodities of China, as the subjects of this now flourishing monarchy have done?

RICHARD HAKLUYT, *Principal Navigations* (epistle dedicatory) 1589

THE SEA

The English Navy

The navy of England may be divided into three sorts, of which the one serveth for the wars, the other for burden, and the third for fishermen which get their living by fishing on the sea. How many of the first order are maintained within the realm, it passeth my cunning to express....Certes there is no prince in Europe that hath a more beautiful or gallant sort of ships than the Queen's majesty of England at this present, and those generally are of such exceeding force that two of them being well appointed and furnished as they ought, will not let to encounter with three or four of those of other countries, and either bouge them or put them to flight, if they may not bring them home. Neither are the moulds of any foreign barks so conveniently made, to brook so well one sea as another, lying upon the shore of any part of the continent, as those of England. And therefore the common report that strangers make of our ships amongst themselves is daily confirmed to be true, which is that for strength, assurance, nimbleness, and swiftness of sailing, there are no vessels in the world to be compared with ours.

WILLIAM HARRISON, *The Description of England* 1587 (2nd ed.)

A Merchant

Believe me, sir, had I such venture forth,
The better part of my affections would
Be with my hopes abroad. I should be still
Plucking the grass to know where sits the wind;
Peering in maps for ports, and piers, and roads;
And every object that might make me fear
Misfortune to my ventures, out of doubt
Would make me sad.

The Merchant of Venice, I. i. 15—22

A worthy merchant is the heir of adventure, whose hopes hang much upon wind. Upon a wooden horse he rides through the world, and in a merry gale he makes a path through the seas. He is a discoverer of countries and a finder out of commodities, resolute in his attempts and royal in his expenses. He is the life of traffic and the maintainer of trade, the sailor's master and the soldier's friend. He is the exercise of the exchange, the honour of credit, the observation of time and the understanding of thrift. His study is number, his care his accounts, his comfort his conscience, and his wealth his good name. He fears not Scylla and sails close by Charybdis, and having beaten out a storm, rides at rest in a harbour. By his sea gain he makes his land purchase, and by the knowledge of trade finds the key of treasure. Out of his travels he makes his discourses, and from his eye-observations brings the models of architecture. He plants the earth with foreign fruits, and knows at home what is good abroad. He is neat in apparel, modest in demeanour, dainty in diet and civil in his carriage. In sum, he is the pillar of a city, the enricher of a country, the furnisher of a court and the worthy servant of a king.

NICHOLAS BRETON, *The Good and the Badde* 1616

A Sailor's Life

The master, the swabber, the boatswain and I,
    The gunner and his mate,
Lov'd Mall, Meg, and Marian and Margery,
    But none of us car'd for Kate;
    For she had a tongue with a tang,
    Would cry to a sailor, "Go hang!"
She lov'd not the savour of tar nor of pitch;
*   *   *   *   *
    Then to sea, boys, and let her go hang!

The Tempest, II. ii. 49—57

Voyages of purchase or reprisals, which are now grown a common traffic, swallow up and consume more sailors and mariners than they breed, and lightly not a slop of a rope-hauler they send forth to the Queen's ships but he is first broken to the sea in the herring-man's skiff or cock-boat, where having learned to brook all waters, and drink as he can out of a tarry can, and eat poor John out of sooty platters, when he may get it, without butter or mustard, there is no ho with him, but, once heartened thus, he will needs be a man of war, or a tobacco taker, and wear a silver whistle. Some of these for their haughty climbing come home with wooden legs, and some with none, but leave body and all behind. Those that escape to bring news tell of nothing but eating tallow and young blacka-mores, of five and five to a rat in every mess and the ship-boy to the tail, of stopping their noses when they drank stinking

255

water that came out of the pump of the ship, and cutting a greasy buff jerkin in tripes and broiling it for their dinners. Divers Indian adventures have been seasoned with direr mishaps, not having for eight days' space the quantity of a candle's-end among eight score to grease their lips with; and landing in the end to seek food, by the cannibal savages they have been circumvented and forced to yield their bodies to feed them.

THOMAS NASHE, *Lenten Stuffe* 1599

The last fight of the Revenge

Antony.   Canidius, we
          Will fight with him by sea.
Cleopatra.   By sea! what else?
Canidius.   Why will my lord do so?
Antony.   For that he dares us to't.

Antony and Cleopatra, III. vii. 27—29

[Many lines of Tennyson's famous poem are taken almost *verbatim* from this account.]

The Lord Thomas Howard, with six of her Majesty's ships, six victuallers of London, the bark *Ralegh* and two or three pinnaces riding at anchor near unto Flores, one of the westerly islands of the Azores, the last of August in the afternoon, had intelligence by one Captain Middleton, of the approach of the Spanish armada. Which Middleton, being in a very good sailer, had kept them company three days before, of good purpose, both to discover their forces the more, as also to give advice to my Lord Thomas of their approach. He had no sooner delivered the news but the fleet was in sight: many of our ships' companies were on shore in the island; some providing ballast for their ships; others filling of water and refreshing themselves from the land with such things as they could either for money, or by force recover. By reason whereof, our ships being all pestered and romaging, everything [was] out of order [and] very light for want of ballast, and that which was most to our disadvantage, the one half part of the men of every ship sick and utterly unserviceable. For in the *Revenge* there were ninety diseased: in the *Bonaventure*, not so many in health as could handle her main sail. For had not twenty men been taken out of a bark of Sir George Carey's, his being commanded to be sunk, and those appointed to her, she had hardly ever recovered England. The rest for the most part, were in little better state. The names of her Majesty's ships were these as followeth: the *Defiance*, which was admiral, the *Revenge* vice-admiral, the *Bonaventure* commanded by Captain Cross, the *Lion* by George Fenner, the *Foresight* by Mr Thomas Vavasour, and the *Crane* by Duffield. The *Foresight* and the *Crane* being but small ships, only the other were of the middle size; the rest, besides the bark *Ralegh* commanded by Captain Thin, were victuallers, and of small force or none. The Spanish fleet, having shrouded their approach by reason of the island, were now so soon at hand, as our ships had scarce time to weigh their anchors, but some of them were driven to let slip their cables and set sail. Sir Richard Grenville was the last weighed, to recover the men that were upon the island, which otherwise had been lost. The Lord Thomas with the rest very hardly recovered the wind, which Sir Richard Grenville not being able to do, was persuaded by the master and others to cut his main sail, and cast about, and to trust to the sailing of his ship: for the squadron of Seville were on his weather bow. But Sir Richard utterly refused to turn from the enemy, alleging that he would rather choose to die, than to dishonour himself, his country and her Majesty's ship, persuading his company that he would pass through the two squadrons, in despite of them: and enforce those of Seville to give him way. Which he performed upon divers of the foremost, who, as the mariners term it, sprang their luff and fell under the lee of the *Revenge*. But the other course had been the better, and might right well have been answered in so great an impossibility of prevailing. Notwithstanding out of the greatness of his mind, he could not be persuaded. In the meanwhile as he attended those which were nearest him, the great *San Philip* being in the wind of him, and coming towards him, becalmed his sails in such sort, as the ship could neither make way nor feel the helm: so huge and high charged was the Spanish ship, being of a thousand and five hundred tons, who afterlaid the *Revenge* aboard. When he was thus bereft of his sails, the ships that were under his lee luffing up also laid him aboard: of which the next was the *Admiral of the Biscaines*, a very mighty and puissant ship commanded by Brittan Dona. The said *Philip* carried three tier of ordnance on a side, and eleven pieces in every tier. She shot eight forth right out of her chase, besides those of her stern ports.

After the *Revenge* was entangled with this *Philip*, four other boarded her; two on her larboard, and two on her starboard. The fight thus beginning at three of the clock in the afternoon, continued very terrible all that evening. But the great *San Philip* having received the lower tier of the *Revenge*, discharged with crossbar-shot, shifted herself with all diligence from her sides, utterly misliking her first entertainment. Some say that the ship foundered, but we cannot report it for truth, unless we were assured. The Spanish ships were filled with companies of soldiers, in some two hundred besides the mariners, in some five, in others eight hundred. In ours there were none at all, besides the mariners, but the servants of the commanders and some few voluntary gentlemen only. After many interchanged volleys of great ordnance and small shot, the Spaniards deliberated to enter the *Revenge*, and made divers attempts, hoping to force her by the multitudes of their armed soldiers and musketeers, but were still repulsed again and again, and at all times beaten back into their own ships, or into the seas. In the beginning of the fight, the *George Noble* of London, having received some shot through her by the armados, fell under the lee of the *Revenge*, and asked Sir Richard what he would command him, being but one of the victuallers and of small force. Sir Richard bid him save himself, and leave him to his fortune. After the fight had thus without intermission continued while the day lasted and some hours of the night, many of our men were slain and hurt, and one of the great galleons of the armada and the *Admiral of the Hulks* both sunk, and in many other of the Spanish ships great slaughter was made. Some write that Sir Richard was very dangerously hurt almost in the beginning of the fight, and lay speechless for a time ere he recovered. But two of the *Revenge's* own company, brought home in a ship of Lima from the islands, examined by some of the Lords and others, affirmed that he was never so wounded as that he forsook the upper deck, till an hour before midnight; and then being shot into the body with a musket as he was a dressing, was again shot into the head, and withal his chirurgeon wounded to death. This agreeth also with an examination, taken by Sir Francis Godolphin, of four other mariners of the same ship being returned, which examination, the said Sir Francis sent unto Master William Killigrew, of her Majesty's privy chamber.

But to return to the fight, the Spanish ships which at-
tempted to board the *Revenge*, as they were wounded and beaten
off, so always others came in their places, she having never less
than two mighty galleons by her sides, and aboard her. So that
ere the morning, from three of the clock the day before, there
had fifteen several armados assailed her; and all so ill approved
their entertainment, as they were by the break of day, far more
willing to hearken to a composition, than hastily to make any
more assaults or entries. But as the day increased, so our men
decreased: and as the light grew more and more, by so much
more grew our discomforts. For none appeared in sight but
enemies, saving one small ship called the *Pilgrim*, commanded
by Jacob Whiddon, who hovered all night to see the success:
but in the morning bearing with the *Revenge*, was hunted like
a hare amongst many ravenous hounds, but escaped.

All the powder of the *Revenge* to the last barrel was now
spent, all her pikes broken, forty of her best men slain, and the
most part of the rest hurt. In the beginning of the fight she
had but one hundred free from sickness, and fourscore and ten
sick, laid in hold upon the ballast: a small troop to man such
a ship, and a weak garrison to resist so mighty an army. By
those hundred all was sustained, the volleys, boardings and
enterings of fifteen ships of war, besides those which beat her
at large. On the contrary, the Spanish were always supplied
with soldiers brought from every squadron: all manner of arms
and powder at will. Unto ours there remained no comfort at
all, no hope, no supply either of ships, men or weapons; the
masts all beaten overboard, all her tackle cut asunder, her upper
work altogether razed, and in effect evened she was with the
water, but the very foundation or bottom of a ship, nothing
being left overhead either for flight or defence. Sir Richard
finding himself in this distress, and unable any longer to make
resistance, having endured in this fifteen hours' fight, the assault
of fifteen several armados, all by turns aboard him, and by estimation eight hundred shot of great artillery, besides many assaults
and entries; and that himself and the ship must needs be
possessed by the enemy, who were now all cast in a ring round
about him; the *Revenge* not able to move one way or other,
but as she was moved with the waves and billow of the sea;
commanded the master gunner, whom he knew to be a most

resolute man, to split and sink the ship; that thereby nothing might remain of glory or victory to the Spaniards: seeing in so many hours' fight, and with so great a navy they were not able to take her, having had fifteen hours' time, fifteen thousand men, and fifty and three sail of men of war to perform it withal. And persuaded the company, or as many as he could induce, to yield themselves unto God, and to the mercy of none else; but, as they had like valiant resolute men repulsed so many enemies, they should not now shorten the honour of their nation by prolonging their own lives for a few hours or a few days. The master gunner readily condescended and divers others; but the captain and the master were of another opinion, and besought Sir Richard to have care of them: alleging that the Spaniard would be as ready to entertain a composition, as they were willing to offer the same: and that there being divers sufficient and valiant men yet living, and whose wounds were not mortal, they might do their country and prince acceptable service hereafter. And (that where Sir Richard had alleged that the Spaniards should never glory to have taken one ship of her Majesty's, seeing that they had so long and so notably defended themselves) they answered, that the ship had six foot water in hold, three shot under water, which were so weakly stopped, as with the first working of the sea, she must needs sink, and was besides so crushed and bruised, as she could never be removed out of the place.

And as the matter was thus in dispute, and Sir Richard refusing to hearken to any of those reasons: the master of the *Revenge* (while the captain won unto him the greater party) was conveyed aboard the General *Don Alfonso Bassan.* Who finding none over hasty to enter the *Revenge* again, doubting lest Sir Richard would have blown them up and himself, and perceiving by the report of the master of the *Revenge* his dangerous disposition, yielded that all their lives should be saved, the company sent for England, and the better sort to pay such reasonable ransom as their estate would bear, and in the mean season to be free from galley or imprisonment. To this he so much the rather condescended as well as I have said, for fear of further loss and mischief to themselves, as also for the desire he had to recover Sir Richard Grenville: whom for his notable valour he seemed greatly to honour and admire.

THE STORY OF THE REVENGE

When this answer was returned, and that safety of life was ｐﾔomised, the common sort being now at the end of their peril, the most drew back from Sir Richard and the master gunner, being no hard matter to dissuade men from death to life. The master gunner finding himself and Sir Richard thus prevented and mastered by the greater number, would have slain himself with a sword, had he not been by force withheld and locked into his cabin. Then the General sent many boats aboard the *Revenge*, and divers of our men fearing Sir Richard's disposition, stole away aboard the *General* and other ships. Sir Richard thus overmatched, was sent unto by Alfonso Bassan to remove out of the *Revenge*, the ship being marvellous unsavoury, filled with blood and bodies of dead and wounded men like a slaughter house. Sir Richard answered that he might do with his body what he list, for he esteemed it not, and as he was carried out of the ship he swooned, and reviving again desired the company to pray for him. The General used Sir Richard with all humanity, and left nothing unattempted that tended to his recovery, highly commending his valour and worthiness, and greatly bewailed the danger wherein he was, being unto them a rare spectacle, and a resolution seldom approved, to see one ship turn toward so many enemies, to endure the charge and boarding of so many huge armados, and to resist and repel the assaults and entries of so many soldiers. All which and more is confirmed by a Spanish captain of the same armada, and a present actor in the fight, who being severed from the rest in a storm, was by the *Lion* of London, a small ship, taken, and is now prisoner in London.

The general commander of the armada was Don Alfonso Bassan, brother to the Marquis of Santa Cruce. The admiral of the Biscaine squadron was Britan Dona, of the squadron of Seville Marquis of Arumburch. The hulks and flyboats were commanded by Luis Cutino. There were slain and drowned in this fight, well near two thousand of the enemies, and two especial commanders Don Luis de Sant John, and Don George de Prunaria de Mallaga, as the Spanish captain confesseth, besides divers others of special account, whereof as yet report is not made.

The *Admiral of the Hulks* and the *Ascention* of Seville were both sunk by the side of the *Revenge*; one other recovered the road of Saint Michels, and sunk also there; a fourth ran herself with the shore to save her men. Sir Richard died as it is said, the second or third day aboard the *General*, and was by them greatly bewailed. What became of his body, whether it were buried in the sea or on the land we know not: the comfort that remaineth to his friends is, that he hath ended his life honourably in respect of the reputation won to his nation and country, and of the same to his posterity, and that being dead, he hath not outlived his own honour.

Sir Walter Ralegh, *The last fight of the Revenge* 1591

The Discovery of Virginia 1576

Adrian. Though this island seem to be desert...uninhabitable and almost inaccessible...it must needs be of subtle, tender and delicate temperance....The air breathes upon us here most sweetly....
Gonzalo. Here is everything advantageous to life.
Antonio. True; save means to live....
Gonzalo. How lush and lusty the grass looks! how green!

The Tempest, II. i. 36—56

Stephano. This is some monster of the isle....If I can recover him and keep him tame, and get to Naples with him, he's a present for any emperor that ever trod on neat's-leather.
Caliban. Do not torment me, prithee....
Stephano. He shall taste of my bottle: if he have never drunk wine afore, it will go near to remove his fit....
Caliban. These be fine things an if they be not sprites.
That's a brave god, and bears celestial liquor:
I will kneel to him....
Hast thou not dropp'd from heaven?
Stephano. Out o' the moon, I do assure thee: I was the man in the moon when time was.
Caliban. I have seen thee in her, and I do adore thee....
I prithee, let me bring thee where crabs grow;
And I with my long nails will dig thee pig-nuts;
Show thee a jay's nest, and instruct thee how
To snare the nimble marmozet; I'll bring thee
To clust'ring filberts, and sometimes I'll get thee
Young scamels from the rock. Wilt thou go with me?

Ibid. II. ii.

The most famous, renowned and ever worthy of all memory for her courage, learning, judgment and virtue, Queen Elizabeth granted her letters patent to Sir Walter Ralegh for the

262

discovering and planting new lands and countries, not actually possessed by any Christians. This patentee got to be his assistants Sir Richard Grenville the valiant, Master William Sanderson, a great friend to all such noble and worthy actions, and divers other gentlemen and merchants, who with all speed provided two small barks, full furnished with all necessaries, under the command of Captain Philip Amidas and Captain Barlow. The twenty-seventh of April they set sail from the Thames, the tenth of May passed the Canaries, and the tenth of June the West Indies: which unneedful southerly course (but then no better was known) occasioned them in that season much sickness.

The second of July they fell with the coast of Florida in shoal water, where they felt a most delicate sweet smell, though they saw no land, which ere long they espied, thinking it the continent: an hundred and twenty miles they sailed not finding any harbour. The first that appeared with much difficulty they entered, and anchored; and after thanks to God they went to view the next land adjoining, to take possession of it for the Queen's most excellent Majesty: which done, they found their first landing place very sandy and low, but so full of grapes that the very surge of the sea sometimes overflowed them: of which they found such plenty in all places, both on the sand, the green soil and hills, as in the plains as well on every little shrub, as also climbing towards the tops of high cedars, that they did think in the world were not the like abundance.

We passed by the sea-side towards the tops of the next hills being not high: from whence we might see the sea on both sides, and found it an isle of twenty miles in length and six in breadth, the valleys replenished with goodly tall cedars. Discharging our muskets, such a flock of cranes, the most white, arose by us, with such a cry as if an army of men had shouted all together. This isle hath many goodly woods and deer, conies, and fowl in incredible abundance, and using the author's own phrase, the woods are not such as you find in Bohemia, Muscovy, or Hercynia, barren and fruitless, but the highest and reddest cedars of the world, bettering those of the Azores, Indies, or Libanus: pines, cypress, sassafras, the lentisk that beareth mastic, and many other of excellent smell and quality. Till the third day we saw not any of the people, then in a little boat three of them appeared. One of them went on shore, to whom we rowed, and he attended us without any sign of fear; after he had spoke much though we understood not a word, of his own accord he came boldly aboard us. We gave him a shirt, a hat, wine and meat, which he liked well; and after he had well viewed the barks and us, he went away in his own boat; and within a quarter of a mile of us in half an hour, had laden his boat with fish, with which he came again to the point of land, and there divided it in two parts, pointing one part to the ship, the other to the pinnace, and so departed.

The next day came divers boats, and in one of them the king's brother, with forty or fifty men, proper people, and in their behaviour very civil; his name was Granganameo, the king is called Wingina, the country Wingandacoa. Leaving his boats a little from our ships, he came with his train to the point, where spreading a mat he sat down. Though we came to him well armed, he made signs to us to sit down without any show of fear, stroking his head and breast, and also ours, to express his love. After he had made a long speech unto us, we presented him with divers toys, which he kindly accepted. He was greatly regarded by his people, for none of them did sit nor speak a word, but four, on whom we bestowed presents also, but he took all from them, making signs all things did belong to him.

The king himself, in a conflict with a king, his next neighbour and mortal enemy, was shot in two places through the body and the thigh, yet recovered: whereby he lay at his chief town six days' journey from thence.

A day or two after showing them what we had, Granganameo taking most liking to a pewter dish, made a hole in it, hung it about his neck for a breastplate: for which he gave us twenty deer skins, worth twenty crowns: and for a copper kettle, fifty skins, worth fifty crowns. Much other truck we had, and after two days he came aboard, and did eat and drink with us very merrily. Not long after he brought his wife and children; they were of mean stature, but well favoured and very bashful. She had a long coat of leather, and about her forehead a band of white coral, and so had her husband; in her ears were bracelets of pearl, hanging down to her middle, of the bigness of great peas. The rest of the women had pendants of copper, and the noblemen five or six in an ear; his apparel as his wives', only the women wear their hair long on both sides, and the men but on one; they are of colour yellow, but their hair is black, yet we saw children that had very fair chestnut coloured hair.

After that these women had been here with us, there came down from all parts great store of people, with leather, coral, and divers kind of dyes, but when Granganameo was present, none durst trade but himself and them that wore red copper on their heads, as he did. Whenever he came, he would signify by so many fires he came with so many boats, that we might know his strength. Their boats are but one great tree, which is but burnt in the form of a trough with gins and fire, till it be as they would have it. For an armour he would have engaged us a bag of pearl, but we refused, as not regarding it, that we might the better learn where it grew. He was very just of his promise, for oft we trusted him, and he would come within his day to keep his word. He sent us commonly every day a brace of bucks, conies, hares and fish, sometimes melons, walnuts, cucumbers, peas and divers roots. This author saith, their corn groweth three times in five months; in May they sow, in July reap; in June they sow, in August reap; in July sow, in August reap. We put some of our peas in the ground, which in ten days were fourteen inches high.

The soil is most plentiful, sweet, wholesome, and fruitful of all other; there are about fourteen several sorts of sweet smelling timber trees; the most parts of the underwood, bays and such like, such oaks as we, but far greater and better...

This discovery was so welcome into England that it pleased her Majesty to call this country of Wingandacoa, Virginia.

CAPTAIN JOHN SMITH, *The Generall Historie of Virginia* 1624

THE SEA

Colonization

(a) Utopia

Gonzalo. Had I plantation of this isle, my lord...
And were the king on't, what would I do?...
I' the commonwealth I would by contraries
Execute all things; for no kind of traffic
Would I admit; no name of magistrate;
Letters should not be known; riches, poverty,
And use of service, none; contract, succession,
Bourn, bound of land, tilth, vineyard, none;
No use of metal, corn, or wine, or oil;
No occupation; all men idle, all;
And women too, but innocent and pure...
All things in common nature should produce
Without sweat or endeavour: treason, felony,
Sword, pike, knife, gun, or need of any engine,
Would I not have; but nature should bring forth,
Of its own kind, all foison, all abundance,
To feed my innocent people.

The Tempest, II. i. 150—171

(b) *Virginia* 1607

It might well be thought, a country so fair as Virginia is and a people so tractable, would long ere this have been quietly possessed, to the satisfaction of the adventurers, and the eternising of the memory of those that effected it. But because all the world do see a defailment, this following treatise shall give satisfaction to all indifferent readers how the business hath been carried: where no doubt they will easily understand and answer to their question, how it came to pass there was no better speed and success in these proceedings.

Captain Bartholomew Gosnoll, one of the first movers of this plantation, having many years solicited many of his friends, but found small assistance, at last prevailed with some gentlemen, as Captain John Smith, Master Edward-Maria Wingfield, Master Robert Hunt and divers others, who depended a year upon his projects; but nothing could be effected, till by their great charge and industry, it came to be apprehended by certain of the nobility, gentry and merchants; so that his Majesty by his letters patent, gave commission for establishing councils,

266

to direct here, and to govern and to execute there. To effect this was spent another year, and by that, three ships were provided, one of a hundred tons, another of forty, and a pinnace of twenty. The transportation of the company was committed to Captain Christopher Newport, a mariner well practised for the western parts of America. But their orders for government were put in a box, not to be opened nor the governors known, until they arrived in Virginia.

On the nineteenth of December, 1606, we set sail from Blackwall, but by unprosperous winds were kept six weeks in the sight of England; all which time Master Hunt, our preacher, was so weak and sick that few expected his recovery. Yet although he were but twenty miles from his habitation (the time we were in the Downs), and notwithstanding the stormy weather, nor the scandalous imputations (of some few, little better than atheists, of the greatest rank amongst us) suggested against him; all this could never force from him so much as a seeming desire to leave the business, but he preferred the service of God in so good a voyage, before any affection to contest with his godless foes, whose disastrous designs (could they have prevailed) had even then overthrown the business, so many discontents did then arise, had he not with the water of patience, and his godly exhortations (but chiefly by his true devoted examples) quenched those flames of envy and dissension.

We watered at the Canaries, we traded with the savages at Dominica, three weeks we spent in refreshing ourselves amongst these West India Isles; in Guadelupe we found a bath so hot, as in it we boiled pork as well as over the fire. And at a little isle called Monica we took from the bushes with our hands near two hogsheads full of birds in three or four hours. In Nevis, Mona and the Virgin Isles we spent some time, where, with a loathsome beast like a crocodile called a gwayn, tortoises, pelicans, parrots, and fishes, we daily feasted.

Gone from thence in search of Virginia, the company was not a little discomforted, seeing the mariners had three days passed their reckoning and found no land; so that Captain Ratcliffe (captain of the pinnace) rather desired to bear up the helm to return for England than make further search. But God, the guider of all good actions, forcing them by an extreme storm to hull all night, did drive them by his providence to their desired port, beyond all their expectations; for never any of them had seen that coast.

The first land they made they called Cape Henry; where thirty of them, recreating themselves on shore, were assaulted by five savages, who hurt two of the English very dangerously.

That night was the box opened and the orders read, in which Bartholomew Gosnoll, John Smith, Edward Wingfield, Christopher Newport, John Ratcliffe, John Martin, and George Kendall, were named to be the council, and to choose a president amongst them for a year, who with the council should govern. Matters of moment were to be examined by a jury, but determined by the major part of the council, in which the president had two voices.

Until the thirteenth of May they sought a place to plant in; then the council was sworn, Master Wingfield was chosen president, and an oration made, why Captain Smith was not admitted of the council as the rest.

Now falleth every man to work, the council to contrive the fort, the rest cut down trees to make place to pitch their tents; some provide clapboard to relade the ships, some make gardens, some nets, etc. The savages often visited us kindly. The president's overweening jealousy would admit no exercise at arms, or fortification but the boughs of trees cast together in the form of a half moon by the extraordinary pains and diligence of Captain Kendall....What toil we had with so small a power to guard our workmen a-days, watch all night, resist our enemies, and effect our business, to relade the ships, cut down trees, and prepare the ground to plant our corn, etc., I refer to the reader's consideration.

Six weeks being spent in this manner, Captain Newport (who was hired only for our transportation) was to return with the ships. Now Captain Smith, who all this time from their departure from the Canaries was restrained as a prisoner, upon the scandalous suggestions of some of the chief (envying his repute) who feigned he intended to usurp the government, murder the council, and make himself king, that his confederates were dispersed in all three ships, and that divers of his confederates that revealed it, would affirm it; for this he was committed as a prisoner. Thirteen weeks he remained thus suspected, and by that time the ships should return they pretended out of their commiserations to refer him to the Council in England to receive a check, rather than by particulating his designs to make him so odious to the world, as to touch his life, or utterly overthrow his reputation. But he so much scorned their charity, and publicly defied the uttermost of their cruelty; he wisely prevented their policies, though he could not suppress their envies; yet so well he demeaned himself in this business, as all the company did see his innocency and his adversaries' malice, and those suborned to accuse him accused his accusers of subornation. Many untruths were alleged against him, but, being so apparently disproved, begat a general hatred in the hearts of the company against such unjust commanders, tnat the president was adjudged to give him two hundred pounds, so that all he had was seized upon, in part of satisfaction, which Smith presently returned to the store for the general use of the colony.

Many were the mischiefs that daily sprung from their ignorant (yet ambitious) spirits; but the good doctrine and exhortation of our preacher, Master Hunt, reconciled them, and caused Captain Smith to be admitted of the council.

The next day all received the communion, the day following the savages voluntarily desired peace, and Captain Newport returned for England with news; leaving in Virginia one hundred, the fifteenth of June 1607.

CAPTAIN JOHN SMITH, *The Generall Historie of Virginia* 1624

Travellers' Tales*

I spake of most disastrous chances,
Of moving accidents by flood and field,
Of hair-breadth 'scapes i' the imminent deadly breach,
Of being taken by the insolent foe
And sold to slavery, of my redemption thence
And portance in my travel's history;
Wherein of antres vast and deserts idle,
Rough quarries, rocks and hills whose heads touch heaven
It was my hint to speak, such was the process;
And of the Cannibals that each other eat,
The Anthropophagi, and men whose heads
Do grow beneath their shoulders.

Othello, I. iii. 134—145

* See also pp. 70, 71.

269

Lepidus. What manner o' thing is your crocodile?

Antony. It is shaped, sir, like itself, and it is as broad as it hath breadth; it is just so high as it is, and moves with its own organs; it lives by that which nourisheth it; and the elements once out of it, it transmigrates.

Lepidus. What colour is it of?

Antony. Of its own colour too.

Lepidus. 'Tis a strange serpent.

Antony. 'Tis so; and the tears of it are wet.

Antony and Cleopatra, II. vii. 47—56

Civis. Gentle master, I cannot tell what to call you, nor of what country you are.

Mendax. Sir, I was born near unto Tunbridge, where fine knives are made; my name is Mendax, a younger brother lineally descended of an ancient house before the conquest. We give three whetstones in gules, with no difference, and upon our crest a left hand, with a horn upon the thumb, and a knife in the hand. The supporters are a fox on the one side, and a friar on the other side. And of late I travelled into Terra Florida, whereas I felt both wealth and woe; the black ox never trod upon my foot before; a dog hath but a day. We are born all to travail, and as for me I have but little to lose. Yet I am a gentleman, and cannot find it in my heart to play the slave, or go to cart; I never could abide it, by the mass.

Civis. You speak like a wise man. I perceive by your behaviour that you have been well brought up. I pray you, where is that land?

Mendax. Many thousand miles beyond Torrida Zona, on the equinoctial line, in the longitude near unto the pole antarctic; it is an hundred thousand miles long, and is in the part named America; and by the way are the islands called Fortunato or Canaria, whose west parts be situated in the third climate.

Civis. It was a dangerous travel into that country. Where landed you? At what place?

Mendax. We sailed to the islands of Portum Sanctum, and then to Madeira, in which were sundry countries and islands, as Eractelenty, Magnefortis, Grancanary, Teneriffe, Palme Ferro, &c. And our captain went with his soldiers to land. And at our first coming near unto the river in one of these islands, as we refreshed ourselves among the date trees, in the land of the palms, by the sweet wells, we did, to the great fear of us all, see a great battle between the dragon and the unicorn; and, as God would, the unicorn thrust the dragon to the heart; and, again, the dragon with his tail stung the unicorn to death. Here is a piece of his horn; the blood of dragons is rich; that battle was worth two hundred marks to our captain. Then we travelled further into Teneriffe, into an exceeding high mountain, above the middle region, whereas we had great plenty of rock alum, and might well hear an heavenly harmony among the stars. The moon was near hand us with marvellous heat; and when we came down at the hill-foot grew many gross herbs, as lovage, laserpitium, acanthus and solanum: and whether it was by the eating of solanum or no, there was a great mighty man naked and hairy, in a deep sleep, whom we gently suffered to lie still. He had a great beard in which a bird did breed, and brought her young ones meat; this man slept half a year and waked not. Our captain declared unto us that the spials had viewed the land, and how that our enemies were at hand. The next day most fearful people painted with sundry colours approached in strange beasts' skins, with flint so were their shafts and darts made, with whom we fought and slew and took some, and yet the people so assaulted us, that with much difficulty we recovered our barks. And then we sailed forth, and chanced to let fall our sounding-lead new-tallowed, whereupon did stick gold. With all speed we sent down our divers, and so within three days we gathered thirty hogsheads of fine gold, besides two butts of orient pearls; all the shore was full of coral. From thence we sailed to the great isle called Madagastat, in Scorea, where were kings, Mahometans by religion, black as devils. Some had no heads, but eyes in their breasts. Some, when it rained, covered all the whole body with one foot. That land did abound in elephants' teeth; the men did eat camels' and lions' flesh. Musk and civet in every place did abound, and the mother of pearl, whereof the people made their platters to put in their meat; they dwell among spice; the ground is moist with oil of precious trees. Plenty of wine out of grapes as big as this loaf; much pepper; they cannot tell what to do with sugar; but that their merchants of Maabar, twenty days' journey off, do come and take of their goods frankly for nothing; but some of them do bring iron to make edge tools, for which they have for one pound twenty pound of fine gold. Their pots, pans and all vessel are clean gold garnished with diamonds. I did see swine feed in them.

Civis. Did you see no strange fowls there and fishes?

Mendax. In the isle called Ruc, in the great Can's land, I did see mermaids and satyrs with other fishes by night came four miles from the sea, and climbed into trees, and did eat dates and nutmegs, with whom the apes and baboons had much fighting, yelling and crying. The people of that land do live by eating the flesh of women. In this land did I see an ape play at tick-tack and after at Irish on the tables with one of that land; and also a parrot give one of their gentlewomen a checkmate at chess. There geese dance trenchmore.

Civis. God keep us from those cruel people.

Mendax. But, sir, as for birds, they are not only infinite in numbers, but also in kinds; some voices most sweet and some most fearful; nightingales as big as geese, owls greater than some horse; and there are birds that do lie in a rock where dragons are, whose feathers on their wings are thirty foot long, the quill as big as a cannon royal. Also I heard parrots dispute in philosophy, fresh[?] in Greek, and sing descant. Also there are a people called Astomii, which live very long, and neither eat nor drink, but only live by air and the smell of fruits. In Selenetide there are women, contrary to the nature of other women, do lay eggs and hatch them, from whom do children come fifty times greater than those which are born of women. There did I see Scipodes having but one foot, which is so broad that they cover all their bodies for the rain and the sun.

Item, I did see men having feet like horse, called Ippopodes.

Item, I did see the Satyrs, half men and half goats, playing upon cornets.

Item, I did see Apothami, half horse and half man.

Item, I played at tables with the people called Fanesii, whose ears were as long as cloaks, covering all their bodies; near them is the great city called O, four hundred miles within the wall; the wall was brass, two thousand gates, six hundred bridges as big as London Bridge; the city paved with gold. Naked men dwell there with two heads and six hands every man. There did I see apes play at tennis.

Civis. I pray you is there any plenty of precious stones?

Mendax, Very many, but hard to come by; but in the island Zanzibar is much plenty of ambergris, that they make clay for their houses withal, there, if we had holden together like friends, we might have gotten a world. When I do remember it, alas, alas, every man is but for himself; you may consider what division is; emeralds, rubies, turkies, diamonds, and sapphires were sold when we came thither first for the weight of iron; a thousand rich turkesses were sold for three shillings four pence, to be short, one with another, after three shillings four pence a peck. Our men gathered up carbuncles and diamonds with rakes under the spice trees.

Civis. How chance you brought none home in to this realm?

Mendax. Oh, sir, we filled two ships with fine gold, three ships with ambergris, musk and unicorns' horns, and two tall barks with precious stones, and sailed by the adamant stones, which will draw iron unto them, and so cast away the greatest riches in Heathenness or Christendom.

WILLIAM BULLEIN, *A Dialogue against the Pestilence* 1573

CONCLUSION

An Elizabethan Day

And then he drew a dial from his poke,
And, looking on it with lack-lustre eye,
Says very wisely, "It is ten o'clock;
Thus may we see," quoth he, "how the world wags:
'Tis but an hour ago since it was nine,
And after one hour more 'twill be eleven;
And so, from hour to hour we ripe and ripe,
And then from hour to hour we rot and rot,
And thereby hangs a tale."

As You Like It, II. vii. 20—28

One of the Clock.

It is now the first hour and time is, as it were, stepping out of darkness and stealing towards the day: the cock calls to his hen and bids her beware of the fox, and the watch, having walked the streets, take a nap upon a stall: the bell-man calls to the maids to look to their locks, their fire and their light, and the child in the cradle calls to the nurse for a dug: the cat sits watching behind the cupboard for a mouse, and the flea sucks on sweet flesh, till he is ready to burst with blood: the spirits of the studious start out of their dreams, and if they cannot fall asleep again, then to the book and the wax candle: the dog at the door frays the thief from the house, and the thief within the house may hap to be about his business. In some places bells are rung to certain orders: but the quiet sleeper never tells the clock. Not to dwell too long upon it, I hold it the farewell of the night and the forerunner to the day, the spirit's watch and reason's workmaster. Farewell.

AN ELIZABETHAN DAY

Two of the Clock.

It is now the second hour and the point of the dial hath stepped over the first stroke, and now time begins to draw back the curtain of the night: the cock again calls to his hen, and the watch begin to bustle toward their discharge: the bell-man hath made a great part of his walk, and the nurse begins to huggle the child to the dug: the cat sits playing with the mouse which she hath catched, and the dog with his barking wakes the servants of the house: the studious now are near upon waking, and the thief will be gone, for fear of being taken: the foresters now be about their walks, and yet stealers sometime cozen the keepers: warreners now begin to draw homeward, and far dwellers from the town will be on the way to the market: the soldier now looks towards the *cour de garde*, and the corporal takes care for the relief of the watch: the earnest scholar will be now at his book, and the thrifty husbandman will rouse towards his rising: the seaman will now look out for light, and if the wind be fair, he calls for a can of beer: the fishermen now take the benefit of the tide, and he that bobs for eels will not be without worms. In sum, I hold it much of the nature of the first hour, but somewhat better. And to conclude, I think it the enemy of sleep and the entrance to exercise. Farewell.

Three of the Clock.

It is now the third hour, and the windows of heaven begin to open, and the sun begins to colour the clouds in the sky, before he shew his face to the world: now are the spirits of life, as it were, risen out of death : the cock calls the servants to their day's work, and the grass horses are fetched from the pastures: the milk-maids begin to look toward their dairy, and the good housewife begins to look about the house: the porridge pot is on for the servants' breakfast, and hungry stomachs will soon be ready for their victual: the sparrow begins to chirp about the house, and the birds in the bushes will bid them welcome to the field: the shepherd sets on his pitch on the fire, and fills his tar-pot ready for his flock : the wheel and the reel begin to be set ready, and a merry song makes the work seem easy : the ploughman falls to harness his horses, and the thresher begins to look toward the barn: the scholar that loves learning will be hard at his

CONCLUSION

book, and the labourer by great will be walking toward his work. In brief it is a parcel of time to good purpose, the exercise of nature and the entrance into art.   Farewell.

Four of the Clock.

It is now the fourth hour, and the sun begins to send her beams abroad, whose glimmering brightness no eye can behold: now crows the cock lustily and claps his wings for joy of the light, and with his hens leaps lightly from his roost: now are the horses at their chaff and provender, the servants at breakfast, the milk-maid gone to the field, and the spinner at the wheel; and the shepherd with his dog are going toward the fold: now the beggars rouse them out of the hedges, and begin their morning craft; but if the constable come, beware the stocks: the birds now begin to flock, and the sparhawk begins to prey for his aerie: the thresher begins to stretch his long arms, and the thriving labourer will fall hard to his work: the quick-witted brain will be quoting of places, and the cunning workman will be trying of his skill: the hounds begin to be coupled for the chase, and the spaniels follow the falconer to the field: travellers begin to look toward the stable, where an honest hostler is worthy his reward: the soldier now is upon discharge of his watch, and the captain with his company may take as good rest as they can.   In sum, I thus conclude of it: I hold it the messenger of action and the watch of reason.   Farewell.

Five of the Clock.

It is now five of the clock, and the sun is going apace upon his journey; and fie sluggards who would be asleep: the bells ring to prayer, and the streets are full of people, and the highways are stored with travellers: the scholars are up and going to school, and the rods are ready for the truants' correction: the maids are at milking, and the servants at plough, and the wheel goes merrily, while the mistress is by: the capons and the chickens must be served without door, and the hogs cry till they have their swill: the shepherd is almost gotten to his fold, and the herd begins to blow his horn through the town: the blind fiddler is up with his dance and his song, and the ale-house door is unlocked for good fellows: the hounds begin to find after the hare, and horse and foot follow after the cry: the

276

traveller now is well on his way, and if the weather be fair, he walks with the better cheer: the carter merrily whistles to his horse, and the boy with his sling casts stones at the crows: the lawyer now begins to look on his case, and if he give good counsel, he is worthy of his fee. In brief, not to stay too long upon it, I hold it the necessity of labour and the note of profit. Farewell.

Six of the Clock.

It is now the first hour, the sweet time of the morning, and the sun at every window calls the sleepers from their beds: the marigold begins to open her leaves, and the dew on the ground doth sweeten the air: the falconers now meet with many a fair flight, and the hare and the hounds have made the huntsman good sport: the shops in the city begin to shew their wares, and the market people have taken their places: the scholars now have their forms, and whosoever cannot say his lesson must presently look for absolution: the forester now is drawing home to his lodge, and if his deer be gone, he may draw after cold scent: now begins the curst mistress to put her girls to their tasks, and a lazy hilding will do hurt among good workers: now the mower falls to whetting of his scythe, and the beaters of hemp give a ho! to every blow: the ale-knight is at his cup ere he can well see his drink, and the beggar is as nimble-tongued, as if he had been at it all day: the fishermen now are at the crayer for their oysters, and they will never tire crying, while they have one in their basket. In sum, not to be tedious, I hold it the sluggard's shame and the labourer's praise. Farewell.

Seven of the Clock.

It is now the seventh hour, and time begins to set the world hard to work; the milk-maids in their dairy to their butter and their cheese, the ploughmen to their ploughs and their barrows in the field, the scholars to their lessons, the lawyers to their cases, the merchants to their accounts, the shop-men to "What lack you?" and every trade to his business. Oh 'tis a world to see how life leaps about the limbs of the healthful: none but finds something to do: the wise to study, the strong to labour, the fantastic to make love, the poet to make verses, the player to con his part, and the musician to try his note: every one in his

277

CONCLUSION

quality and according to his condition, sets himself to some exercise, either of the body or the mind: and therefore since it is a time of much labour and great use, I will thus briefly conclude of it: I hold it the enemy of idleness and employer of industry. Farewell.

Eight of the Clock.

It is now the eighth hour, and good stomachs are ready for a breakfast: the huntsman now calls in his hounds, and at the fall of the deer the horns go apace: now begin the horses to breathe and the labourer to sweat, and, with quick hands, work rids apace: now the scholars make a charm in the schools and *ergo* keeps astir in many a false argument: now the chapmen fall to furnish the shops, the market people make away with their ware, the tavern-hunters taste of the t'other wine, and the nappy ale makes many a drunken noll: now the thresher begins to fall to his breakfast and eat apace, and work apace rids the corn quickly away: now the piper looks what he hath gotten since day, and the beggar, if he have hit well, will have a pot of the best: the traveller now begins to water his horse, and, if he were early up, perhaps a bait will do well. The ostler now makes clean his stables, and, if guests come in, he is not without his welcome. In conclusion, for all I find in it, I hold it the mind's travail and the body's toil. Farewell.

Nine of the Clock.

It is now the ninth hour, and the sun is gotten up well toward his height, and the sweating traveller begins to feel the burden of his way: the scholar now falls to conning of his lesson, and the lawyer at the bar falls to pleading of his case: the soldier now makes many a weary step in his march, and the amorous courtier is almost ready to go out of his chamber: the market now grows to be full of people, and the shopmen now are in the heat of the market: the falconers now find it too hot flying, and the huntsmen begin to grow weary of their sport: the birders now take in their nets and their rods, and the fishermen send their fish to the market: the tavern and the ale-house are almost full of guests, and Westminster and Guild Hall are not without a word or two on both sides: the carriers now are loading out of town, and not a letter but must be paid for ere it

278

pass: the crier now tries the strength of his throat, and the bear-ward leads his bear home after his challenge: the players' bills are almost all set up, and the clerk of the market begins to shew his office. In sum, in this hour there is much to do, as well in the city, as the country: and therefore to be short, I will thus make my conclusion: I hold it the toil of wit and the trial of reason. Farewell.

Ten of the Clock.

It is now the tenth hour, and now preparation is to be made for dinner: the trenchers must be scraped and the napkins folded, the salt covered and the knives scoured and the cloth laid, the stools set ready and all for the table: there must be haste in the kitchen for the boiled and the roast, provision in the cellar for wine, ale and beer: the pantler and the butler must be ready in their office, and the usher of the hall must marshal the serving-men: the hawk must be set on the perch, and the dogs put into the kennel, and the guests that come to dinner must be invited against the hour: the scholars now fall to construe and parse, and the lawyer makes his client either a man or a mouse: the chapmen now draw home to their inns, and the shopmen fall to folding up their wares: the ploughman now begins to grow towards home, and the dairy maid, after her work, falls to cleansing of her vessels: the cook is cutting sops for broth, and the butler is chipping of loaves for the table: the minstrels begin to go towards the taverns, and the cursed crew visit the vile places. In sum, I thus conclude of it: I hold it the messenger to the stomach and the spirit's recreation. Farewell.

Eleven of the Clock.

It is now the eleventh hour, children must break up school, lawyers must make home to their houses, merchants to the exchange, and gallants to the ordinary: the dishes set ready for the meat, and the glasses half full of fair water: now the market people make towards their horses, and the beggars begin to draw near the towns: the porridge, put off the fire, is set a cooling for the plough folk, and the great loaf and the cheese are set ready on the table: colleges and halls ring to dinner, and a scholar's commons is soon digested: the rich man's guests are at curtsy, and "I thank you": and the poor man's feast is "Welcome, and God be with you": the page is ready with his knife and his trencher, and the meat will be half cold, ere the guests can agree on their places: the cook voids the kitchen, and the butler the buttery, and the serving-men stand all ready at the dresser: the children are called to say grace before dinner, and the nice people rather look than eat: the gates be locked for fear of the beggars, and the minstrels called in to be ready with their music: the pleasant wit is now breaking a jest, and the hungry man puts his jaws to their proof. In sum, to conclude my opinion of it, I hold it the epicure's joy and the labourer's ease. Farewell.

Twelve of the Clock.

It is now the twelfth hour, the sun is at his height, and the middle of the day: the first course is served in, and the second ready to follow: the dishes have been read over, and the reversion set by: the wine begins to be called for, and who waits not is chidden: talk passeth away time, and when stomachs are full discourses grow dull and heavy, but after fruit and cheese say grace and take away: now the markets are done, the exchange broke up, and the lawyers at dinner, and Duke Humphrey's servants make their walks in Paul's: the shopmen keep their shops, and their servants go to dinner: the traveller begins to call for a reckoning, and goes into the stable to see his horse eat his provender: the ploughman now is at the bottom of his dish, and the labourer draws out his dinner out of his bag: the beasts of the field take rest after their feed, and the birds of the air are at juke in the bushes: the lamb lies sucking while the ewe chews the cud, and the rabbit will scarce peep out of her burrow: the hare sits close asleep in her muse, while the dogs sit waiting for a bone from the trencher. In brief, for all I find of it, I thus conclude in it: I hold it the stomach's pleasure and the spirit's weariness. Farewell.

Midnight.

Now is the sun withdrawn into his bedchamber, the windows of heaven are shut up, and silence with darkness have made a walk over the whole earth, and time is tasked to work upon the worst actions: yet virtue being herself, is never weary of well doing, while the best spirits are studying for the body's rest: dreams and visions are the haunters of troubled spirits,

while nature is most comforted in the hope of the morning:
the body now lies as a dead lump, while sleep, the pride of ease,
lulls the senses of the slothful: the tired limbs now cease from
their labours, and the studious brains give over their business:
the bed is now an image of the grave, and the prayer of the
faithful makes the pathway to Heaven: lovers now enclose
a mutual content, while gracious minds have no wicked imaginations: thieves, wolves and foxes now fall to their prey, but
a strong lock and a good wit will aware much mischief: and
he that trusteth in God will be safe from the Devil. Farewell.

The Conclusion.

And thus to conclude, for that it grows late, and a nod or
two with an heavy eye makes me fear to prove a plain noddy,
entreating your patience till to-morrow, and hoping you will
censure mildly of this my fantastic labour, wishing I may hereafter please your senses with a better subject than this: I will in
the mean time pray for your prosperity, and end with the English phrase, " God give you good night."

NICHOLAS BRETON, *Fantastickes* 1626

Be cheerful, sir:
Our revels now are ended. These our actors,
As I foretold you, were all spirits and
Are melted into air, into thin air:
And, like the baseless fabric of this vision,
The cloud-capp'd towers, the gorgeous palaces,
The solemn temples, the great globe itself,
Yea, all which it inherit, shall dissolve
And, like this insubstantial pageant faded,
Leave not a rack behind. We are such stuff
As dreams are made on, and our little life
Is rounded with a sleep.

The Tempest, IV. i. 147—158

GLOSSARY AND NOTES

Acarum vulgare. Common myrtle.

Aconitum. Monkshood.

Adamant. Loadstone, magnet.

Admirals, i.e. flagships.

Agaric. A purgative made from fungi.

Ale-conner, or Ale-taster, an officer appointed to test the ale and bread in a parish or town. Shakespeare's father was made ale-conner of Stratford in 1557.

Alleyn (Edward). 1566-1626. One of the greatest actors of the age. Founder of Dulwich College.

Almain, i.e. German.

Angel. Gold coin, about 10/-.

Antic. Buffoon, contortionist, òr grotesque pageant.

Antic-woven. Fancifully embroidered.

Apuleian ears, i.e. asses' ears.

Arcadian and Euphuized gentlewoman, i.e. talking the fashionable jargon of Lyly's *Euphues* or Sidney's *Arcadia*.

Argent. Money, silver.

Arimaspi, i.e. the Arimaspians, a mythical one-eyed people of Scythia always at war with the Gryphons (= Grips).

Aristolochia longa. The clematis.

Armados, i.e. Spanish vessels.

Arming doublets, i.e. military doublets.

Arts-vanishing. p. 132. McKerrow suggests "so skilfully that the art is concealed."

Assize. Standard measurement.

Atomies. Atoms, motes.

Augurate. To divine.

Aurum potabile. A legendary medicine largely composed of gold. Possibly denotes in Elizabethan times a fashionable quack drug.

Avoid. To turn out, empty or clear away.

Baby-caps. ?Toy-caps.

Bale. The set of dice for any special game, usually three.

Bandogs, i.e. band-dogs, tied up in order to make them fierce.

Bank, i.e. the South side of the Thames.

Barbarian fleeces. ?Cloaks from Barbary.

Barns. Children.

Barred. See False dice.

Bastinado. A thorough thrashing.

Bastone. = bastinado.

Battle. ?Put into the common stock.

Beagle, i.e. to smell out like a dog.

Beaver. Visor. Piece of cloth across the mouth.

Beggar's bush. A notorious spot by the roadside between Huntingdon and Caxton where beggars kept rendezvous.

Berayed. Defiled.

Beseen. Dressed.

Besmeared. Befouled.

Bethlehem, i.e. the asylum of St Mary of Bethlehem, now called Bedlam.

Bird-eyed. Quick to see or imagine danger.

Bit. Cant term for money.

Biting (of a bullet). It was customary to bite the bullet in order to raise ridges upon it and so prevent it falling out of the gun.

Bittorn, or Bittour. Bittern.

Black-jacks. Leather bottles.

Black ox trod upon my foot. Proverbial expression meaning "trouble came upon me."

Block. Mould for a hat.

Blue-coats, i.e. servants.

GLOSSARY AND NOTES

Borders. Plaits or braids of hair worn round the forehead or temples.

Boss. To cover with bosses or knobs.

Bouge. To bilge, stave in the ship's bottom.

Bowdled. With feathers ruffled.

Bridewell. A house of correction for women.

Bridges'. ?Bridget's, i.e. his wife's.

Britanny, i.e. Britain.

Broker, i.e. pawnbroker.

Bucklersbury. A street in London chiefly inhabited by druggists.

Budge. Lambskin with the wool dressed outwards, a very cheap fur.

Budget. Leathern bag.

Bug. Bogey.

Bum card. A raised or otherwise marked card, used for cheating at play.

Bush, i.e. ivy-bush outside a tavern. A bunch or tuft of hair.

Calabrian flood. A contemporary pamphlet foretold the advent of floods from the appearance of certain stars in Calabria.

Calicut. Town in India near Madras.

Calms. Frames.

Cambyses. The chief character in an early Elizabethan tragedy, proverbial for rant.

Campanus, i.e. Campani, a 15th century Italian writer of Latin epigrams.

Campo. ?The playground.

Canaries. Spanish dance.

Cantharides. Spanish flies used for blistering.

Cap-case. Bag or wallet.

Caraways. Sweetmeats containing carraway seeds.

Carbonado. To cut open and slash with a knife for grilling. To grill.

Carcanet. Necklace or ornamental collar.

Card. Guide, directory.

Carted, i.e. taken to Tyburn for execution.

Carted, i.e. exposed like a criminal to public ignominy.

Casual marts. ?Chance bargains.

Caterpillars, i.e. brokers, extortioners.

Caul. Net.

Chained. p. 10. The meaning of the passage seems to be that the country gentleman made himself ridiculous at court by appearing with a gold chain, which was the mark of a steward.

Challenge. Claim.

Chamber. ?City treasury.

Chandler's treasure. p. 13. ?A large store.

Changeling. p. 102. Idiot, madman. The passage is apparently a reference to the shaving of madmen when in confinement.

Charenton bridge, i.e. Charenton-le-pont on the Maine. It has a famous bridge of ten arches.

Chase. p. 257. Porthole at the bow.

Cheapen. Buy, bargain for.

Cheats. False dice.

Checkmate. p. 46. "Go checkmate with justice and coin out countenance ofttimes equity" = make friends with the judges and often win the case by means of influence.

Children. Boy-actors.

Clarissimoes. Grandees of Venice.

Clause. Conclusion.

Cledgy. Cledge = clay.

Club. ?Bat.

Clyster. Enema.

Cockatrice. Mistress, harlot.

Codiniac. Quince-marmalade.

Cofferer. Officer in royal household, next to controller.

Coffin. p. 227. i.e. pie.

Combust. p. 46. "Faces being combust with many fiery inflammatives." One form of a common Elizabethan pun upon a writ known as "fieri facias."

Commacerate. To harass, torment.

Commodity. Convenience. p. 120. "Commodities of proclamations," etc. In order to circumvent the laws against usury, money-lenders were in the habit of selling for a small sum some worthless commodity to needy persons, who

GLOSSARY AND NOTES

immediately resold it to the usurer at a high price.

Commorant. Resident.

Complexion. Humour, disposition.

Composition. To bring to composition=to bring to terms.

Consort. A band of musicians, choir.

Contrivitions, i.e. contrivances.

Cordelier. A Franciscan friar.

Cornelis of Chelmsford. I can find nothing about this gentleman.

Corn-trees, i.e. cornel tree or cornelian cherry.

Cosset. Pet lamb.

Cot-house. Shelter, shed.

Counter. Debtors' prison. One of these stood in the Poultry, Cheapside.

Counterfeit crank. A rogue who feigns illness or disease.

Counter-tenor. Male alto voice.

Court-cupboard. Movable sideboard.

Cozen. Substantive=a dupe. Verb =to cheat.

Crank. One suffering from a disease.

Crayer. Small vessel.

Creak. "To cry creak." p. 20. =to yield.

Cross. A coin. Misfortune.

Crossbar-shot, i.e. expanding bullets or cannon balls.

Culling. Cuddling, hugging.

Cullion. Mean wretch.

Cullis. Meat broth.

Cup-shotten. Intoxicated.

Curst. Shrewish.

Cut and long-tail, i.e. all sorts of dogs.

Dagswain. Coarse coverlet of rough shaggy cloth.

Dawcock. Jackdaw, silly fellow.

Decard, i.e. discard.

Decoy. A card game.

Derrick. A hangman of the period.

Descant. Musical variations.

Desperate. p. 10. Reckless.

Difference. p. 270. Heraldic term: an alteration in a coat of arms to distinguish a junior branch from the main line of the family.

Dismal day. p. 29. i.e. one of the *dies mali* (=dismal) Jan. 1st and 25th, the unlucky days upon which the plagues of Egypt were supposed to have taken place.

Dispend. Spend.

Disquisition. Inquisition.

Divulge. Publish.

Dizard. A talkative fool.

Dodkin, i.e. a doit.

Dor. Drone, beetle.

Doubt. p. 225. Hesitate, scruple.

Drab. Harlot.

Dragon-water. A popular medicine of the age.

Drawer. Tapster.

Duchy, i.e. Cornwall.

Duke Humphrey's servants. Poor gallants who could not afford to dine and so spent the dinner-hour loitering near Duke Humphrey's monument in St Paul's Walk.

Eleoselinum. Mountain parsley.

Embraiding. Embroidering.

Embusk. To raise the bosom by tight-lacing.

Engines. Instruments of torture.

Ensnarl. Entangle.

Erra Pater. A famous almanac of the period entitled "The prognostication of Erra Pater, a Jew born in Jewry." The astrologer's name is probably an invention.

Euphormio, i.e. *Euphormio Satyricon*, a satirical novel in Latin by John Barclay, published c. 1603.

Even and odd. A dicing game.

Exemplify, i.e. correct the proof by the copy.

Factors. Agents, assistants.

Falling-sickness. Epilepsy.

False dice. *Barred cater-treys*= dice which never turn up the 3 or the 4. *Barred cinque-deuces*=dice which never turn up the 5 or the 2. *Barred six-aces*=dice which never turn up the 6 or the 1. *Flat cater-treys*=dice which always turn up the 3 or the 4. *Flat cinque-deuces*= dice which always turn up the 5 or the 2. *Flat six-aces*=dice which

GLOSSARY AND NOTES

always turn up the 6 or the 1. *Bristle dice*, i.e. dice in which bristles were fixed to influence the throw. *Contraries*: some form of loaded dice. *Demies*: nature or purpose not clear. *Fullam* or *fulham*: a die loaded at the corner. A "high fullam" cast a high number and a "low fullam" a low number. *Gourd* (from O. French =a swindle): nature not clear. *High men or low men*: dice so loaded as to cast high or low numbers. *Light graviers*: possibly dice which were light on one side and heavy on the other. *Long dice*: i.e. with two sides smaller than the others. *Quarters*: possibly dice loaded so as to throw 4.

Farthingale. Hooped petticoat.

Fatist. Fatalist.

Ferula. Ruler.

Fetch over. p. 87. To deceive.

Fire-drake. Fiery dragon, or ? will o' the wisp.

First-man. p. 87. ?i.e. claims a prior right to his fellow waterman to take a fare on board.

Five and five. p. 255. i.e. five make a meal off one rat.

Flankard. ?Wound in the side.

Flat. See **False dice**.

Flat-cap. These caps were once fashionable but now ridiculous.

Flawn. A kind of custard.

Fleer. Grin, mock.

Flews. Large hanging chaps.

Florentine. Kind of meat-pie.

Flush. Fledged.

Foins. Fur trimmings made of beech-marten's skin.

Foist. "A sleight to carry dice easily in the hand" in order to introduce them into the game when the cheater desired.

Forgetive. Inventive.

Fray. Frighten.

Frets. The stops of a musical instrument which regulate the vibration of the strings. Lines on the face.

Friends. p. 247. Relatives, ancestors.

Frounced. Curled, frizzed.

Gage. p. 248. "Laid to gage" i.e. pawned.

Gallery commoner. One who paid a penny for a seat in the gallery of the playhouse.

Galliard. A lively dance.

Galligaskins. Slops. Loose breeches.

Gallimaufry. Medley, hodge-podge.

Gallislops. Galligaskins (q.v.).

Garnish. Money extorted from a new prisoner to buy drink for the other inmates.

Gascoins. Galligaskins (q.v.).

Gazet. Small Venetian coin.

Geason. Rare.

Gellif. Jelly.

Gins. Tools.

Girder. Scoffer.

God's cope. Proverbial expression for a very large sum.

Gorboduc. The earliest regular English tragedy. Produced 1562 by Sackville and Norton. Closely modelled upon Seneca's tragedies; hence Sidney's admiration.

Green-sickness. Chlorosis.

Grips. Gryphons. See **Arimaspi**.

Grogram. Coarse fabric of silk, mohair and wool.

Groundling. One who stood upon the floor of the playhouse, under the open sky.

Gulled. Full of ruts, worn away.

Gulling. Swallowing.

Had-I-wist. Vain hope or supposition.

Hanger. Short sword. Strap suspending a sword from the belt.

Harlots (used of men). Worthless fellows.

Hazard. A game of dice in which the chances are complicated by a number of arbitrary rules.

Headborough. Parish officer, petty constable.

Herb of grace. Rue.

Hilding. Menial, servant.

Hippocras. A mediaeval drink, made of wine flavoured with spices.

Historians, i.e. playwrights.

GLOSSARY AND NOTES

Histories, i.e. plays.
Ho. p. 255. "No ho with him"=
no stopping him.
Hobby-horses. p. 120. Toys, trash.
Hockey. Seedcake distributed at
harvest home.
Hooker. See p. 241.
Hopharlot or hapharlot. Coarse
coverlet made of shreds.
Horn thimble. A thimble used by
cut-purses.
Horse-lock. Padlock.
Huke. Cape, hooded cloak.
Hull. To drift before a storm.
Humour. Moistures of the body of
any kind. Oddities of mind and
disposition.

Imposition. Command.
Indentures. Deeds, contracts. The
scrivener drew up such contracts in
duplicate on a single sheet of paper,
the two copies being then severed
(on the same principle as a tally)
along a zigzag line. Hence "pair
of indentures," and the origin of
the word "*indent*ure" itself.
Infants. Boy actors.
Ingle. p. 66. "An ingle to gold
hat-bands"=a catamite to young
bloods at the university.
Interprets to the puppets, i.e.
does the talking in a puppet show.
Irish. A game like backgammon.

Jack of Lent. A figure of a man
set up to be pelted, like Aunt
Sally, during the Lenten season.
Jagging. An indented border or
fringe.
Jerk. Stroke, blow. Verb=to beat.
Jeronimo and Isabella. The prin-
cipal characters in Kyd's *Spanish
Tragedy*, a very popular play.
Jet. Walk pompously.
Jew's trump. Jew's harp.
Joined bed, i.e. bedstead, considered
a luxury at this period.
Jollop. The wattle of a cock.
Jolly Robins. A favourite expression
with Lodge, but the meaning and
origin are unknown to me. (Not
found in *N.E.D.*)

Journey-man. Hired workman,
one who has ceased to be a prentice
but has not become a master-crafts-
man.
Juke. "At juke (or juck) together"
= chirping or clucking to each
other.
Jump. Exactly.

Kecherman. (1571–1609). A learned
German logician and philosopher.
Ketches. Catches, songs.
Kind. p. 247. "Have by kind'
i.e. inherit.
Knell (Thomas), fl. 1585, an Eliza-
bethan actor.
Knots. Designs.

Latitat. A writ which assumed
the defendant to be lying concealed
and summoned him to the King's
Bench.
Launder. Washerman.
Law-day. Sheriff's court session.
Laystow or laystall. A place where
refuse is put.
Leasings. Lies.
Lecture. Sermon by perambulating
preacher without cure, called a
"lecturer." *Lecture-day.* p. 62.
?The day on which one of these
sermons was delivered.
Leger. Resident ambassador.
Let. Hesitate, prevent.
Lewd. Wicked.
Liberties. The boundaries of the city.
Lightly, i.e. as a general rule.
Lin. To stop.
Lipsius. Justus Lipsius (1547–
1606), a Belgian writer on politics.
Lockram. Coarse linen stuff.
Looking-glasses in the pave-
ment. Polished oak floors.
Louvain. The celebrated Catholic
university founded in 1426.
Luff. To turn the ship towards the
wind.
Luneburg table. Lüneburg, a town
in Hanover. In one of its churches
there was a table of gold from
which, according to legend, a queen
of England had had her crown
made.

GLOSSARY AND NOTES

Make-shifts. Rogues.
Maltworm. A tippler.
Mandilion. A loose kind of overcoat.
Manured. Cultivated, tilled, handled.
Marchpane. Marzipan.
Mean. Middle voice part in music, alto or tenor.
Merchants by the great. p. 8. Wholesale merchants.
Melilot. A herb like clover.
Melpomene. The muse of tragedy.
Midden-hills. Dung-hills.
Mistress. The "Jack" in bowls.
Mithridate. An antidote.
Momus. Carper.
More and no more, i.e. talks without saying anything original.
Morrow-mass. Morning mass.
Mow. To grimace.
Mumchance. A dicing game resembling hazard, apparently played in silence.
Mure. Wright: *Dialect Dict.* gives "husks of fruit from which the juice has been squeezed." Perhaps an old spelling of myrrh.
Muse. Hole in the hedge.
Musk melon. The common melon.

Nappy, i.e. drinks strong enough to cause sleep.
Naturals. Fools.
Neck. p. 117. ?Nick. Perhaps a reference to nicking or marking cards.
Nest, i.e. set (as we say "nest of drawers").
New-spade. See Spade.
Novem or **Novum.** A dice game played by five or six persons, the two principal throws being nine and five.
Noverint-maker. Scrivener.
Nunchion. Snack taken between meals, generally at noon.
Nuncius. Nuntius, messenger.

Obligation. Contract, bond.
Occupy. Traffic in, cultivate.
Ofter offensive. p. 227. i.e. **more** often dangerous than the knife.

Orange-pills. Orange peel.
Ordinary. Eating house. Public feast.
Orient. Bright.
Otto, the Marquess. I have not been able to discover anything about this person.
Oyer and determiner. Court of a judge on circuit.

Packs. Evil confederacies.
Pacolet's horse. Pacolet was a magician in an old romance who made an enchanted horse which could transport him through the air.
Paetum. A corruption of the Brazilian *petum* = tobacco.
Painted cloths. p. 144. Hangings often found on the walls of alehouses (cp. p. 106). Here the word is used to signify the alehouse itself.
Painted sheath. ?Gallant exterior.
Pakers. Vagrants, strollers.
Parcel-gilt. Partly gilded.
Parker, Martin. A famous ballad writer.
Pass. p. 143. "Better to pass," i.e. better off.
Passage. A dicing game played by two persons using three dice.
Peise. To poise, weigh.
Penner. A case to hold pens.
Penniless-bench. Roadside seat.
Pentaphyllon. Cinquefoil.
Perpetuana. A durable wool fabric.
Persian lock. p. 168. ?Misprint for "Parisian."
Pettifoggers. Petty legal practitioners.
Pick. To knock down. To pierce.
Piecing. Patch.
Pilch. A leather coat.
Pilcher. Scabbard.
Pilliwinks. An instrument of torture for pinching the fingers.
Pinch. A pleat in a skirt.
Pique de vant. ? A braggart's beard.
Pitch. p. 82. Aim (an expression derived from falconry).

Plant. To colonize.
Plaudities. Applause.
Players' bills. Placards announcing the play for the day.
Plumping. Padding.
Point. "To the point," i.e. exactly.
Polypus. Octopus, cuttle-fish.
Poor John. Salted hake.
Portingal. Portuguese.
Posy. Motto or verse.
Potable. Drinkable.
Pottle. Tankard containing two quarts.
Pounce. To powder.
Preeches. "You must be preeches" =you must be breeched (flogged).
Prick. A dot or mark.
Prick in. Implant, embroider.
Primero. Very popular card game in the 16th century, generally played by four persons.
Print. "In print" p. 174. i.e. to a nicety.
Proclamations, i.e. waste paper.
Proctor. One who held a licence to collect alms for "spital-houses."
Proof. Result.
Prunes. p. 100. "House where they set stewed prunes before you" =a brothel.
Pudding-prick. Skewer.
Puling. Whining.
Pullin. Poultry.
Punk. Harlot.
Purchase. Booty.
Purl. An embroidered border.

Quean. Jade, hussy.
Quern. Mill.
Quetch. Stir.
Quietus. Settlement of an account.
Quit. Repay.

Race. Root.
Raddles. Laths.
Raisins o' the sun. Dried grapes.
Rampier. Rampart.
Rase. Scratch.
Rash. Inferior kind of silk.
Rear-banquet. Collation taken after supper or dinner.
Reredos. Brick or stone back of a fireplace.

Reversion. Scraps left over, remnant.
Riddle. A large kind of sieve.
Rifts. Strips of oak wood.
Roarer, or roaring boy. A cant name for a swaggering bully.
Rochet. A bishop's vestment.
Rock Monday. The Monday following Twelfth Day. Rock=distaff.
Rodulphus Agricola (1442–1485). A learned German scholar and scientist. Agricola, of course, means husbandman, hence the "mere scholar's" mistake.
Rogues. *Rufflers*: see p. 239. *Hookers*: see p. 241. *Wild rogues*: those born rogues. *Palliards*: beggars in patched cloaks. *Abrams*: see p. 238. *Dummerers*: beggars pretending dumbness. *Swadders*: pedlars. *Demanders for glimmer*: female beggars pretending to have lost all that they had by fire. *Morts*: female beggars not legally married. *Dells*: female beggars who are still maidens. *Uprightmen*: the highest rank of rogues. *Rogues*: beggars pretending to seek kinsmen: see p. 242. *Priggers of prancers*: horse-stealers. *Fraters*: pretended proctors (q.v.) with false licences. *Freshwater mariners*: pretended shipwrecked sailors. *Drunken tinkers*: thieves posing as tinkers. *Jarkmen*: clerkly rogues who make false licences and unite their comrades in wedlock. *Bawdy baskets*: female pedlars. *Autem morts*: legally married female rogues. *Doxies*: mistresses to rogues. *Kinching morts*: young female rogues. *Kinching coes*: young male rogues.
Roscius and Aesop. Two Roman actors fl. B.C. 70.
Rousy. Riotous, noisy.
Rumaging. At sixes and sevens.
Running over. p. 150. i.e. till the reader has run through it.
Rutter. Trooper.

Sacring-bell. Bell used at the mass.
Saint or Saunt. Corruption of the

GLOSSARY AND NOTES

word "cent," a card game like piquet.

Saint Lawrence. Martyred by roasting on a gridiron.

Scant. Scarcely.

Sconce. Protection, bulwark.

Scores him. p. 119. ?Writes him down as in his debt.

Searced. Sifted through a very fine sieve.

Sear-cloth. Cerecloth.

Secretary hand. Style of handwriting used for engrossing.

Sergeant. Police officer.

Sharers. The members of the company who ran the theatre.

Sherris sack. The same as modern sherry.

Shift. p. 76. Avoid. p. 163. Change their clothes.

Shifting. Deceitful.

Shoeing-horn. i.e. shoe-horn, but often used in Elizabethan English to mean anything that would induce or "draw on" thirst.

Shot. Bill, reckoning.

Shoulder-clapping. Arrest.

Shrode. ?Married to a shrew.

Shrovings. Festivities at Shrovetide.

Sign of the smock, i.e. the brothel-house.

Sir-reverence. p. 127. =saving your reverence.

Sium. Yellow watercress.

Slawata. William Slawata (1572–1652), a great traveller, High Chancellor of the Empire.

Slipper-merchants. Slippery customers.

Slop. p. 255. i.e. Sailor. Cp. **Galligaskins**

Slot. Track of a deer.

Snort. Snore.

Snuff. "To take in snuff"=to take offence.

Solanum somniferum. Nightshade.

Sorteth to. Results in.

Sound. p. 171. "Just upon the third sound": as we should say "just when they are ringing up the curtain."

Spade. To cut a beard in the shape of a spade.

Spending. p. 17. Utterance.

Spent. p. 3. Consumed.

Spials. Spies.

Spoie. p. 92. If we read "spoil" it would appear that Brown, a cutpurse, intentionally provoked a quarrel in order to collect a crowd from which he and his accomplices might reap a harvest.

Sprag. Active.

Squirting. Upstart.

Standard. The Standard in Cheapside was a conduit, upon which were portraits of kings and queens.

Stauling-ken. A house that will receive stolen goods.

Stave and tail. Bear-baiting term; to stave=to beat back the bear; to tail=to hold back the dog.

Still. Always, ever.

Stoop. p. 116. This word seems to be used figuratively here=to alight as a bird. The cheaters are of course the fowlers.

Stoves. Houses for hot vapour baths.

Strangate. ?Strand-gate.

Strangury. Difficulty in discharging the urine.

Strength of his horses. p. 80. The number of his horses.

Suburb shadow. The suburbs were the most disreputable quarters of London in which the houses of ill-fame stood.

Suckets. Sweetmeats or sugarplums.

Summoner. One who summons to the ecclesiastical court.

Swag-bellied. With a large overhanging belly.

Sword and buckler. Went out of fashion about 1580. Frequent contemptuous references of them occur in Elizabethan literature. Apparently associated with thieves. Cp. 1 *Henry IV*, I. iii. 230.

Syrups, i.e. medicines (cp. **Treacle**).

Systema. The point is, I suppose, that the "mere scholar" takes *systema* (i.e. *Systema Logicum*=a system of logic) to be the name of the author of the book.

Tables. p. 64. Backgammon.

GLOSSARY AND NOTES

Take it of merit. Take as their due.

Talbot. Great English general of the time of Henry VI. cp. 1 *Henry VI.*

Tarlton (Richard). Died 1588. A famous Elizabethan comic actor, said to be the original of Yorick in *Hamlet.*

Tawe out. Extort.

Tax idle circumstance. Censure trivial matters.

Telephus. The wound of Telephus could only be cured by rust from the spear of Achilles, which had inflicted it.

Term. p. 146. "Attend the end of every term"; the end of the law terms was the busiest season for publishers.

Termagant. An imaginary god of the Mahomedans, who figured in the old miracles and morality plays as a violent character.

Terminate. Determine.

Testor or **teston.** Sixpence.

Thales Milesius. He fell into a ditch while looking at the stars.

Tick-tack. A game like back-gammon.

Toucher. The bowl lying nearest the "Jack."

Trade. Manner, custom, practice.

Travel for a stomach. Walk to get an appetite.

Traverses. Crosses, misfortunes.

Treacle. Medicine.

Treads. Steps, measures.

Treen. Wooden.

Trenchmore. A popular dance tune.

Troll. To move round.

Trump. A card game very much like whist.

Try. p. 2. Refine.

Truss. Breeches. Verb = tie up the "points."

Twelve, the. ?The signs of the zodiac.

Twisks. ?Twists, i.e. threads.

Unlettered. p. 80. "No unlettered man," i.e. he carries letters.

Untruss. See **Truss.**

Utter. Deliver, speak.

Veney. Bout.

Verdures. ?Green hangings.

Verucae, i.e. Verrucae = warts.

Vice. The chief comic figure in the old morality play.

Voiders. Trays or plates for broken meat.

Waiters. Attendants.

Wap. Sheep-dog.

Warden. A kind of pear.

Warrener. Keeper of poultry and rabbits.

Watshod. ?Some kind of silk.

Weasel-beaked. With a sharp thin face like a weasel.

Welt. Strip, border: (verb) to patch.

We three. A well-known inn-sign representing two fools and inscribed "We three." The third fool of course is the man who looks at the picture. Cp. *Twelfth Night*, II. iii. 17.

Wheel and reel. i.e. for spinning.

Whetstone. p. 270. Given as a prize for the biggest liar.

Whirligig-jacks. Spinning jacks.

Wings. Shoulder knots or epaulettes.

Wool-packs. p. 13. cp. p. 87.

Yerk. Jerk (q.v.).

Zany. A clown whose business on the stage was to imitate foolishly the actions of the principal clown.

INDEX OF AUTHORS

INDEX OF AUTHORS